Vision to Legacy

The Great Clips Story

Shelby Yastrow

with Steve LeBeau

Kirk House Publishers
Minneapolis, Minnesota

Vision to Legacy
The Great Clips Story

Shelby Yastrow with Steve LeBeau

Published under the auspices of Great Clips, Inc., 4400 West 78th St., Suite 700, Minneapolis, MN 55435 (www.greatclips.com).

Library of Congress Cataloging-in-Publication Data

Yastrow, Shelby.
    Vision to legacy : the Great Clips story / Shelby Yastrow with Steve LeBeau.
         pages cm
    ISBN 978-1-933794-66-2 -- ISBN 1-933794-66-6
    1. Great Clips (Hair salon chain)--History. 2. Beauty shops--Management. 3. Franchises (Retail trade)--United States. I. LeBeau, Steve. II. Title.
    TT965.Y37 2013
    363.72'99068--dc23

                              2013007374

Kirk House Publishers, PO Box 390759, Minneapolis, MN 55439
www.kirkhouse.com
Manufactured in the United States of America

Contents

Part Four: Fractures

Part Five: Aiming High

Part Six: Ready—Aim—Fire!

Part Seven: A New Beginning

Part Eight: Time to Smell the Flowers

It is my considered opinion that the hairdresser
is the most influential person in any community.
When the public goes to a hairdresser,
something happens to them.
They feel safe, they relax. . . .
I tell you that a clever, thoughtful, ambitious hairdresser
wields a power beyond comprehension of most people.

John Steinbeck, *The Hairdresser*

Foreword

The barber shops and beauty salons that dotted our landscape in the 1960s and 1970s had come a long way from their antecedents, which have been traced back to the very beginning of the Bronze Age (circa 3500 BC) in ancient Egypt. The profession later developed in Greece, then Rome, and eventually throughout the entire world. In their earliest days, barbers (from the Latin word *barba,* meaning beard) were highly respected, often enjoying the role of priests. The religious connotation had to do with the idea that evil spirits entered and left the body through the hair, and the manner in which the hair (including beards) was cut, shaped, scented, or even dyed influenced the passage of these spirits in and out of the body.

Over time, the barber's place in society became broader. In early Athens, for example, his shop was a likely gathering place for exchanging social, political, and sporting news.

The role of the early barbers was later expanded into medicine, and it was they who were often society's doctors, dentists, and surgeons before modern medicine and anesthetics opened the door to practitioners more closely akin to today's doctors and dentists. Indeed, the modern "barber shop pole" depicts the rack used by early bloodletting barbers to dry bandages that had been used (and re-used) on their hapless patients after the application of leeches for the then-common bleeding treatment meant to cure any and all maladies.

By the mid-1970s, the United States would have over 250,000 barber shops and beauty salons. Virtually all were sole proprietorships, and an owner seldom had more than one location. It might be in a storefront, but it was just as likely to be in the owner's living room, back porch, or garage. At a time when society was much less mobile than it is today, a typical man had "his" barber and a typical woman had "her" beautician. Customer loyalty was strong—not only to the establishment but to the specific person doing the hair. While there was variety in terms of price, services offered, ambiance, and number of chairs, there was one overriding similarity: The customer and the person cutting the hair were likely to be on a first-name basis, and the relationship lasted for years.

But the business was about to undergo a mighty change. The intimate, customized shops of the early 1970s—especially barbers—were about to be steadily replaced by lower-cost chains and franchised operations where a customer might not have ever been in the salon or seen the stylist before, but could get the haircut expected, in the time expected, and for the price expected. Because these new operations were larger—more stylists, more chairs, more customers—the total number of barber shops began to decline.

This transformation of an industry, taken alone, would hardly merit an entire book. But, when viewed in the context of the company that helped pioneer the change through franchising and now leads the entire industry, the story takes on an incredible human-interest dimension that is not taught at Harvard Business School. That company is Great Clips, Inc.

By any acceptable measure, however, Great Clips should never have happened!

To be sure, the two men who actually started the company, and the third they brought in a short time later, had skills that seemed to complement one another, and on paper there was a synergy that bode well for success in the haircare business. One had cut hair for years, one had been an operations director in a small chain of hair salons, and the third was a CPA who had once worked for a company that did national franchising.

However, collectively they lacked the three ingredients that one would think were necessary to launch any business, let alone a business that would soon dominate its industry. *They had no money; they had no entrepreneurial experience; and they had no new ideas or products.* Indeed, in 1983, the year after they started their business, there were already nineteen chains that had franchised more than 2,000 hair "salons"—a term that was steadily replacing "shops" and "parlors."

Add to that the fact that the three owners disagreed on virtually everything relating to how the business should be run!

In the beginning, the disagreements were not serious and reflected little more than the normal give and take in any business relationship. Over time, however, these differences of opinion grew into resentment, then festered further, and eventually led to an "all or nothing" showdown!

That the company survived this unseemly birth is remarkable; that it grew into the company it is today is, in a word, miraculous.

Introduction

Minneapolis, Sunday afternoon, September 30, 2012.

For the past twenty-four hours, thousands of people have been arriving at seven different hotels and finding twenty-four smiling greeters there to answer questions, meet their every need, and make them feel like kings and queens.

Since this morning, long lines have been forming at the various registration stations.

Excitement and good cheer fill the air. People who haven't seen each other in months or years are exchanging kisses, bear hugs, and high-fives.

Last-minute touches are being put on dozens of exhibition booths as technicians race around with headsets and clipboards busily checking connections, plugging in amplifiers, concealing wires, and whispering into phones, as harsh voices are crackling through the receivers on their belts.

Scores of people have spent the night stuffing papers into folders, stapling handouts, sorting name badges, and rearranging stacks of paper—all the while checking their computers and smartphones.

In isolated rooms, far above the tumult, executives accustomed to giving directions are nervously polishing their scripts and rehearsing their lines.

Unseen trucks are delivering tons of food, chefs are preparing to cook it, and servers are preparing to serve it.

Professional speakers and entertainers, including a nationally well-known television comedian, are en route to Minneapolis to educate and entertain everyone now starting to crowd the halls.

Hidden away in various places are hair stylists eagerly awaiting the hair-cutting competition that will draw the cheers of everyone in attendance.

And young people, perhaps on their first trip out of Iowa or Georgia, are craning their necks and wondering what all the fuss is about.

These thousands of people are here to participate, one way or the other, in the 2012 convention of the Great Clips franchise network. And a big event it is, for this is the thirtieth anniversary of the founding of Great Clips,

The Great Mural created by seven Twin Cities' artists at the 2012 30th Birthday Convention, inspired by hundreds of text messages sent in by Convention attendees.

Inc., the world's largest salon brand, and the franchise system it created. The convention is hailed as the "30th Birthday Convention."

In a matter of hours, there will be announcements reconfirming the success of the system—the record numbers of hair salons, franchisees, sales, and profits.

The numeral "3" will be seen and heard over and over again: The *30th* anniversary. Over *3,000* attendees. Over *3,000* salons. Over *30,000* stylists working in those salons. All traceable back to the original *three* owners.

The numeral "1" will also reverberate through the halls: "We are the *No. 1* haircare brand in the world!" "Within a year we will have annual system-wide sales of *$1 billion*!"

While this is not the first Great Clips convention, it is surely the biggest and glitziest. Indeed, except for the genuine esteem and respect that everyone has for everyone else, any similarity between this gala and the first convention in 1988 is purely coincidental:

- This year over 3,000 people are attending the convention. In 1988, there were 80 in attendance.

- This year, a major metropolitan convention center and seven hotels are needed to accommodate the people and events. In 1988, everything and everyone were in a single hotel with plenty of room to spare.

- This year, twenty-four greeters are on hand. In 1988, it was the three early owners who greeted everyone in the lobby of the one hotel, and it was they who directed the attendees to the coffee shop, meeting room, elevators, and bathrooms.

- This year, over sixty vendors and suppliers have booths spread throughout a 30,000 square-foot space—nearly three-quarters of an acre. In 1988, there were five booths in a single meeting room.

- This year features high-tech computerized and synchronized videos, music, voice-overs, lighting, and giant multiple monitors. In 1988, the vice president of human resources hand-fed slides into a projector to be shown on a single, portable screen. Her three children hand-printed the name badges for everyone who attended. This year, computers and printers have been spitting out the badges along with reservation confirmations, room assignments, agendas, programs, and announcements.

- This year, everything is being coordinated by professional event planners and their well-trained staffs. In 1988, it was the company office staff who pitched in to handle reservations, haul boxes, hang decorations, set up the few props that were used, and plug in the microphones.

As with most conventions, especially festive ones such as this, a theme has been assigned:

IT'S GONNA BE GREAT!

No one familiar with the Great Clips system would challenge the accuracy of this theme. But it tends to obscure another undeniable fact:

IT *HAS* BEEN GREAT!

PART ONE

Before the First Haircut

CHAPTER 1

The Stage Is Set

During the 1970s, two forces collided that set the stage for a dramatic change in the history of haircare. On the one hand, the long hair that men preferred in the sixties was giving way to a much different preference. More men now wanted their hair *shaped*—not *cut*. This gave rise to the unisex salons that catered to both men and women, and where a standard haircut—which typically included a shampoo, razor cut, and blow dry—would cost upwards of $16. On the other hand, it was also during this time that the country was undergoing spiraling inflation and a stagnant economy, intensified by a severe energy crisis. Not everyone could afford $16 haircuts.

Suddenly, the marketplace was demanding lower-priced haircuts, but to deliver them the salons had to bring down costs or give faster haircuts—or both.

Among the first to respond to this demand were Dennis and Ann Ratner who, in 1974, opened a low-cost salon called Hair Cuttery in West Springfield, Virginia. About the same time, Sam Ross launched Fantastic Sams, a similar concept, in Memphis, Tennessee. In both of these models, a faster, less expensive haircut was offered with no frills. If the customer wanted a shampoo, razor cut, or blow-dry, he or she had to pay extra for it. In the following year, 1975, Frank Emmett and Geoffrey Rappaport opened their first low-cost, no-frills Supercuts salon in the San Francisco Bay Area. All three of these enterprises enjoyed customer acceptance and strong growth from the beginning.

Soon, such operations were springing up in other parts of the country. The price of haircuts in these salons was typically about $6—a fraction of the price charged at the full-service establishments.

In 1979, a Canadian named James Tucker visited a Supercuts salon in California. This was his first visit to one of the newer low-cost, no-appointment operations, and he was immediately struck by the opportunities it offered. He could see that the low price (coupled with the shampoos, razor cuts, and blow-dries being offered only as higher-priced options) would lead to faster haircuts, happier customers, and repeat business.

Also, because the customer could not make an appointment with a particular stylist, there were no "favorites." Thus, Tucker could see, the stylists were not working against the owners by building up their own clientele. This minimized the age-old hazard of stylists leaving to open their own salons and taking their customers along.

Tucker was so taken by the concept that he immediately asked for a Supercuts franchise for Canada, but the owners weren't interested. So he returned to Canada and, with his brother Brian and a stylist named Bud Cowan, founded Super Clips, Ltd. in 1980, with headquarters in the Toronto area. Their low-cost Super Clips salons, which closely replicated the Supercuts in California, had immediate success, and soon they began opening more profitable salons in Canada. Capitalizing on this momentum, they turned their eye to the south to find regional franchisors in the United States.

Since regional franchising becomes a short-lived but very important factor in the story that follows, the concept should be briefly explained. In the standard arrangement, the *franchisor* sells a franchise directly to a *franchisee* to open an outlet (which may be a hair salon, a restaurant, a motel, or virtually any other business). The contract between them is the franchise agreement. If the franchisee later has a problem, he picks up the phone and calls the franchisor. If the franchisee violates the terms of the franchise agreement, the franchisor may be able to terminate it.

In a regional franchise arrangement, on the other hand, there is a middleman who goes by different names depending on the company. For convenience, that middleman will be referred to here as a "regional developer." The primary franchisor contracts with the regional developer to sell franchises within a specific territory or region.

At the risk of over-simplifying, the main advantage of having regional developers is that it facilitates faster and less expensive growth. Instead of paying a large team of sales people to go out and find franchisees, the franchisor contracts with these developers to sell franchises in specifically defined territories. The franchisor spends almost nothing; the regional developer earns his money from the fees paid by the local franchisee, which are then shared with the primary franchisor. By having, say, twenty regional developers, huge areas can be developed simultaneously with virtually no investment from the franchisor.

The main *disadvantage* of using regional developers is that the franchisor gives up important controls, such as choice of locations, oversight of the franchisee's actual operations, and, to some extent, the right to throw a non-performing franchisee out of the system. And, in some of these arrangements, the franchisor has little or no input on the selection of the ultimate franchisees. If the franchisor can't enforce standards and control the operations impacting the public or approve the franchisees, it can lead to inconsistency, a confused image, and a weaker brand.

In short, using regional developers works well for a franchisor that is looking for fast and inexpensive growth. Traditional franchising works better for the franchisor who wants more control over the people who deliver the brand and who is willing to pay more—and forego faster development—in return for that control.

In the spring of 1982, the Tuckers, in pursuit of their desire to move into the United States, placed a call to Joe Francis in Minneapolis. Francis was the founder and owner of The Barbers Hairstyling for Men & Women, a local chain of about 135 upscale, unisex salons. Some of The Barbers salons were franchised while others were owned and operated by the company. The purpose of the call was to enlist Francis as a regional developer to sell Super Clips franchises in the United States.

Francis had little enthusiasm for the Tuckers' proposal. He was proud of his elegant, full-service salons with private, wood-paneled booths and stylists trained to give European razor cuts. Why would he be interested in operating these new no-frills salons and selling discount haircuts? And from a practical viewpoint, he had his hands full trying to expand The Barbers in the middle of a recession. Interest rates were hovering around 20 percent, making it difficult to borrow the money he needed for his *existing* business. For him—or potential franchisees—to find the money needed to start a totally new venture was next to impossible.

Despite his skepticism, Joe Francis could not totally ignore the Tuckers' call. If they were having success in Canada and wanted to expand to the south, they could influence the haircare business in the United States. As it was, low-cost salons were already popping up here and there. *Better check this thing out*, Francis told himself. He put together a small task force from

The Barbers to drive to Winnipeg, Manitoba, to visit a few Super Clips salons and bring back a report. Heading up the task force was Steve Lemmon, The Barbers' director of operations.

Fortuitously, Steve Lemmon, like James Tucker, had already visited the Supercuts salons in California a few years earlier, and those visits sold him on the potential of low-cost haircare. "I got three haircuts in two trips and visited every Supercuts in the area," Steve recalled. "I found out that they hired beauticians and barbers and trained them to give fast—but totally professional—haircuts, and at a fraction of the price of most of the competition."

He returned from California to Minneapolis to promote the low-cost concept to Joe Francis, but his report fell on deaf ears. Francis was committed to expanding his upscale salons, and Steve's pitch was little more than a diversion that didn't warrant his attention. But that was a few years earlier; now the public's acceptance of the low-cost concept, together with the recent call from the Tuckers, aroused Francis's curiosity.

Joining Steve on The Barbers' task force was David Rubenzer, a longtime stylist who had worked for Francis and was now a franchisee of a Barbers salon. Unlike Steve, David had not previously looked into low-cost hair operations and had no idea what to expect from the trip to Winnipeg.

Even though Steve and David went to Canada merely to "kick the tires," they were immediately hooked on the Super Clips operation. It was a virtual carbon copy of the Supercuts concept that had impressed Steve on his earlier trip to California—not surprising since James Tucker had used Supercuts as his model for the design of Super Clips. If Steve loved Supercuts, well, why *wouldn't* he love Super Clips? And David was stunned! As he later recalled, "Here we were at The Barbers charging $16 for a haircut, and these guys were doing just as good a job for a third of the price and in a fraction of the time." According to David, "It was like looking into the future and seeing something that many customers would certainly prefer—especially in those tough times."

Returning to Minneapolis, Steve told Joe Francis that, by all means, The Barbers and Super Clips, Ltd. should form an alliance to franchise the low-cost concept in the United States. They could organize a new company under an Americanized name—something like Super Clips USA. Steve envisioned himself in charge of this endeavor, and the more he thought about it the more he wanted it.

Joe Francis still wasn't convinced—he wanted more data. To add to his briefing from the Winnipeg trip, he now sent Steve and David to the Super Clips headquarters in Toronto to learn what they could about the company itself and how it functioned. Steve and David took along Tom Cook who did marketing for The Barbers.

The contingent from The Barbers was welcomed by the Tuckers who freely answered any and all questions about their operation. As with Steve and David, Tom Cook was impressed with what he saw and heard. More importantly, all three were overwhelmed with the Tucker brothers, personally and as solid businessmen, and they could plainly see the advantages of an alliance between Super Clips and The Barbers.

Killing time over cocktails at the Toronto airport on the way home, they started brainstorming. No doubt because Steve was an operations guy, David was a barber, and Tom was in marketing, the discussion focused more on the salon than on corporate organizational issues.

Coming from The Barbers where the stylist worked in an enclosed wood-paneled booth, the wide-open design of the Super Clips salons was a definite turn-off. To them, the customer would want a little more privacy, but they couldn't afford to duplicate the paneled booths at the lower prices they'd be charging. Ideas were tossed back and forth regarding inexpensive but serviceable barriers or partitions. What would work?

Suggestions ranged from freestanding partitions to blinds, even to bamboo curtains, and with each drink the trio became more creative. Eventually, Tom Cook started playing around with the name "Super Clips" which, with a little contrivance and rearrangement of letters, conjured up the image of "clipper ships." As soon as he said it aloud, it struck a chord with Steve who had always loved sailing, and both of them almost simultaneously declared "sails" to be the ideal partition. On the flight back to Minneapolis, Tom was already making sketches of sails and thinking of ways to construct them.

Interestingly, the fact that this discussion was taking place signaled the naiveté of these three gentlemen regarding franchising. The hallmark of franchising is consistency of appearance as well as operations. The strength of the franchise concept is a recognizable brand that consistently meets the customer's expectations, and there is a value in that reliability. For that reason, décor is nearly always standardized, and the franchisor universally demands approval of even the slightest change in décor and signage as well as operations. The Tuckers could hardly be expected to permit significantly different décor among Super Clips salons, but, as it turned out, ignorance was bliss. As we will see, the alliance between the Canadians and Americans was later abandoned, with the Americans creating an entirely new business; Great Clips. And today 33,000 sails serve as attractive and functional privacy barriers in Great Clips salons throughout North America.

The enthusiasm of the three-man task force was short-lived. Just as after the earlier trip to Winnipeg, Joe Francis remained cool to the idea of the low-cost concept. To punctuate his own resolve that it was a good idea, Steve Lemmon drew a line in the sand: "If The Barbers doesn't do it, then I'll do it myself." Joe took him at his word—he fired Steve Lemmon the very next day!

And Steve *was* as good as his word. With no job and no money, he immediately contacted the Tuckers in Canada, got the go-ahead to introduce Super Clips in the United States, and incorporated Super Clips USA, Inc.—the company that was later to become Great Clips, Inc.

It was 1982, and Steve Lemmon was off to the races!

CHAPTER 2

A Company Is Born

There's no telling how he would have fared as a professional boxer, but he would have made a hell of a cage fighter! Steve Lemmon exuded a feistiness that would never let him back down from a confrontation. Add to that some of his other attributes—brains, ambition, energy, and guts—and we have the makings of a driven entrepreneur. All he needed was the right vehicle to kick-start and put into gear, and he found it in Super Clips USA.

Steve's first job out of college was with Investors Diversified Services in Minneapolis, and from there he went to New York to become a stockbroker.

In the 1970s, one of his clients persuaded him to leave the brokerage business and take a partnership interest in a then-abandoned gold mine in the High Sierra Mountains in northern California. Characteristic of his daring, Steve took the challenge and abandoned stocks and bonds to hunt for gold. He was able to recruit some investors but, like so many of the gold mine ventures, it didn't pan out. The experiment ended with the sale of the mine to a Canadian company which, luckily, enabled Steve and his investors to recoup most of their money.

He next took a job with The Barbers where, after only four years, he was supervising their thirty-five corporate-owned salons. The company revenues doubled, and no one doubted that Steve was instrumental in the newfound success. "It was easy," he recalled. "I simply gave more authority to the managers to run their salons. This gave them a sense of ownership that translated into better-run salons, and that naturally led to greater sales and higher profits." In that short, simple statement, Steve encapsulated what he knew instinctively, but which franchise and chain organizations too often forget: Finding good managers and empowering them to act beats micromanaging them from a far-removed corporate headquarters. Ironically, Steve himself later vacillated on this basic idea, and, as we will learn, it became a point of serious contention at the new company.

Steve's original intent when he incorporated Super Clips USA, Inc. was to open company-owned salons; franchising was not on his radar screen at the time. In other words, his company would own and operate the United States salons itself as the franchisee of the Canadian Super Clips.

One of his first decisions to that end proved to be a good one. He invited David Rubenzer to join him in the venture. "I knew I could find the real estate and run the business end of things," Steve explained, "but I needed someone to find and train the stylists. It was hard to find people to cut hair in those days, and those we found had to be trained to give faster and more standardized haircuts. That way we could keep the price down but make it up in volume." As already noted, many of the stylists working at the time were giving customized haircare, and the cuts often included "the extras" that had to be dispensed with in a low-cost operation. According to Steve, "David was the perfect guy to re-train them to give faster and less expensive haircuts."

Steve's decision to recruit David was bolstered by the knowledge that David might be able to help raise capital. Steve himself had no money, and, even if he could afford the astronomical interest rates that the banks were charging, there was no way a bank would be interested in a thinly capitalized start-up venture by a guy with no resources and no track record for owning and operating a business. David was receptive to making an investment and joining the business, and he was willing to let Steve have control with 51 percent of the stock. This was a big plus for Steve—any other investors would likely demand either majority control or, at the very least, enough restrictions to limit the autonomy that Steve so dearly wanted.

So, between David's ability to recruit and train the stylists, his access to some needed capital, and his willingness to give ultimate control to Steve, he seemed to be exactly the person Steve was looking for.

CHAPTER 3

The First Barber

No one who knew David Rubenzer before 1980 would have predicted the force he would become in the haircare industry.

The adjectives that best described him, then and since, are all warm and fuzzy—adjectives such as fun-loving, humorous, compassionate, and likeable. That tall man with a ready smile, when matched with the shorter, quick-tempered Steve Lemmon, evokes images of the Odd Couple.

David had originally planned on a career in nursing, an ambition born when he was working as an orderly at Miller Hospital in St. Paul, Minneapolis's twin city. It was there where he met his future wife, Mary Alice, who was a nurse. To raise the tuition money for nursing school at North Hennepin Community College, David first went to Brooks Barber College, and nine months later began cutting hair at a Barbers salon in downtown St. Paul.

He had never given thought to barbering as a permanent career, but Mary Alice convinced him that he'd enjoy it more than nursing. In her view, his creativity and engaging personality were certainly better suited for barbering than for nursing. She was right; he absolutely loved it!

In 1974, David was promoted to manager of one of The Barbers salons, and soon thereafter became manager of a second one. His newly acquired managerial skills, coupled with his recognized talent as a stylist, would prove to be valuable assets in the years to come.

Steve Lemmon had been promoted to director of operations of The Barbers

David Rubenzer at the Great Clips Convention in 1997.

in 1978, and he became David's supervisor. Although they soon developed a personal friendship, the relationship was not always easy. "Steve was this no-nonsense, in-your-face kind of guy," recalls David. "But hairstylists tend to be more touchy-feely and do better in a warmer and more personal setting."

In the following year, 1979, David changed hats. He bought The Barbers salon in Northfield, Minnesota, and exchanged his role as an employee/manager for a Barbers franchisee. He joked that he did it to get out from under the controlling Steve.

Because of their mutual respect for one another, Steve and David got along well in spite of their different personalities. There were, however, set-backs—like the time the two of them almost got into a fight when they were playing on opposite sides of a volleyball game at a company picnic. What had been a friendly, competitive game morphed into a hostile battle. An argument ensued, then some jostling, and that led to David shoving Steve. Steve fell backwards, but quickly jumped up into a fighting stance. David prudently backed off, and an ugly situation was averted.

After David became a Barbers franchisee, Adrienne Olson, a long-time stylist who had worked under David, replaced him as manager of The Barbers salon known as Diamond Head. It was apparent from the beginning that she was better than David at getting along with Steve—so much so in fact that Steve married Adrienne the next year, 1980! Steve had a previous marriage but, judging from everything he and Adrienne had in common, this one looked like it was for keeps. By the time of their marriage, Adrienne had purchased the Diamond Head salon from The Barbers and, like David, had become a Barbers franchisee.

So, when the unemployed Steve approached David to join him in the Super Clips USA venture, David and Steve's wife both had business rela-tionships with The Barbers—no longer as employees but as franchisees. It infuriated Joe Francis to learn that two of his franchisees were joining Steve, his former director of operations, to take an interest in competing salons.

Francis issued a simple warning to David: *Stay away from Steve. He's trouble*! David ignored the warning. He was impressed with what he saw on his two visits to Canada. Equally important, he said, "Steve already had all the numbers figured out. He knew what it would cost to rent space, build out a salon, and hire staff." David remembers Steve telling him, "We could open a salon for $15,000, whereas it was costing about $100,000 to open a single Barbers salon." David knew that it could take two years before a Barbers salon could earn any profit, but the lower-cost Super Clips could show earnings almost from the start.

Tragically, the person who had convinced him to become a barber in the first place, Mary Alice, had died of breast cancer the preceding winter, so David had to make this decision on his own. And he went for it! Between the remaining life insurance proceeds from Mary Alice's death and a second mortgage on his home, he raised $30,000 and bought a 49 percent interest in Super Clips USA. This left Steve with the 51 percent control he wanted from the beginning.

The partnership was forged.

CHAPTER 4

Laying the Groundwork

Although the new company started by Steve and David was intended to be a franchisee of the Canadians, the idea that they might be sub-franchising others to open Super Clips in the United States was never far from their minds. By that time, franchising had become a popular way of doing business.

Prior to the late 1950s, the concept of franchising retail businesses in the United States was virtually unheard of. Until then, the word was essentially limited to governments giving *franchises* to operate railroads or public utilities, or sports organizations giving *franchises* to operate professional teams, such as the New York Yankees or Boston Celtics, to compete within that organization.

Retail franchising, as we know it today, sprung up primarily in fast food—particularly with McDonald's, which opened its first franchise in 1957 in Des Plaines, Illinois. The concept soon became commonplace in countless other industries from pet grooming to dentistry, from hardware stores to equipment rental, and everything in between. This popularity was a result of a "marriage" between two groups, each in need of a partner. On one side were the people who had great ideas and expertise but no money, and on the other were people who, *collectively*, had large amounts of capital and were looking for businesses to run for themselves. Subway and Kentucky Fried Chicken (KFC) could never have opened thousands of outlets throughout the world without franchisee money, and the franchisees could never have achieved their success without Subway or KFC leveraging that money to produce greater know-how, purchasing power, site evaluation, supply lines, mass marketing, training, research, and personnel.

The success of the early franchisees produced a strong demand by people wanting to buy franchises, and the rush was so great that the would-be franchisees were downright reckless in what they bought. Inevitably, many unscrupulous franchisors were only too happy to meet that demand. Back-room franchise scams popped up daily to fleece these naive investors. Many franchisors took the franchisees' money and gave little in return; and many others took the franchisees' money and disappeared!

As greed follows money, legislation follows greed. The federal government and several states quickly reacted to protect the gullible franchisees by requiring franchisors, before offering franchises, to disclose vast amounts of information about the company and themselves, backed up with certified audits. The cost to comply with these regulations was high, and the penalties for non-compliance were higher.

Minnesota, like many other states, required the public filing of such disclosure statements before franchises could be offered for sale in the state. As of 1982, Super Clips, Ltd. in Canada had not made such a filing in Minnesota, and as a result could not yet issue a master franchise to Super Clips USA. Not letting such a technicality get in their way, Steve and David decided to open salons without a formal franchise agreement, and it was agreed that they would escrow money to pay fees and royalties to the Canadians later when all the paperwork was completed. The Americans would likewise be precluded from selling sub-franchises in Minnesota without disclosure statements on file, but this was not a problem because their intent was to start by opening only company-owned—and not franchised—salons.

In reality, the decision to start with company-owned salons had nothing to do with filing legalities. For one thing, Steve and David had integrity, and they wanted to test the concept thoroughly—working out the kinks—before asking franchisees to risk an investment. For another, "We wanted to be sure that there was enough positive cash flow to support a franchise fee, marketing fee, and royalties," Steve later explained. "The franchisee would need a 20 percent gross profit before these costs in order to afford them. We could do all the calculating and estimating, but we had to see what happened in an actual salon to know for sure."

Even though the Canadians could not yet issue a master franchise in Minnesota, David and Steve made another driving trip to Winnipeg to collect materials such as training videos and brochures, and to get as much information as they could on payroll, staffing, scheduling, and running the salons. On this trip, they were joined by Steve's wife, Adrienne, and Katie Lagieski. Katie had been Steve's operations assistant at The Barbers, and was now to become the first employee of Super Clips USA—another burr under Joe Francis's saddle! In those early days, her job was to handle a myriad of administrative tasks and the endless details that needed attention to get a new business started.

For its first "office," the fledgling company operated out of a small screen structure in Steve's backyard. He ran in a phone line and even had some meetings in those close confines. Much of his time was spent designing the future salons, sourcing furniture and equipment, and, of course, figuring out how to build and install the sail dividers that exc ted him.

A breakthrough on the sail problem came in the course of a conversation Steve had with a friend who happened to make canvas equipment bags for high school hockey teams. After the friend had stockpiled an oversized inventory in preparation for a large sale, the deal fell through and he was stuck with stacks of ten-foot canvas rolls in various colors. Steve now had the material he needed, and at a good price! In short order, he found someone to do the heavy-duty sewing and add a colorful accent stripe through each finished sail. Later he figured out how to use PVC piping for the masts and framework.

To complete the nautical look he wanted, he came up with the idea for stylists' uniforms with red and white striped tops and navy blue slacks or skirts. That led him to his close friend, Tom Kivo, who worked at the Garland Sweater Company in Minneapolis, which became the source for the tops.

To celebrate how well things were falling into place, and to stand back from the intensity to catch their breath, Steve, David, Adrienne, and Katie erected one of the sails outside the backyard office, and the four of them had a little party. They reviewed all they had accomplished, and toasted their future success. And, as happened at every opportunity, they discussed the progress of their first salon which was to be at the University of Minnesota. A lot—maybe everything—was riding on that first salon, and they didn't want to leave anything to chance.

Every conversation about that first salon inexorably led to speculation as to what would follow. If it failed—well, they didn't want to talk about that. But what would be their goal if it succeeded as planned? "We were hoping to open up seventy-five salons in the Twin Cities area, and then retire ridiculously wealthy," David said. "That was both Steve's and my grand plan. That was the extent of our ambition—seventy-five salons!"

They thought they were shooting for the moon, and secretly doubted that such a goal was attainable. Little did they know that the wee venture hatched in that backyard would become a behemoth, a leader in the hair-care industry, with well over 3,000 salons in less than thirty years. Their goal of seventy-five salons in their *lifetime* would be dwarfed by the still embryonic company that in later years would open that many salons in fewer than six months!

CHAPTER 5

A Shot Across the Bow

The euphoria felt at that backyard party was about to be dampened. The four celebrants were soon to learn that Joe Francis of The Barbers was out to torpedo their dreams with a low-cost brand of his own. It wasn't clear whether he was having second thoughts about the viability of the low-cost concept or whether he had *personal* reasons to stop these amateurs in their tracks. After all, he had employed and trained them, and now they had defected and were using what they had learned to compete with him.

He called an impromptu meeting at his lakeside home, inviting key people from The Barbers staff and several of his franchisees. He wanted their input and asked which of the franchisees present would take the chance of opening and running a low-cost, no-frills operation.

Only one franchisee spoke up and volunteered to buy the first franchise, but that was all Francis needed to unleash his attack. Moving full-steam ahead, he opened his first salon using a name that left little doubt as to what the customer could expect, "Cost Cutters." *And he did it a full two weeks before Steve and David opened their first salon!* Moreover, if there had been any question whatsoever that Joe Francis had a personal agenda, it was put to rest when he located his first Cost Cutters in Savage, Minnesota, within three miles of both David's and Adrienne's Barbers' salons. Because of their non-compete clauses, neither David nor Adrienne would have been permitted to open salons at that location to compete against Joe Francis, but now *he* was opening a salon at that location to compete against *them*! Obviously, he was making good on something he had said when Steve left The Barbers: *If you try to get into the hair business around here, I'll drive you into the ground!*

The battle was on! David and Adrienne both terminated their Barbers' franchises under an arrangement where they were allowed to operate their salons under a different name. David's became "Plaza Hair," and Adrienne's became "DH Hair." Adrienne immediately switched to the Super Clips concept at DH Hair by lowering prices, giving no-frills cuts, and no longer accepting appointments. David, for the time being, retained the full-service concept at his salon.

Carla Fryar, a stylist at DH Hair, remembers that the regular customers were shocked when the prices suddenly dropped from $16 to $6. "They would ask me, 'Am I still getting the same haircut?' I told them, 'Well, it's still me cutting your hair, isn't it? I'm not going to shampoo it, blow-dry it, or curl it. If you want any of that you will have to pay extra, but it's not part of the regular visit anymore.'"

The other three stylists at DH Hair, not comfortable with the low-cost concept and fearing a loss of income, resigned and went to full-service salons. This exodus created an opportunity for Carla who was soon moved into the manager's position. "My promotion to manager really changed my parents' attitude toward my career," she said. "They had wanted me to go to college, but any misgivings they had disappeared when I became a manager just nine months after finishing cosmetology school."

The success of the DH Hair changeover was both instant and dramatic, and it prompted David to make the switch at Plaza Hair where he, too, saw a marked improvement in business. And he likewise heard comments from incredulous customers when the prices were slashed. "So, have you been ripping me off all these years?" some would joke, or, "Do I get a refund for all those years I paid $16?"

Although DH Hair and Plaza Hair did not operate under the Super Clips name, David and Steve used them as training grounds to perfect the new concept.

One advantage of the Joe Francis's Cost Cutter threat was that it helped define the image that Steve and David wanted to portray to their customers. Cost Cutters operated in a wide-open space without dividers or partitions between the stations, and they were painted in a garish combination of yellow and red. Because their prices would be the same, Steve and David made the décor a point of differentiation. The sails, which provided both privacy and more appealing colors, were perfect! They wouldn't be competing on price, but they held the aces when it came to comfort and ambience; and they were committed to offering better haircuts. According to David, "If there was going to be a Kmart and a Target in this business, we were going to be the Target. We were going to give great haircuts in nicer surroundings, and with better-trained stylists."

For the record, Cost Cutters remains in business and continues to sell franchises to this day. In 1999, it was sold to Regis Corporation which owns several haircare brands. Despite the concerns it caused with its first salon, Cost Cutters never posed a threat to David and Steve.

CHAPTER 6

The Star of the Show: The Haircut

In the final analysis, a successful salon is all about the haircut. At the new company, the haircut was all about David Rubenzer.

There are cosmetology schools throughout the country to train aspiring stylists; however, in-school training is only the beginning of what a good stylist has to know. John Halal, director of education at Tricoci University of Beauty Culture in Oak Brook, Illinois, sums it up this way: "Our students aren't finished learning when they graduate. They are just beginning. Good schools provide a solid foundation, but we have to rely on the salons to continue with the ongoing education our graduates need to be successful."

The haircut that David and Steve needed to generate greater customer turnover—and customer satisfaction—didn't just happen. It had to be created using definite criteria. Standardization was critical, but not to the point where all customers walked out looking alike. Speed was critical, but not to the point where the stylist rushed and the customer *felt* rushed. And eliminating the frills was critical, but not to the point where customers weren't getting their money's worth. Achieving this with customers who were accustomed to slow, fancy, and expensive haircuts would require a master stroke, especially since it had to be achieved in a single visit or the customer would never be seen again—and it had to be achieved with a stranger cutting their hair!

David was the perfect person to develop and teach the technique that would do the trick. By this time, he had been cutting hair for twelve years, and his experience at The Barbers included training others. He was blessed with a natural creativity to explore, invent, and improvise. More important, he had a friendly and outgoing personality that, as if by osmosis, was absorbed by those he trained. Through his training, and by his example, the stylists delivered just the right experience for the new salons—professional, comfortable, efficient, and friendly.

The importance of "friendly" can't be overstated. For one thing, the customer and the stylist are in very close contact for the duration of the haircut, and having at least some conversation is only natural, even if it is only about the weather. For another, friendliness can instill confidence—*the customer is there because he or she wants to look better, and therefore must be made to feel confident that the stylist can make that happen.* Every stylist learns early on that the customer's vanity is a high standard to meet. Even after a great haircut, none of us looks as handsome or as beautiful as we think we are!

A patient undergoing medical treatment may not know for a long time, if ever, just how successful that treatment was, but the person getting a haircut is still in the chair when assessing both the haircut and the person giving it. These assessments are more positive when the customer has good vibes about the stylist.

Engendering a relationship between the stylist and the customer presented a risk! As noted earlier, in the full-service salons where the customers had their own preferred stylists, the stylists tended to build a clientele that would follow them if they left to go elsewhere. David's challenge was to figure out how to ensure that the customer's loyalty was more toward the salon—the brand—than to the individual stylist. To do this, he had to develop a more or less standardized "experience" so that the customer would receive the same professional cut and the same friendly treatment regardless of whose chair he or she was assigned.

Standardization began with the greeting and the "consultation" when a few questions were asked as to what the customer wanted in terms of length, shape, or style. This was as essential a part of the training as the haircut itself. Initially the standardized system included ten steps, but it has since evolved into a five-step process beginning with a warm greeting and ending with the customer confirming their satisfaction and being invited back. The entire process is continuously reinforced at training sessions and operational reviews.

To train for the cut, David initially relied heavily on videos and other materials created by the earliest pioneers of low-cost haircare, Supercuts and Super Clips, Ltd. The focus was on five basic but different haircuts. From there, he perfected a fast and efficient process that fit the bill for what he and Steve Lemmon wanted.

"He taught us to follow a certain cutting order, so there was no guessing," recalled Pam Keller who was hired as a stylist for the second salon. "Less experienced stylists don't always know the best approach for any particular haircut." David's system was simple but, at the same time, very specific as to the precise technique—and sequence—for each of the cutting steps *and* for each of the basic styles. Only then could there be consistent cuts from stylist to stylist, a goal essential in a no-appointment, low-cost salon. As explained by Yvonne Lopez, a current training manager at the company, "Just like everything else, when we have a definite system or process for completing a task, consistency is better, efficiency is higher, and the ability to teach and learn is easier."

David proved his special genius by creating the perfect haircut for the intended business model. While the technique was standardized, the results were not. Every head of hair is unique, and David's limited number of basic haircuts for an unlimited variety of heads yields an infinite number of final results. Thus, while the technique and the quality are consistent, the appearance is not.

This discussion should not be construed to imply that a customer's choice of haircut is limited, or that a customized cut is unavailable. On the contrary, recent feedback received online from John M., a customer in Fort Wayne, Indiana, is enlightening:

"Your people and your service are GREAT! I had let my hair grow for eight months to get the length I wanted, and then went to Great Clips. I told them I wanted my hair to look like Owen Wilson's, the movie star, and they did it perfectly! I was amazed. GREAT bunch of people—and fast!!"

To teach a new system to a beginning stylist is one thing; to teach the system to an experienced stylist from a full-service salon is quite another. By its very nature, hairstyling is a creative profession, and stylists tend to think of themselves as artists. Like the adage about old dogs and new tricks, the longer one has been doing it, the harder it is to change to a more streamlined, no-nonsense technique.

In the old paradigm of the full-service salons, a stylist might spend an hour or more on each customer. The process might even be extended further by adding extras—shampoo, blow-dry, color services, curling—whatever it took to increase the price. The higher the final price, the better. But the new paradigm for the low-cost salon was just the opposite. The goal here was to provide a quality haircut in about fifteen minutes, thus serving three or four customers per hour: Give a faster, high-quality haircut at a low price, and serve more customers in the course of a day. Reduce the margin but increase the volume.

To that end, a shampoo or other extra was not *offered*, even though it was available *upon request* for a charge. Both the salon and the stylist would be better off by passing up the extra charge and saving time, and staying at the lower cost would maintain the price differentiation from most of the competition.

This was a tough concept to grasp for stylists trained to "sell the extras." However, with solid basic training, the stylists adapted to the new process, and they were soon delivering low-cost haircuts to happy customers—and at a profit! Better yet, the greater number of customers served generated more tips for the stylists than fewer customers paying higher prices.

Even with as many as four haircuts per hour, however, the low price would not produce enough profits to support a salon—unless there were several stylists doing it at the same time. And if the need for increased staffing was not obvious before Steve and David opened their first salon, it became brutally clear almost immediately after the doors opened.

PART TWO

Open For Business!

CHAPTER 7

Showtime!

September 22, 1982! No better words than "instant success" could describe the grand opening of the first Super Clips USA salon!

Located in a small storefront on Washington Avenue near the University of Minnesota, next to a Kinko's, the site posed a problem from the beginning: There was no off-street parking. This alone would have nixed almost any salon, but David and Steve went with the site because of the high pedestrian traffic from the university. And, they figured, if anyone would take a chance with a $6 no-frills haircut, it would be a college student or someone else associated with a state university.

Although Steve hired an independent designer to oversee the décor, Katie Lagieski skillfully supervised the build-out of the salon. The sails were finally erected for the first time! The crisp white canvas with stripes of various colors perfectly fulfilled their intended purpose—privacy—and at the

Salon interior at the University of Minnesota salon (which was originally opened under the name Super Clips) showing the early Classic design with the signature sails, ropes and décor that included plants.

same time presented a unique atmosphere. The PVC "masts" were attached to the floor with flanges and anchored to the walls. To add to the sailing motif, the sails were linked together with a nautical rope that ran all the way to the rear of the salon. Glass shelves at each station held such items as gels and sprays, along with small containers for the stylist's shears, clippers, combs, and other tools. A chair rail ran along the perimeter of the salon, topped with brackets to support more glass shelves. A blue accent stripe lined the walls just below the ceiling line, another subtle hint of blue sky and fair weather for sailing. Facing each customer entering the salon was a receptionist sitting at a white desk; behind the receptionist were the stylists in their nautically-inspired uniforms. Punctuating the entire ambience was a plethora of artificial plants.

As anyone who knew them would expect, David and Steve didn't leave the opening day customer count to chance. On the contrary, they employed guerrilla marketing—*literally*! They hired a guy in a gorilla costume to interact with the people walking by, letting them know that the first fifty haircuts were free.

Students took the bait and swamped the salon, and when it was filled others waited out on the sidewalk. So successful was this free haircut ploy that it became standard for openings to follow. Adrienne and David were standing by to help with the cutting if the customers showed up in the hoped-for numbers, and it was a good thing that they did!

That first salon opened with a bang. There would be no looking back.

CHAPTER 8

The First Problem of Success

David and Steve tried to anticipate every conceivable problem they might encounter and then deal with it before it struck. The success of the first grand opening, however, highlighted a problem that they hadn't expected.

Their initial calculations confirmed that, because of lower prices, more stylists per salon would be needed to produce the volume necessary to make a profit. But the unexpectedly high demand for haircuts in their first salon increased this need exponentially. They would need even more stylists than they had realized, and finding them would not be easy.

Most of the available stylists were accustomed to working in full-service salons. Adrienne and David had hired and trained the stylists for the new salon, and they saw that the idea of unbundling the services and going to an *à la carte* menu was hard to accept for stylists who had spent their careers working in full-service salons. Experience had taught them that the way to add money was to add features—not subtract them. "We preferred not to hire anyone who worked full-service because they resisted our concept," Adrienne reported. "And most of the kids coming out of school wanted to work at fancier places." Nevertheless, shrewd recruiting attracted a number of outstanding stylists. Some moved up to enjoy careers in key positions in the company, and many others have become franchisees. Clearly, different stylists succeed in different environments. As John Halal of the Tricoci University of Beauty Culture observed: "Our graduates may work at one or more different salons before they realize that the right place for them is with a low-cost chain."

Finding enough good stylists has been an on-again-off-again problem in the haircare business, at least since the introduction of large, multi-chair salons and chains. Before that, a high percentage of barber shops and beauty salons had one chair, and it was often serviced by the owner. If there was a second or third chair, it was likely serviced by someone who had worked in the salon for years. Hiring, training, and turnover were not serious problems in those salons.

But the newly-arrived chains meant finding, hiring, and training non-owner and non-family stylists, stylists whose tenure at the salon was often short and who had to be replaced many times over. Finding stylists was difficult, particularly during strong economic times when people were not desperate for jobs. All kinds of creative incentives were used to secure and retain them. One such incentive was to reimburse the stylist for part of the cost of cosmetology school. Retention bonuses were another. But when unemployment was high and jobs were scarce, it was much easier to find and retain stylists. Interestingly, one reason for this was that many privately-owned salons were forced to close during hard times, and the owners themselves were looking for work at the chains. Another reason was that licensed stylists who had left the industry were coming back and looking for work.

A valuable recruiting tactic was to convince the would-be stylist that he or she could actually make more money at a low-cost salon than at one providing full service for a higher price. Under Super Clips USA's original compensation plan, the stylist received minimum wage or $1.65 per haircut, plus tips. A busy stylist and the owner would *both* make more money with three or four small tickets over one hour than with one big ticket at a full-service salon during the same hour. Thus simple math, in addition to customer demand, dictated the need for more stylists.

Recruitment can be a two-way street in the field of haircare. In one direction, salons recruit stylists from various cosmetology schools throughout the country; in the other, these schools depend on salons and others in the haircare industry to refer potential students to them. Mez Varol, founder and president of International Academy in Daytona Beach, Florida, is quick to cite this symbiotic relationship. "The salons are constantly recruiting at our school," he explains, "and every salon out there should be a recruiting center for people to come to our schools to learn to be stylists."

CHAPTER 9

Three Salons and an Office— a Chain

In October 1982, a month after the first opening at the university, salon number two opened at the Silver Bell Center in Eagan, a Twin Cities suburb. In spite of a traffic-generating McDonald's, the center had a number of vacant storefronts and by any measure was a questionable site. Yet, with one small newspaper ad and a repeat of the grand opening guerrilla marketing tactic offering free haircuts to the first fifty customers, the new salon opened with a rush of customers and became another big success. In fact, this salon became the anchor that helped revive the Silver Bell Center.

With winter right around the corner, the screened-in office in Steve's backyard was a problem. He solved it by walling off the back of the Silver Bell location for a new corporate office; fortunately, the total space was three times larger than necessary for a salon.

The next problem would be to furnish this newly created "executive suite." While the initial money from David was not yet exhausted and the first two salons were looking good, David and Steve were not about to waste precious funds on plush furnishings. Steve fashioned a makeshift desk using a hollow-core door strategically placed over two file cabinets. "It made an excellent desktop," he boasted. Instead of the popular, multi-lined office phones that also serve as intercoms, they installed two simple black phones, each with a separate phone number. They completed the bare-bones décor by slapping some gray paint on the concrete floor and adding a folding table and a couple of cheap couches.

The office space served as a meeting room, storage site, and training area for stylists and managers. It was here where many brainstorming sessions took place and where crucial decisions were made that determined the future of this budding venture. *More importantly, it was here where the uniquely egalitarian culture of the company was born.* No one was disqualified from offering opinions and fighting for his or her ideas, whether the subject was scheduling, cutting hair, how to keep wait times short, or how to keep track of sales. Ideas were respectfully and thoughtfully debated before being rejected or adopted. This atmosphere encouraged comment without fear of ridicule. Even though he was an owner and had special rank, it was usually David who took notes and was constantly running back and forth to the copier to ensure that everything was circulated.

"It was very exciting to be part of this," according to Roxie Poliak, a Great Clips franchisee whose long, successful career with the company began when she was hired as a stylist at Silver Bell. "I was young and full of energy. The whole concept was new and seemed to offer a wonderful opportunity to those of us starting on the ground floor. We were made to feel like pioneers of something great. David was the personality of Super Clips, and he made it fun. Our motto was, "We work hard and we play hard." We often worked long into the evenings to get the training materials just right. Looking back, it was quite an adventure."

Experimentation never stopped. Steve even tried installing a tanning bed inside the Silver Bell salon. The idea misfired. Although the stylists enjoyed using it during their breaks, the customers had no interest. That ended the tanning experiment!

Marybeth Callahan, who likewise began a rewarding career at the company as a part-time stylist at Silver Bell and went on to become a successful franchisee, recalls the pressure of always having the bosses so near. She had an intimidating encounter one day when Steve came to her for a haircut. Whether it was just his nature or a way to test her, he sat down in the chair and said, "I want one-sixteenth of an inch off the sides, one-eighth of an inch off the top, and one-quarter of an inch off the back." Not knowing whether he was serious, she nervously began cutting. As Marybeth laughingly remembers, "All of a sudden he picks a piece of hair off his lap and complained, 'This is more than one-quarter of an inch!' I replied, 'Well, the last haircut you had was so crooked that I had to even it up.' It must have worked because he didn't say another word."

Until then, Steve and David had planned to open two salons and then put future expansion on hold until they could assess the situation. However, even before the opening of the second salon at Silver Bell, they were approached by a gentleman who owned two salons in the Twin Cities area that were operated as franchises of a chain of upscale salons based in Texas. Wanting to get out of what for him was a terrible investment, he told Steve and David, "We are literally drowning in red ink. If you just take over my leases, I'll cancel my franchises and give you both salons and everything in them. All I want is out."

Steve and David couldn't resist. They figured that the equipment alone was worth as much as $50,000 and the locations were good. They converted the first salon immediately, complete with a new sign and the hoisting of their signature sails. It opened as their third Super Clips on November 11, 1982—their third salon in less than two months! Once again the "fifty free haircuts" promotion clicked, and salon number three was off and running. Meanwhile, Steve had found a location that intrigued him. It was on France Avenue in one of the most affluent neighborhoods in the Twin Cities. Would these upper-income people come in for a $6 haircut when they were accustomed to paying $20 or $30? There was only one way to find out. However, developing this location as well as any others would have to be put on hold. Capital was tight, or, to be more accurate, the founders of this skyrocketing enterprise were now flat-out broke!

CHAPTER 10

The First Outside Investors

Even though the openings of the first three salons exceeded their wildest dreams, Steve and David were stymied for lack of funds. Building out new locations was expensive; their original stake was depleted, and the profits from the first salons were insufficient to finance more growth. They didn't have the credit worthiness for banks and, in any event, the prevailing commercial interest rates would strangle them. By default, they turned to friends and relatives.

David was the first to strike pay dirt. During a dinner with his late wife's family, he tried out his pitch on his two brothers-in-law, Tom and Pete Schneider. He enthusiastically described the success of the first three openings, but confessed to the lack of funds needed to capitalize on this early success. When he finished, he sat back and put the question directly to Tom and Pete: "Are you guys interested in buying in? We only need $16,000."

Both brothers-in-law were intrigued by the idea, but they likewise didn't have that kind of money. They discussed David's proposal with others who gave no encouragement whatsoever. One of Tom's friends, a financial planner, offered this advice: "Don't even *think* about doing this! It's the dumbest idea I ever heard."

Despite the bad reception they were getting, the Schneider brothers were not dissuaded. They had known David for the many years since he had begun dating their sister, Mary Alice. They genuinely liked and respected him, and they had confidence that he would turn his dreams into reality. As Tom put it, "There was almost a magic with David. Everything he touched seemed to work." Pete agreed. Both bothers knew that David, having grown up on a farm, had a strong work ethic and a fierce determination. To him, failure was simply not an option. They later met Steve, and they liked what they saw. That settled it.

After being turned down by a bank, the brothers, as a last resort, went to their father, Urban Schneider. Probably more out of familial loyalty than business considerations, the elder Schneider loaned each of his sons $8,000. For their $16,000, the brothers together took a 50 percent non-operating interest in the company's fourth salon in December 1982. It was on France Avenue in the upscale neighborhood that Steve had targeted.

Tom and Pete were the first outside investors in the new venture, even though their interest was in only one salon and, as non-operating partners, they had no managerial or other responsibilities. They would keep their jobs—Tom as an architect and Pete as an insurance agent—and leave the haircare business to Steve and David. Like the three before it, that one salon was successful and generated enough profits to enable the repayment of the entire $16,000 to Tom and Pete in a

Pioneer franchisees Pete and Tom Schneider were the first outside investors in Super Clips USA. They are pictured here in the mid-1990s with a staff member at their France Avenue salon in the Twin Cities.

matter of months, with which they repaid their father. They retained their 50 percent silent interest in the salon but made only rare appearances—a situation that delighted them.

CHAPTER 11

Exit Super Clips—Enter Great Clips

In December 1982, two lawyers representing the California Supercuts paid a visit to Steve Lemmon. They explained that Supercuts was preparing a lawsuit against Super Clips, Ltd. of Canada. The case would allege trademark infringement and commercial misappropriation of trade practices, arising out of James Tucker's duplication of the Supercuts salons he had first seen in California.

The lawyers inspected the Minnesota salons opened by Steve and David, and concluded that the décor was significantly different from that of Supercuts. If Steve and David would simply change the name of their salons, the lawyers said, they would be in the clear. Steve wasn't sure what to do, but the decision became obvious when he called the Tuckers in Toronto. Perhaps due to the threatened lawsuit, they told him that they were planning to change their name to First Choice Haircutters. Furthermore, they said, they had abandoned the idea to franchise in the United States.

This was good news for Steve and David. The success of their first four salons convinced them that they didn't need a franchise from the Canadians. Better yet, for the past few months they had been putting franchise fees and royalties into escrow in anticipation of the Super Clips franchise, but now they could close the escrow and use the money for their own business—and they needed it!

Now, what to do about a new name? Steve and David did not want to discard the four existing signs that prominently displayed the name SUPERCLIPS. These signs were expensive, and buying new ones was out of the question on their budget. It occurred to them, however, that instead of *replacing* the signs they may be able to *change* them by substituting enough of the letters to keep the Supercuts lawyers at bay. Retaining "CLIPS" was a must because of the sailing motif, so the focus was on replacing "SUPER" with another five-letter word that would fit in its place.

After tossing suggestions back and forth, one of them suggested "GREATCLIPS." Eureka! They both liked the way it sounded and the image it created. It was as easy as that! Steve filed a name change with the

Exterior façade following removal of the "Super" portion of the signage in 1983.

Minnesota Secretary of State's office, and on February 12, 1983, the company name was officially changed from Super Clips USA, Inc. to Greatclips, Inc. The four signs were immediately changed to GREATCLIPS.

There is an anomaly in the name that, to this day, no one can fully explain. While the original *corporate* name had Super Clips as two words, the signage had SUPERCLIPS as one word. When the corporate name was changed to Greatclips, Inc., it was presumably to be consistent with the signs that had ten letters with no space. However, some time in late 1983, the new signs showed GREAT CLIPS as two words, and the older signs were likewise changed over time. Yet, it wasn't until 1991 that the corporate name was officially changed to Great Clips, Inc., separating the two words to match the signs. (In the interest of convenience, the company will hereafter be referred to as Great Clips, even during the time when the official name was Greatclips.)

CHAPTER 12

Thoughts of Franchising — and a Call to Ray Barton

Steve Lemmon and David Rubenzer were the ideal pioneers for starting Great Clips as a solid, locally-based chain. That was, in fact, all they had set out to do. As already noted, their ambitions were limited to developing about seventy-five salons, then retiring to live off the earnings. While the initial salons were intended to be company-owned, Steve and David knew that franchising was a definite possibility for future expansion.

In mid-1982, even before they opened their first salon at the university, Steve had called Ray Barton who had been a Barbers franchisee. Ray was a CPA, and Steve knew that registering to sell franchises required a certified audit. Further, Ray had worked with a franchising company, Century 21 Real Estate, and his insight from the franchisor's point of view would be invaluable. In Steve's mind, Ray would be an ideal employee. He could handle the company's accounting and, at the same time, investigate the pros and cons of franchising.

But Ray Barton had other attributes beyond his work experience that made him uniquely qualified for the challenges that lay ahead.

A man of average size, Ray's energy and ambition are without limit. His methodical and detailed approach to any problem is complemented by persistence (or stubbornness, depending on the judge), and once he decides to take a risk he'll do so fearlessly. He is not easily distracted by day-to-day pressures or annoyances. A pleasant, polite, and soft-spoken gentleman, Ray could get feisty when necessary—a trait he inherited from his mother, Alice. A psychologist would probably classify him as a "Type A," if only because he never walks slowly and never sits back in a chair.

Hard work was no stranger to Ray Barton. Having grown up in near-poverty in Des Moines, Iowa, he attended Catholic elementary school where the nuns taught him that he could achieve his dreams of success through hard work and education. He took that lesson seriously. While the other kids were enjoying recess, Ray washed dishes to pay for the hot lunches his parents could not afford.

The habit of working for what he wanted became part of his DNA. If he wanted a baseball mitt or bicycle, he knew he'd have to earn the money to pay for it. So, from the age of ten, and without complaint, he began delivering newspapers twice a day, seven days a week, and mowed grass in the summer and shoveled snow in the winter.

A youth so dedicated to working for what he got could hardly be expected to have a career in the arts, so when Ray went to college, he studied accounting—a field more in line with his ambitions to move up the economic ladder.

He graduated from San Diego State in December, 1972 with a bachelor's degree in accounting, went on to pass the CPA exam, and began a five-year stint with the Alexander Grant Company in Minneapolis. He and his co-workers would talk about eventually having their own businesses, and his pet model was McDonald's which in 1974, after barely fifteen years in business, had a higher market capital than U.S. Steel. McDonald's franchising success was based on giving good value for a low price, providing convenience, being consistent, and giving the public what they wanted—a simple formula that became a beacon for Ray in the years to come. In later years, Ray would buy many copies of two books about the fast food chain, *Grinding it Out: The Making of McDonald's* and *McDonald's: Behind the Arches*, and give them to colleagues.

In 1978, Ray was introduced into the world of franchising when he became treasurer of a regional franchisee for Century 21 Real Estate. That company oversaw more than 150 Century 21 franchises in four north central states. The job provided a unique vantage point from which to see the challenges—and opportunities—of both the franchisor and franchisee. It provided valuable learning for all that followed.

His earlier dedication to working hard and saving continued. Once in the workforce, Ray began investing every extra dime in residential rental properties—houses and duplexes. There were often months when he spent far more than he brought in, but he was adept at the discipline of delayed gratification. He could be patient and grit his teeth as long as he could see a financial pay-off down the road.

On St. Patrick's Day in 1978, a fire caused substantial damage to one of Ray's duplexes. Repairs were completed in July, and that's when a new tenant arrived in the person of Mary Lou Stevens. Ray was smitten, and the feeling was mutual. Courtship and then marriage and a family followed, and to this day Ray calls the fire his "lucky" St. Patrick's Day fire.

In late 1980, while still with Century 21, Ray decided to invest in a Barbers franchise but was told that only stylists would be qualified to be franchisees. Ironically, Mary Lou was a salesperson for Wallace Business Forms, and The Barbers was one of her customers. When she later learned that The Barbers was considering changing its policy to allow non-stylists to become franchisees, she ran home to tell Ray and Ray re-applied. He was accepted and became their first "test case" franchisee without prior haircare experience.

Ray didn't give up his "day job" and he didn't personally manage the salon. His salon opened on February 2, 1981, an easy day for him and Mary Lou to remember because their daughter Annie was born the same day, joining Katie and Jason—Katie was Mary Lou's daughter and Jason was Ray's son from their former marriages.

After observing the operation, Ray became convinced that having haircare experience was unnecessary for owning and operating a salon. He figured that The Barbers could expand faster by seeking more franchisees that had no haircare background, and he tried to sell the idea to Joe Francis through a detailed presentation. Joe nixed the idea; he was not persuaded that it was a good general strategy to have inexperienced franchisees. Perhaps Joe was right in this case. It turned out that Ray, his test case, wasn't able to make a go of his Barbers franchise; it wasn't long before he cried "uncle" and sold it back to the company.

Although Ray's experience with The Barbers was short-lived, it fortuitously brought him into contact with Steve Lemmon—and that changed both their lives forever.

CHAPTER 13

The Third Owner

When Steve Lemmon made that first call to Ray Barton to ask him to come to work at Great Clips, he was turned down. Ray had recently left his Century 21 job and had just taken a new position with Questex Energy, an oil and gas exploration company. He had no interest in leaving.

The remarkable success of the first salons convinced Steve that they had a concept that they could franchise. So he once again called Ray whose franchise and accounting experience was just what they needed to explore that path. He made that second call in the fall of 1982, about the time the third salon was opening.

This time Ray showed a sudden interest. What Steve didn't know, and Ray didn't mention, was that Ray was about to lose his job at Questex. The company was in trouble because of a drop in the price of oil, just as Steve's gold mine earlier had suffered from a drop in the price of gold. As Ray tells the story, "I can laugh about it today, but I was a three-time loser. I failed as a Barbers franchisee, I was demoted at Century 21 and quit, and I got fired at Questex—all within six months! The only reason I ever got involved with Great Clips was because I was out of work and needed a job."

In discussing the job offer, Ray made it clear to David and Steve that he would take the job only if the company was getting into franchising, a business concept he thoroughly understood. They agreed to that condition, but Ray believes that they weren't as fully committed to the concept as he was at the time. He accepted the offer and began work in late 1982; his job description was to handle the books and prepare whatever was needed to start franchising.

Almost immediately he became even more convinced that franchising was perfect for the Great Clips concept. It had many characteristics that would appeal to potential franchisees: It was not a complicated business that would be hard to understand; it didn't require nearly as much start-up capital as, say, a fast food restaurant with its grills, fryers, ovens, ice-makers, plumbing, and ductwork; there would be no inventory or seasonality concerns; the franchisee would not have to find and train stylists—that would be the responsibility of the franchisor; and the franchisee would not have to give up his or her existing career. From the company's point of view, franchising provided the means to open outlets with the franchisees' money, and the market for potential franchisees was broad.

As we will see, not requiring close hands-on management from the franchisee would, over the next several years, become a serious issue—both within the company and with the franchisees.

From his stint at Century 21, and from observing successful companies such as McDonald's, Ray could see that simplicity and consistency of operations were the keys to successful franchising and a strong brand. Nothing has happened to change his mind, and to this day he still calls it the "Power of Consistency."

Ray immediately began the process of getting the books in order. He also started the documentation for all of the filings that would be required to franchise salons to others. These filings were embodied in a Uniform Franchise Offering Circular (UFOC) mandated by the Federal Trade Commission as well as by many states in which franchises would be offered for sale. As noted earlier, Minnesota was such a state. The UFOC is now called the Franchise Disclosure Document (FDD).

It was during this time that the company name was officially changed from Super Clips USA, Inc. to Great Clips, Inc.

The more Ray delved into the franchising opportunity, the more his enthusiasm infected Steve. What had been an interesting possibility now became a goal not to be denied. Steve was also observing Ray's skills, creativity, and work ethic, and he knew that the future of the business would be brighter if Ray were more than a hired hand. To that end, in early 1983 Steve invited Ray to become a third owner of the business.

Ray's first step in deciding whether to buy in was to run the idea past his lawyer, recalling that when he had sold his Barbers' franchise back to the company he had agreed to a limited non-compete clause. Under no circumstances, Ray told the lawyer, would he violate the non-compete clause, both as a matter of law and a matter of honor. He also told the lawyer that he didn't have any money, but might be able to borrow against the duplexes he owned.

The lawyer leaned back and shook his head. "Let me get this straight," he asked. "You want to hock everything you own to invest in a new, struggling business in which you will have a minority position, and by doing so, you will be opening yourself up to the possibility of a lawsuit from The Barbers. Do I have that right?"

Ray nodded sheepishly, leading the lawyer to give the same assessment that the Schneider brothers previously heard from *their* experts: *This is a dumb idea! Don't do it.*

Although he respected the advice, Ray wasn't about to give up on Steve's offer. He had already spent a few months familiarizing himself with the numbers, and all he could see was the huge potential that he knew was out there waiting for him. What he wanted now was a customer's perspective. He and Mary Lou were living near the France Avenue salon, so he sent Mary Lou over there to get haircuts for Katie and Jason, their two older children. She carried out the mission and was definitely impressed with what she saw.

"I was absolutely blown away," Mary Lou reflects. "The salon looked great, the kids loved it, and only $6 for a haircut! We just walked in without an appointment, were warmly greeted, and the kids got great haircuts. I even went back two days later and got my own hair cut. When Ray first told me about these places I thought he was crazy, but after that first visit I was sold."

An interesting footnote to this story is that the two stylists who cut the Bartons' kids' hair that day were Ruth Ann Grimsley and Roxie Poliak, each of whom today owns multiple Great Clips salons!

Mary Lou's endorsement was all Ray needed to hear! He called Steve to confirm his interest in moving forward, but a "minor obstacle" presented itself: *David had not yet agreed to have Ray join the ownership team!*

Actually, David and Ray hardly knew each other at the time. When Ray was a Barbers franchisee, he had little contact with David; and, since Ray had been working for Great Clips, David was busy with the training and haircutting side of the business while Ray had been working on the financial details with Steve. Ultimately, Steve persuaded David to accept Ray as an owner because of his background in franchising. Steve again explained to David how franchising was the ideal vehicle for their expansion and why Ray was the guy who could make it happen. As for Ray, he had no interest in being a minority owner of a few salons in Minnesota. His vision saw Great Clips as a national brand, and franchising was the way to get there.

David was soon on board with both decisions—franchising and having Ray as a co-owner—and Ray joined the team. Realizing that Ray would be the "face" of the company to potential franchisees and investors, it was agreed that he would have the title of chief executive officer, with Steve as president and David as executive vice president.

Ray's investment to become an owner of the business was a strange one indeed. It's worthwhile to take a look at the details of that investment. It's not only interesting, but it also provides an insight into the different ways the three owners approached the business. And that, in turn, serves as a preview of greater differences that would soon overshadow—and all but destroy—their relationship.

First, Ray paid a grand total of only $505 to buy 505 shares of company stock. With Steve giving up a few shares, each of the three owners now held 505 shares, and each had an equal one-third ownership of the company.

For the rest of his "investment," Ray agreed to pledge some of his rental properties to secure two loans for a total of $35,000—$20,000 in the form of a line of credit for the company and $15,000 which he would borrow and then personally re-lend to the company. (David also agreed to loan the company $15,000.) But where could Ray raise $35,000?

From his days with Century 21, Ray remembered Cindy Darling, vice president for commercial loans at Park National Bank. They had belonged to the same breakfast club. Hoping she might be able to provide the line of credit, he called her to arrange a meeting. "What I remember most," Cindy said, "was his enthusiasm and his confidence in the company's future. That made it easy to believe in him and enabled the loan, even though the company didn't have a track record." She added: "And as a CPA, he presented his case very carefully and concisely, just as he always has."

The relationship with Park National Bank endured, and the bank thereafter increased the line of credit from $20,000 to $200,000. Furthermore, the bank later financed about thirty franchisees in developing their own salons. This proved to be a major factor in the success of the company and its franchisees.

Of the three owners, it was Ray who maintained the financial relationship with Park National. The bank trusted his figures and projections, and his penchant for never over-promising. Banks will often say that they don't deal with *companies*, they deal with *people*, and to Park National Ray Barton was Great Clips.

Steve Lemmon and David Rubenzer, on the other hand, had little inter-action with Park National. Steve, in fact, had no interest in meeting with Cindy or anyone else at the bank. And even though Ray risked his personal real estate holdings to secure the loan, Steve wouldn't share even his personal financial statements with the bank. "Steve didn't seem to understand that the bank and the company were on the same side." Cindy said. "Sure, we wanted our loan paid back, but we also wanted the company to succeed and grow as Ray had envisioned. That would be in our interest as well as theirs."

CHAPTER 14

Joe Francis Strikes Again!

Ray's lawyer's concerns about Joe Francis and The Barbers were well founded.

Ray, David, and Steve had all been involved with The Barbers. Thus, all three of the owners of Great Clips were directly or indirectly bound by non-compete agreements not to open any salons for two years within a specified radius of any of their past or present Barbers salons. Ray remembers how careful they were to comply with those restrictions. "We had a map with pins at the locations of our Barbers salons. Mine had been in downtown St. Paul, and David's and Steve's wife's were in Burnsville. We drew circles around each location to show the restricted area and vowed not to put a Great Clips salon within any of those circles for two years. There was no way we would violate those agreements."

Despite their compliance with the non-compete agreements, Joe Francis wasn't going to sit back and calmly watch these three pirates open salons in "his" market. He had assumed that his earlier preemptive strike with Cost Cutters would be enough to thwart the ambitions of these pests, but apparently they had not learned their lesson! *They're actually going ahead with their plans to compete head-to-head with me. They have to be stopped!*

The mileage limitations in the non-compete agreements meant nothing to Joe Francis. Foregoing the niceties of pre-litigation negotiations, he filed suit against Great Clips and his former franchisees without any notice. Even though no Great Clips salons had been opened within any of the restricted territories, the suit alleged that Steve, Ray, and David had developed their new venture by using "trade secrets" and other proprietary or confidential information presumably stolen from The Barbers. The suit not only asked for money damages and legal fees, *it also actually sought to put Great Clips out of business.*

It fell upon Ray to retain a lawyer to defend them. For this, he needed a skilled trial lawyer as opposed to a business lawyer who seldom, if ever, saw the inside of a courtroom. After several inquiries and interviews, he retained

Jeff Keyes who was one of those rare trial lawyers whose legal advice was blended with good business judgment.

"I never thought that The Barbers had much of a case," Jeff Keyes recalls. "I investigated the facts carefully and saw nothing close to a misuse of confidential information. But rather than call Joe Francis and his lawyers to discuss it, we put up a vigorous defense to let them know that these guys weren't going to fold. Sure enough, Francis never pushed back, and the case was put on the back burner. No significant rulings were made, and the case was finally dismissed. We never heard another word from Joe Francis."

There was one silver lining to the litigation. Jeff Keyes went on to do outstanding legal work for Great Clips, giving valuable counsel enabling the company to avoid or prevail in sensitive skirmishes over the years. His services to Great Clips continued until 2008 when he was appointed as a United States Magistrate Judge.

CHAPTER 15

Paperwork

By the spring of 1983, shortly after Ray bought into the company, he had completed and filed a Uniform Franchise Offering Circular (UFOC) and all of the other documents required for the sale of franchises. Getting to that point had been hard work as well as an exercise in creativity.

Typically, legal fees for preparing these documents and getting clearance from the Federal Trade Commission and the various state regulatory agencies, even for a small company, could easily run to $75,000, and it often cost much more than that. This kind of expense was out of the question for this new enterprise, so Ray and Steve improvised.

Steve would run back and forth to the Secretary of State's office in St. Paul with sacks of quarters to make copies of all of the filings by other franchisors. He already had the filings from Supercuts, The Barbers, and Century 21, and was now spending hours at a 25-cents-per-page copy machine duplicating the UFOCs from a variety of other franchisors that could be helpful. Then he would bring back the still-warm copies to Ray who would cut, paste, and edit various parts and pieces into a document that fit for Great Clips.

There was a wide variance among franchisors regarding initial franchise fees, service fees (commonly called royalties), advertising or marketing fees, and so on. Picking and choosing the right fees was critical because the term of a franchise agreement might be anywhere from five to twenty years, and therefore the numbers were binding (on both sides) for several years. Service fees were generally around 6 percent of sales, so it was an easy decision for Great Clips to arrive at that number.

Selecting an advertising fee was a little more challenging. At first, Ray planned to use 2 percent of sales as the number because that's what Century 21 used, but then he saw that Supercuts charged 5 percent. "I just thought that if they had a 5 percent advertising contribution, then we should have 5 percent too," he said. "It was one of those things that you don't know for sure what's right at that particular moment, so you more or less guess. But this was about the luckiest guess I ever made. Using the 5 percent number has produced a very significant advertising fund, and it's been a powerful tool for promoting our brand."

The 6 percent service fee and 5 percent advertising contribution have remained constant at Great Clips over the years, as has the ten-year initial franchise term. However, the franchise fee, initially set at $10,000, has varied, as have renewal and transfer fees that started at $500.

To put the final touches on the UFOC, Ray turned to Bob Zalk, a lawyer who did work on the Century 21 documents. Bob made some minor edits here and there, corrected some of Ray's legalese, and gave his official "blessing" to the document. The entire process had cost the company $5,500, a fraction of what it would have cost if they hadn't done so much of it themselves, and the three months it took them was far less than it ordinarily takes.

According to the first Great Clips filings in 1983, the entire cost for a franchisee to open a salon, including all fees, build-out, working capital, pre-marketing, and a grand opening, ranged from $28,700 to $43,400!

Even today, Great Clips has managed to dodge the long delays and the large legal fees paid by most franchising companies for these documents. In 1988, the company hired Carolyn Bastick who, over the ensuing years, has filled many critical positions. Early in her

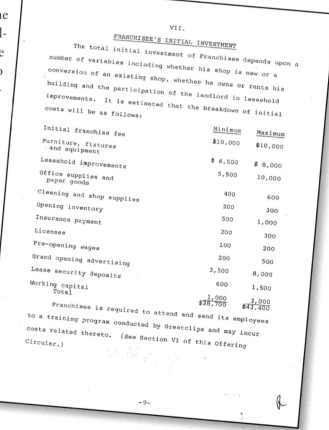

VII.

FRANCHISEE'S INITIAL INVESTMENT

The total initial investment of Franchisee depends upon a number of variables including whether his shop is new or a conversion of an existing shop, whether he owns or rents his building and the participation of the landlord in leasehold improvements. It is estimated that the breakdown of initial costs will be as follows:

	Minimum	Maximum
Initial franchise fee	$10,000	$10,000
Furniture, fixtures and equipment	$ 6,500	$ 8,000
Leasehold improvements	5,500	10,000
Office supplies and paper goods	400	600
Cleaning and shop supplies	200	300
Opening inventory	500	1,000
Insurance payment	200	300
Licenses	100	200
Pre-opening wages	200	500
Grand opening advertising	3,500	8,000
Lease security deposits	600	1,500
Working capital	1,000	3,000
Total	$28,700	$43,400

Franchisee is required to attend and send its employees to a training program conducted by Greatclips and may incur costs related thereto. (See Section VI of this Offering Circular.)

-9-

Initial Investment page from Great Clips, Inc.'s first Uniform Franchise Offering Circular (UFOC)—May 1983.

career, she convinced Ray that she could save the company time and money if he allowed her to handle the preparing and filing of the UFOC without outside experts—a heavy responsibility for a young lady with no legal training. To this day, Carolyn still reviews all of the disclosure documents before they are finally approved for filing by Sandra Anderson, Great Clips' chief legal officer.

As already noted, the Uniform Franchise Offering Circular (UFOC) is now called the Franchise Disclosure Document (FDD).

It was March 1983, and Great Clips was now ready to franchise!

PART THREE

Franchising and Growing Pains

CHAPTER 16

The First Franchisee

The process for selecting franchisees is often complex—and always critical—and it varies from company to company. Obviously, a proven, successful franchise system will be in high demand, and the standards for selection may therefore be very high. By contrast, a new franchisor with an unknown reputation will be tempted to take any franchisee that walks in the door, but that is a temptation that must be resisted. It can take ten outstanding franchisees to offset the damage done by one bad choice.

Some franchisors require that the franchisee has experience in the particular industry. Some don't. Some require that the franchisee be intimately involved in the day-to-day operations. Some don't. When deciding on the criteria for Great Clips franchisees, Steve and David were in lockstep on these two issues. They would not require that franchisees have haircare experience, and they would not require daily involvement in the operations of the salon. In fact—and this would surprise anyone familiar with franchising —*they actually preferred that their franchisees have no background in haircare and stay as far away from the salon as possible!*

Steve and David's rationale was straightforward. Great Clips, as franchisor, would train the stylists and oversee the operations, mostly through the franchisee's own managers who would be hired and trained by Great Clips. The franchisee's presence would at best be unnecessary and at worst a distraction. Stated another way, as Steve and David saw it, the franchisee was needed only for their capital and not for their managerial expertise. They were to be passive investors only; Great Clips would run the salons.

Ray was not entirely in accord with Steve and David. While he accepted the idea that a franchisee need not have previous haircare experience—a point he tried to make with Joe Francis of The Barbers—he definitely believed that the franchisee should be more involved with the day-to-day operations. He saw the value of "hands-on" franchisees at Century 21, and, in any event, it just seemed right that a franchisee with a hard-earned personal investment in the salon should have a say in the daily management.

Despite Ray's tendency to be persistent when he thinks he's right, he reluctantly went along with Steve and David on this issue. In fact, he then persuaded them to accept his choice for the first franchisee: his wife, Mary Lou, and their close friends, Roger and Marylu Ledebuhr.

Roger had previously been a Century 21 franchisee in Bismarck, North Dakota, but in 1979 he sold his franchise and moved to the Twin Cities to work in the Century 21 regional office. His friendship with Ray was a warm one, but marked with a lot of ribbing—mostly from Ray. For example, one day Roger walked into a Century 21 meeting proudly wearing a new suit with a bold, plaid pattern, prompting Ray to ask, "What did you do, kill a couch?"

Embarrassed by the ensuing laughter, Roger went home for lunch and changed to a different suit. He handed the plaid one to his wife, Marylu, saying, "Here, take this to Goodwill." As it happened, someone from Roger's church bought the suit and wore it on Sundays, a grim reminder of Ray's barb.

The friendship between the Bartons and Ledebuhrs grew even closer over the years and included their children who were of the same ages. The families even vacationed together.

Although Ray convinced Steve and David to accept Mary Lou and the Ledebuhrs as franchisees, he had not yet convinced *them*! But he was determined that they would own the very first Great Clips franchise, and he began his pitch in a highly unorthodox way. He knew from their close association that Roger regularly went to bed fairly early and was nearly always asleep before 10:00 p.m. Waiting until a little later than that, Ray started making nightly calls to Roger, waking him with the same question: "Good evening, Roger, would you like to buy a Great Clips franchise?" Roger had no interest whatsoever. After doing this several times, Ray added a new element: "Would you do it if Mary Lou became your partner? If you say 'yes' I'll stop calling you."

Without missing a beat, Roger reacted to the new twist. "Okay, we'll do it if she will. Now let me go back to sleep."

The only remaining problem was that Mary Lou hadn't agreed to it either! "I had no thoughts of becoming a franchisee," she said. "I had a full-time job and liked it. But Ray was using Roger to persuade me to agree, and later I learned that he had used me to persuade Roger to agree. Anyway, Ray kept talking up the potential and when he promised that I wouldn't have to give up my job, I gave in. And that was that."

The first Great Clips franchisees Mary Lou Barton, Marylu Ledebuhr, and Roger Ledebuhr (not pictured) open the first franchised salon in Brooklyn Center, Minnesota, on July 16, 1983.

To raise the money needed to buy the franchise and build out the salon, the Bartons put a second mortgage on another duplex and the Ledebuhrs refinanced their home. Their salon, the first *franchised* Great Clips salon, opened for business on July 16, 1983, in the Minneapolis suburb of Brooklyn Center.

Mary Lou and the Ledebuhrs have remained Great Clips franchisees to this day. *In fact, in 2011, the Ledebuhrs opened the 3,000th Great Clips salon.*

CHAPTER 17

Family + Friends = Franchisees

Although Great Clips opened four salons during its first few months of existence, granting a franchise to Mary Lou Barton and the Ledebuhrs in mid-1983 had the effect of injecting a growth hormone. By the end of 1986, only three-and-a-half years later, there were 132 Great Clips salons, most of them franchised—a growth rate of about three salons per month! Even more amazing, the growth extended far beyond the Twin Cities, including Atlanta, Tampa, and Orlando to the east, Denver and Phoenix in the west, and Des Moines, Kansas City, Omaha, and Indianapolis in the central part of the country.

However, while the expansion in those first few years seems extraordinary *looking back*, it was in fact an arduous, step-by-step process marked by hard work, disappointments, and even mistakes. Any new franchising company has difficulty finding and then persuading franchisees to make the leap of faith. Great Clips was hardly a household name at the time, and no one had even heard of the company in most of its new markets. But Steve, David, and Ray found that they could kick-start their franchise sales by continuing to tap into two rich sources—family and friends.

Soon after Mary Lou and the Ledebuhrs became franchisees, Steve convinced his parents, Howard and Sally, to take a franchise in the northern Twin Cities suburb of Anoka. His lawyer, Bob Levine, became one of the early franchisees and even served on the Great Clips Board of Directors for a short time.

In those early years, the company was using Whitney Peyton, a commercial real estate agent, to find locations, and he was so impressed with what he saw that he convinced his wife, Nancy, to become a franchisee. It wasn't a problem that Nancy was pregnant and otherwise employed at the time, because franchises were being sold as passive investments.

Shortly thereafter, Steve formed a partnership with his friend Tim Lawless and several other investors to open salons in Indianapolis where Great Clips was then offering franchises.

David and Mary Lou Barton were likewise busy bringing franchisees into the system. One night, David bumped into a couple of friends, Mike and Kris Barcelow, at a TGIF restaurant, and made a spur-of-the-moment pitch: "All you have to do is give us a check, and we'll take care of everything else." Mike soon teamed up with Nathalia Ciresi (now Nathalia Faribault), a friend of Mary Lou and Ray, and together they opened a salon in the Twin Cities in 1984. The following year, Mike's brother Kris opened a salon in St. Louis.

Dee Tibbetts, one of David's customers, also took the bait. At first, she rejected the idea out of hand, claiming she knew nothing about business. David made the same assurance he made to the Barcelows: "Don't worry, we'll handle everything." Dee moved to Colorado, opened a salon in the Denver market, and took a job as a ski instructor at Copper Mountain. Today she owns several Great Clips salons.

Tom and Pete Schneider, David's brothers-in-law, didn't need any convincing. They were happily collecting checks from the France Avenue salon where they were the first outside investors, and they wanted more! They later bought total ownership of the France Avenue salon from the company and in addition opened other franchises in Minneapolis, Omaha, and Des Moines.

The Schneider brothers were also good salesmen for the company. Through them another of their brothers-in-law, Mike Testa, became a franchisee and bought from the company the original Great Clips salon located at the University of Minnesota.

Subsequently, Pete Schneider was boasting about his Great Clips investments to one of his insurance company clients, Bill Divine. Bill, who worked at a glass company, was impressed with the numbers. "I looked at it and I'm thinking, 'I don't know anything about the hair business.' But then I realized it's a service business, just like the glass business, and that I know." He bought a franchise and, in his words, "It went very well." Indeed it did! Bill went on to open several successful salons.

When it came to selling franchises to family, Ray likewise played his part. Soon after Mary Lou and the Ledebuhrs opened the first franchised salon, Ray sold another franchise in Minneapolis to Mary Lou's brother, Pat Stevens. Pat later opened more salons and eventually became a leader of the Great Clips community of franchisees.

Ray's sister, Regina Finkelstein, having great confidence in her brother, wanted to get in on the game. When she asked to buy a franchise, Ray's initial reply was curt: "Absolutely not!" He was concerned about his sister taking such a risk. But Regina, having the Barton "persistence gene," would not be deterred. She persuaded their mother, Alice Barton, to be partners with her and her husband, Steve. Ray, outnumbered and knowing his mother's previous business experience, yielded; they opened their first franchise in Minnetonka, a well-to-do suburb west of Minneapolis.

Of course, the three owners understood the risks of relatives becoming franchisees, and they were careful never to "over promise." Ray said to them, "If this doesn't work out, I hope you'll still have me over for Thanksgiving dinner."

Although by 1984 Great Clips finally had "outsiders" who were franchisees—people who were neither family nor friends—with so many friends and family on board, the three owners wisely adopted two policies to ensure fairness and to avoid even an appearance of favoritism.

The first policy: No deals! No relative, friend, or stranger was allowed to negotiate any part of the arrangement. The fees and franchise terms were the same for *everyone*, and there was no wavering from this rule. There were unquestionably times when special circumstances seemed to warrant an exception, but there was no yielding on this point. While the three owners could be miles apart on many issues, none of the three ever compromised his ethics or reputation for fair dealing. When specific terms seemed wrong, unfair, or obsolete, they would be addressed when the next UFOC was filed, and changes would be made going forward.

The second policy: The creation of a real estate priority list for each market. Every existing or new franchisee wanted the best sites. To remove competition and possible arguments over site selection, franchisees were given priority based on the date they signed their franchise agreements. Generally, Great Clips would find the sites for the franchisees, and when one was available it would be offered to the first franchisee on the priority list. Being a relative or a friend had nothing to do with it. If the first franchisee on the list turned it down, it would be offered to the next one. The franchisee accepting the site would then be free to enter into the lease with the landlord; and, if they couldn't agree on the final terms, or if the franchisee was not acceptable to the landlord, the next one on the list would be given the opportunity for the site.

Securing sites often presented a dilemma. If Great Clips found a good site, the landlord might be reluctant to take it off the market and "hold" it for a franchisee whose identity and credit he didn't yet know. But if the site *wasn't* taken off the market, there was a good chance that it would be gone by the time a franchisee agreed to the site and came to terms with the landlord. To address this, Great Clips often found itself in a hectic three-way mating dance—the company racing back and forth between the landlord and franchisee trying to get them together before another tenant showed up, with the company keeping one or two more franchisees waiting in the wings.

Franchisees did have the option of finding their own sites, provided the corporate office agreed to the sites. This gave the enthusiastic franchisee an opportunity to bypass the waiting list. A case in point was Pat Stevens. When Pat was ready to open his first salon, he discovered that he had the sixth position on the real estate priority list. Not having the patience to wait, he took steps to find his own location.

Having worked with chemically dependent teenagers, he knew many of the neighborhoods in and around the Twin Cities, and he soon focused on the fast-growing city of Blaine. He found a promising location there, but when he presented it for corporate consent he met resistance from Steve who wasn't impressed with the area. Company attorney Bob Levine then told Steve how Bob's own family, who had owned Penny's grocery stores, had a store in Blaine that was out-performing their others in the Twin Cities. When he mentioned that the Blaine store sold extraordinary quantities of meat and potatoes, Steve gave the go ahead, figuring that a neighborhood consuming so much meat and potatoes must be filled with solid, working class folks—an ideal market for Great Clips. As with so many others, the salon had success right from the beginning and produced enough profits to enable Pat to open additional salons. Indeed, that salon still operates at the same site and continues to be successful.

Pioneer franchisee Pat Stevens receiving the Franchisee of the Year Award from David Rubenzer and Ray Barton at the Great Clips Convention in 1991.

CHAPTER 18

The First Seeds of Dissension

It's only natural that the owners of a business will have differences in opinion from time to time, and when there are three owners, it will often come down to two against one. This was true in the early days of Great Clips, when the "two" were nearly always Steve and David and the "one" was Ray. Mary Lou Barton, Ray's wife, described it as Steve and David often "ganging up" on Ray, and that "while Ray didn't like to bring these problems home with him, I could see that he was frustrated and angry. As time went by, it seemed to be getting worse. Little everyday differences were becoming serious issues."

David, who usually shared Steve's thinking, was by far the more restrained of the two. The more assertive Steve was always ready to take off the gloves and go at it with bare knuckles. In fact, prize fighting may be an apt metaphor to describe the way the owners handled their differences—differences that were minor in the beginning but later grew in frequency and intensity. In one corner was Ray, sitting alone and calmly sizing things up; in the other corner was Steve, waiting for the bell with fire in his eyes. More often than not, David was in Steve's corner behind the ropes. When the bell rang, Steve scored points by throwing punches; Ray racked them up by bobbing and weaving.

The first visible point of difference had to do with the involvement of the franchisees in their salons. Steve and David, as already noted, did not want the franchisees meddling in the day-to-day operations. Their role was as passive investors while the company, as franchisor, oversaw training and management. Ray went along with this thinking at the beginning but, after seeing the situation through the eyes of his wife and the Ledebuhrs, realized that it was a mistake. To Ray, the franchisees had an investment and were therefore entitled to manage the business. Besides, they were on the scene and could therefore do it better. The more he lobbied for more franchisee involvement in those early years, the more adamant Steve and David became.

David Rubenzer, Steve Lemmon, and Ray Barton at a planning meeting in 1984.

Looking back, this difference of opinion seems minor. As the company grew there would be bigger disagreements over an endless array of subjects, almost always with the same "two against one" scenario. A recurring point of contention had to do with profit distributions. Ray preferred the strategy of reinvesting profits to grow the business for long-term rewards, and he was willing to sacrifice short-term distributions. David and Steve also had their eyes on the future, but they didn't share Ray's patience when it came to enjoying the fruits of their labors.

For example, as related in the following chapter, all three agreed that remote markets should be developed in a manner that required considerable investment. However, when these investments meant that profits could not be distributed, David and Steve shared a frustration that often rose to the surface.

But Ray was determined. He was convinced that building a *national* brand demanded a disciplined, specific, market-by-market development plan. This was expensive. Each market had to have a training center and offices for personnel to train stylists and support franchisees. Further, marketing costs would be incurred introducing the brand in the market, and travel and relocation expenses were unavoidable. Ray's strategy would wipe out the possibility of short-term distribution of profits to the owners but, he knew, would produce a national presence with greater returns for all of the owners in the long run.

The debate over balance of long-term distributions with long-term growth become even more heated some years later when there was talk of "going public"—offering Great Clips stock on the open market. The price of shares for an initial public offering (IPO) is generally based in large part on a multiple of earnings—the higher the earnings at the offering date, the higher the share price; and the higher the share price, the more money for the owners. When Steve and David decided that they wanted a public offering, they fought to increase *short-term* earnings by cutting back on the development costs of opening new markets. Ray, however, could not be dissuaded from his goal of *long-term* growth, and for that the development costs could not be avoided. As expected, Ray fought for his position—strenuously and constantly—and managed to keep the company private.

It was becoming obvious that the managerial differences extended far beyond day-to-day salon operations. The owners were battling over basic long-term goals and strategies. In time, these disagreements would attract the attention of Great Clips' employees, franchisees, and new board members.

Something would have to give, and eventually it did!

CHAPTER 19

Expansion Considerations

Expansion at Great Clips is a continuing process that has never slowed down and continues to evolve. Thus, an accurate chronology of the company would require a mention of expansion in every chapter, if not on every page. However, for the sake of clarity, a pause is in order to present a brief overview of the Great Clips philosophy of growth.

In the very broadest sense, there were two approaches to developing new markets—one was the "shotgun" and the other was the "rifle." With the shotgun approach, salons would be built wherever a franchisee chose; a franchisee who liked Texas might find a site in Dallas or San Antonio—it was his choice. Expansion would be influenced mainly by franchisee preference. The rifle approach, on the other hand, involved developing individual markets in a systematic sequence, and this was the approach that Great Clips chose.

Once a market was selected, the first step was to build a company-owned salon. This established a foothold in the market and served as a model to show potential franchisees what a Great Clips salon looked like and how it operated. This first salon would be large enough to house the market training center and be the base of operations for district managers and trainers (who at the beginning were often the same person). Having such a support system for future franchisees in the market proved to be invaluable, and it would not have happened if expansion followed the shotgun mode.

The second step was to open enough franchised salons to create market-wide recognition of the Great Clips brand, and to do so as quickly as the right sites and franchisees could be found. These new salons made cumulative contributions to the advertising fund, enabling significant advertising and marketing to produce still more brand recognition. In franchising circles, this synergy of many franchisees working together is referred to as "leveraging the brand," and, when reduced to its most basic terms, this is what franchising is all about.

The third step was to continue to add more salons until the market was fully developed. Defining "fully developed" is more an art than a science, and it may mean one thing to a franchisor and quite another to the franchisee. To illustrate, a franchisor might believe that one more salon in a market would make a lot of sense and generate more customers, but if even a few of those customers at that new salon had already been customers of another Great Clips salon, the owner of that other salon will cry "encroachment" or, more likely, "cannibalism." As will be explained later, *these charges of "stealing my customers," whether legitimate or imagined, create more grief, distrust, and litigation than any other single issue in franchising.*

At what point does a market—or an area within a market—become "saturated" so that further development should be put on hold? When has development reached the point of diminishing returns? That question will forever be asked and debated, but it never will be resolved with any certainty.

The Great Clips owners initially calculated that it would take a population of 75,000 to support one salon, since most of the population would be going to competing salons, barber shops, and beauty salons. So, based on the Twin Cities population of 2.1 million in 1980, it was assumed that the Minneapolis-St. Paul market could support a maximum of 28 salons. An interesting analysis—*except that thirty years later there were nearly 140 salons in that market!*

No franchisor has solved this puzzle of knowing how many customers it takes to support an outlet. Even McDonald's, with all of its experience in market development, continues to revise its thinking on how many people are needed to support one of its restaurants. Nearby population was the earliest determinant. Later consideration was expanded to nearby "stomachs"—not only residents—because so many patrons pass through rather than live in the area. This led to more restaurants in shopping areas, and the introduction of the drive-thru enabled profitable highway restaurants to be built in areas with virtually no population. Then too an entire "market" might consist of only one large office building—an area of much less than one square block—or a sports arena. Obviously, therefore, the number of residents in the area is not a reliable guide.

The rifle approach to expansion required discipline. A new company has to swallow hard when turning down a franchisee who has cash but wants to go to a market of his choice. A case in point: In May 1983, just months after the partners agreed to this approach, a man appeared at the Great Clips office in Minneapolis to inquire about a franchise. Ray and Steve drove him to see several salons, and the man said he was definitely interested. Excited, the two owners offered him a choice of the markets where Great Clips already had a presence—Minneapolis, Omaha, or Des Moines. He replied that he was interested only in having a salon in his Midwestern hometown, which was nowhere near any of those markets. Ray explained that wouldn't work—there would be no training facility and no support staff, and with only one salon there would not be enough marketing strength to leverage the brand. Being stubborn, the man sent Ray a tempting $10,000 check for the franchise fee the following week, again insisting on a salon in his hometown. Equally stubborn, Ray returned the check. He knew the young, struggling company could dearly use the $10,000 to meet payroll the following Friday, but he refused to abandon the strategy they had chosen for rifle expansion. Ray describes this as long-term thinking—choosing long-term success over short-term gain.

As explained earlier, the rifle approach was costly. Putting in the first company-owned salon large enough to accommodate a training center and offices for staff to train and support franchisees could easily cost several hundred thousand dollars. Additionally, there were hiring and relocation expenses, and a marketing campaign had to be launched before an advertising fund was up and going.

Steve and David had agreed with Ray that the rifle approach was the better route to follow—but only in principle. In practice, this approach meant reinvesting profits, and this would later add fuel to the embers of discontent by dashing hopes that they harbored for profit distributions. By the late 1980s, those embers were becoming flames.

As for Steve, his demands for profit distributions in lieu of reinvestment were not isolated to the company. He later had become a partner with Tim Lawless and others in the ownership of salons in Indiana. When Tim and the other partners wanted to reinvest profits to add more franchises, Steve objected because he wanted to take the profits for personal use. Great Clips requires that any person holding at least 10 percent of a franchisee partnership must sign new franchise agreements, so Steve—who owned a greater than 10 percent interest in the partnership—simply refused to sign agreements for additional salons. By that simple refusal, he blocked the partnership from expanding. In order to grow their Great Clips business, Tim and the other partners were forced to buy Steve out of the partnership.

Having seen how markets are *developed*, it's worthwhile to see how those markets are *selected*.

Actually, as with so many other significant decisions, chance often plays a larger role than studied analysis. In the very beginning, Des Moines was selected mainly because Ray was familiar with the area. He had once lived in Des Moines, and he had family in the vicinity. Omaha became a market because a franchise was sold to a friend of Steve's who lived there.

Six more markets opened in the next two or three years, and four more opened by the end of 1985. Looking back, Ray can't explain today exactly why each market was selected for development at the time, but he will confess that it had little to do with sophisticated market research or study of detailed demographics.

CHAPTER 20

A Culture of Fairness Is Born

The Great Clips policies to avoid favoritism regarding terms and locations were motivated by ethics and fair play—traits that came naturally to Ray, Steve, and David alike. While the three owners would often disagree, and with more intensity as time went by, they did so openly and without deceit. It was a subject on which all three agreed, and it wasn't something they even had to discuss. It was this early practice of treating franchisees fairly and with respect that came to define the unique culture of Great Clips.

The three owners probably didn't even know it at the time, but franchisees universally have a better internal communication system than even the best of the famous prison "grapevines." If one franchisee believes that he or she has been mistreated, every other franchisee in the market will hear about it, often before the sun sets. Conversely, if one franchisee were to get a special break, he or she wouldn't be able to resist telling the other franchisees—often just to rub it in. In either event, the credibility of the franchisor suffers, and the resulting ramifications are limitless: Franchises get harder to sell because existing franchisees cease to be supporters of the system; franchisees become wary of the franchisor and won't participate in marketing programs or operational enhancements. As a result, the outlets—whether they are stores, restaurants, or salons—begin to look and perform differently from the others in the same system.

A national brand requires consistency and reliability. The customer has to know what experience to expect, regardless of whether she is in Omaha or Tampa, and the franchisee has to deliver that experience. Indeed, that is the essence of franchising. It can be described as harmony, with the franchisees likened to musicians being guided by the franchisor/conductor. Everything is beautiful when they follow the maestro and play from the same score. But if they ignore the maestro's baton and substitute their own sheet music for his score, the symphony becomes cacophony—and the audience flees.

Because Great Clips has maintained its credibility with its franchisees through fair dealing, reasoned guidance, and good listening, the harmony has been right and the audience has grown.

CHAPTER 21

"May I Recommend a Conditioner, Sir?"

Every salon must maintain an inventory of haircare products to sell, such as shampoos, conditioners, gels, and sprays. This is not only a convenience to the customer, it provides a source of revenue to the owner of the salon, results in added royalties for the company, and can boost the stylist's take-home pay. Sourcing these products and figuring out how to get them delivered to the salons proved to be a bigger logistical problem than the three owners anticipated.

At first, Ray, Steve, and David wanted Great Clips to have its own private label for these items, and they contracted with a major manufacturer of beauty products, Tyrol, to produce a Great Clips line of products. Tyrol was not interested in shipping to individual salons because each shipment would be so small. The original plan, therefore, was to have Tyrol ship in bulk to Great Clips, and Great Clips would then repackage the items and ship them to the individual salons. As the number of salons started to grow, however, the owners could see that the handling, re-packaging, re-shipping, and billing would become a nightmare. "The more we would do," Ray lamented, "the more money we would lose." His conclusion: "We're not distributors. We've got to find someone else to distribute the product for us."

Steve Lemmon, knowing about product distribution from his years with The Barbers, was not optimistic. His prediction to Ray was, "You can try, but you won't find anyone who will be willing to do it. The small amount of sales to each individual salon is just not worth it to anyone, and if they charged enough to make it worthwhile it would be too expensive for the salons. They'd have to charge more for the stuff than the customers would pay."

Ray welcomed the challenge and went to work on it. He learned that many franchisors supply merchandise and products to their franchisees as an added source of revenue, but he came to see that this introduced a serious conflict of interest. The franchisee wants to pay as small a price as possible, but the franchisor (in its dual role as supplier) would want the price to be as high as possible. Also, the franchisee should be able to rely upon the franchisor to screen for quality, but if the franchisor were the supplier there would be a temptation to be lax on quality control.

The more Ray thought about it, the more convinced he became that Great Clips should not provide product for sale in the salons. He believed that it was their responsibility to find the best prices, the best quality, and the best value for equipment and products going to the salons, and that responsibility too easily could be compromised if the company was itself the supplier. *How can we police ourselves?* he would ask. Further, Ray recalled his days as a franchisee of The Barbers who *did* act as a supplier, and how irritated he was whenever he had to write an extra check to The Barbers for product. He vowed that the Great Clips franchisees would never feel that same irritation.

With his trademark tenacity, Ray set out to find a supplier. He started by calling the main beauty supply companies—National Beauty Supply, Beauty Craft, Cardinal, and others. None was interested because Great Clips was simply not large enough at that time—it was 1983 and there were only 12 salons in the system. Not easily discouraged, Ray went to the Yellow Pages and began making calls alphabetically to all "Beauty Distributor" listings. It was one rejection after another; Great Clips was too small.

Finally, after working his way almost through the entire alphabet, he got to Warehouse Beauty Supply. The owner, Bob Hanson, answered and after a minute or two said, "Come on over. Let's talk about it."

When they got together, Ray discovered that Bob was also a CPA and that he ran the beauty supply business as a sideline. Bob understood the franchise issues because he owned six Edie Adams Cut 'n Curl franchises, a full-service salon concept that had about 350 salons nationwide at the time.

"We had a lot in common," Bob said, "and hit it off immediately. We trusted each other and, right there, shook hands on the deal."

That handshake was the only "contract" Bob Hanson ever had with Great Clips. Thirty years later his company continues to enjoy enormous success as a major supplier to Great Clips salons, supplying essential items such as tools, capes, and brushes in addition to the "wet line" products that include shampoos, gels, conditioners, and sprays. The company name has been changed to Salon Innovations and is now owned by Bob's children, son-in-law, and Margaret Stone, the president of the company.

Salon Innovations management team at the Great Clips corporate offices memorializing their nearly thirty years of doing business with Great Clips, all done on a handshake. Back row (left to right) Jo Anne Todd, Sam Hanson, Margaret Stone. Front row (left to right) Bob Todd, Bob Hanson, Rhoda Olsen, and Ray Barton (2012).

This is not the only long-standing "handshake deal" that Great Clips has with vendors and suppliers. In its very earliest days, the company gave a modest printing job to Andy Olson, a representative of a printing company. Andy since became the owner of Ideal Printing in the Twin Cities and today, with no formal contract, Ideal continues to meet the ever-growing printing needs of Great Clips and its franchisees.

In the Great Clips lexicon, suppliers are generally referred to as vendors. To this day, Great Clips has not been a vendor to its franchisees—at least not in the traditional sense. However, to "leverage the system" to ensure lower prices, better quality control, and more reliable distribution, the company now buys and then re-sells some equipment, fixtures, and other items to the franchisees, but makes no money in the process. According to Tom Schuenke, the director of facilities & office management, "The Great Clips purchasing model provides our franchisees with the lowest cost and the best service and warranties they could possibly get." The model includes modest margins for the company that don't even offset the costs associated with that function.

Salon Innovation sells its "wet line" products and salon supplies directly to the salons. Great Clips receives nothing for these items, other than a small royalty on the Great Clips private label product.

CHAPTER 22

Sweat Equity

Every franchising company wrestles with the interminable question of which outlets should be franchised, and which, if any, should be company owned. It would seem that there would be an easy answer to the question but, if there is, no one has found it!

The factors to consider are endless: Does the company have the financial wherewithal to build out and staff the outlet? Can it find a competent on-site manager? How would the profits compare with the fees and royalties paid by a franchisee? How will the outlet "compete" with existing or future outlets in that market—for customers, employees, and sites? Is there a franchisee who believes that he or she is "entitled" to that location? Could all the employment issues be controlled?

For Great Clips, an additional consideration was the real estate priority list. Did the company have to go on the list and wait its turn with the other franchisees on the list? If not, credibility would be destroyed.

To add some real-case reality to these considerations, a brief mention of McDonald's history on this subject is in order. McDonald's has dealt with the problem longer than any other franchisor, and its experience is both interesting and educational. The giant fast food chain started in the late 1950s by franchising, but soon also was opening company-owned restaurants known internally as McOpCos (for McDonald's Operating Company). Almost from the beginning, the ratio was maintained at about 75 percent franchised and 25 percent McOpCo. In later years, the ratio changed closer to 85 percent franchised and 15 percent McOpCo. Why the change, and what did McDonald's learn?

The clearest lesson learned, and one that should be the most obvious, was this: Other things being equal, a franchisee with "skin in the game"— that is, one with his own hard money invested—will do a better job than a salaried manager who may not have long-range plans to stay with the business. This was proven so often and so regularly that McDonald's soon began to require that its franchisees live within an hour's drive of their restaurants. Having skin in the game was important, but it was meaningless if the franchisee was 500 miles away on the golf course.

In fact, so important was it that the franchisee be actively involved in the operation of the restaurant that McDonald's adopted another rule in its early days: The restaurant must be the franchisee's primary vocation. No franchises would be issued to doctors, lawyers, or business people who wanted to dabble in fast food while actively pursuing their "main" careers. McDonald's was able to be that selective because its franchises were extraordinarily successful from the beginning and the demand for its franchises was so great that there were plenty of applicants who were willing to give up other careers for a McDonald's franchise.

Such rigid standards for hands-on management are particularly necessary for a fast food chain where more than 500,000 customers are served at *each restaurant* every year, where a maze of high-tech equipment has to be constantly monitored and fine-tuned, and where scores of employees are relatively unskilled. While writing a check could produce financial equity, it's the franchisee's daily involvement in the restaurant—the *"sweat equity"*—that so often makes the difference between success and failure. While a haircare salon may not have the same issues as a fast food restaurant, the difference is only one of degree—and not enough to negate the need for the franchisee's presence.

There has been another change in the franchising universe that demands even more hands-on management from franchisees. More and more outlets are being opened in non-traditional venues such as schools, hospitals, sports arenas, inner cities, interstate highways, airports, and even within larger operations such as Walmart. These venues present *unique* problems in such areas as marketing, staffing, scheduling, opening and closing times, which can be handled better by an on-site owner than by someone trained to deal with these issues in the traditional way. Unique problems require unique solutions.

Great Clips also foresaw other problems if company-owned salons shared markets with franchised salons. Some of these problems were real and some were perceived, but the difference is inconsequential because with franchising, as with everything else, perception is reality. Many franchisees hate to share markets with their franchisor because, in their mind, the company takes the best sites, hires the best managers and staff, and can afford the best marketing. Sometimes they are right and sometimes they aren't.

There is, however, one area in which the franchisees have a realistic (if not legitimate) complaint: pricing. In most franchised systems, company-owned outlets have lower prices than franchised outlets. The explanation for the pricing differential depends on who is giving it, but it always comes back to what franchisees see as a conflict of interest. Since franchisee royalties and fees are based on a percentage of *gross sales*, the franchisor makes more money as *gross sales* increase—even if *profits* take a nosedive. Thus, the franchisees maintain, the franchisor is always pushing for low prices to drive up gross sales. The franchisee, on the other hand, couldn't care less about gross sales if, at the end of the day, he's losing money. "No wonder they want me to sell pizzas for three bucks," a fast food franchisee will bemoan. "I'll sell a million of 'em, pay a fortune in royalties and fees, and go broke in the process!"

In reality, franchisors are not that narrow-minded or selfish. Great Clips advocates lower prices, but makes a strong case that it is strictly for the benefit of the *franchisee*. "We are a business built on volume," Ray explains, "and a franchisee can't make money with low customer counts. A salon giving 600 haircuts a week at $12 each will be much more profitable than one giving 400 haircuts at $14 each, and the fastest way to get those extra customers is with a lower price." Ray insists: "We make price recommendations for the franchisee, not for us. In the final analysis, the better they do, the better we do."

Great Clips started with company-owned salons, but soon came to recognize the problems of having those salons share markets with franchised salons. Actually, Ray had been convinced since joining the company that it just made better business sense to franchise exclusively. But much more important, all three owners were acutely sensitive to the possibility of conflict of interest accusations, and maintaining their credibility with the franchisees was too important to risk. So the owners agreed—at least for the time being—to put all their eggs in the franchise basket by selling off their company-owned salons. This had the added advantage of generating capital needed for developing new markets.

The company thereafter operated salons only temporarily after buying them from one franchisee and selling them to another. And to implement the rifle approach to market development, the company typically would introduce the brand with a company-owned and operated salon. This salon would also be used as a training base. However, once it served its initial purpose the salon would be sold to a franchisee.

That said, the issue never entirely went away, and until the late 1990s there would be heated discussions about having company-owned salons in specific markets.

At the end of the day, the best cost accountants in the world will disagree as to whether a franchisor will make more money by owning or franchising an outlet. As long as there is franchising, there will be debate on this question. A possible answer, however, might lie in this observation: Companies sell more company-owned outlets *to* franchisees than they buy *from* them!

CHAPTER 23

"Not My Fault— Must Be Your Fault"

We live in an age when people seldom take responsibility for their own conduct: A man carelessly steps in front of a taxi and sues for his injuries. A woman smokes for fifty years and blames the tobacco companies for her cancer. A family moves near an airport and then complains that the noise of the planes is annoying. And the man who stammers shouts "discrimination" when turned down for a job as a newscaster.

So, too, one must look far and wide to find a franchisee who will acknowledge that the poor performance of his or her franchise has anything to do with the way it's managed! It's usually the franchisor's fault—poor marketing, inadequate training, lousy sites (when found by the franchisor), or a bad product. Secondary excuses include bad weather, bad economy, the price of gasoline, or strong local competition. Some excuses are heard so often that they could be put to music.

The Great Clips owners were already starting to hear these refrains when, in early 1984, Ray heard it again—this time from his own wife and best friends! Mary Lou and the Ledebuhrs came to Ray's office to report that the sales of their Brookdale Center salon were disappointing and they weren't making any money. Roger Ledebuhr put his feet up on Ray's desk and announced: "This isn't working, Ray. Your marketing stinks!"

He was talking to the wrong guy. Ray raised his hand to stop Roger from going further. "The marketing is great," he replied. "I'd say that your operations are lousy!"

Finger pointing solves nothing. There had to be some way to determine when poor sales can be traced to poor operations—or to other sources beyond the control of the franchisee. If the franchisee and the salon staff are all doing their jobs well, and sales are still slow, then it's reasonable to re-examine the location or the marketing. It's very tricky to assess operations objectively, but Ray came up with an idea that helped solve the problem.

His idea was primitive—almost laughable—in terms of today's highly sophisticated, computerized methods of conducting research. He devised a "survey" (more accurately, a sheet of paper) that sat on the front desk of the salon, and each customer was asked whether this was a first or a repeat visit. Then, by reviewing the results at several salons over a period of time, the company could start to see trends and compare the salons.

It's generally recognized that the franchisor's job is to get the customers into the store the first time, and it's the franchisee's job to get them to come back for repeat visits. Ray's very simple survey was an excellent start at measuring how the franchisor and the franchisee were doing their respective jobs. A high number of first visits suggested a good location and/or good marketing, and that implies that the franchisor was doing its job. A high percentage of repeat visits indicated that the customers had a good experience and were willing to return, and this spoke well for the franchisee.

The information learned from this rudimentary survey was put into a report, the name of which was far more complicated than the survey itself: the Salon Performance Operating Tracking Report. It was referred to by its acronym, the SPOTR, *and it worked!* This was the company's first tool for identifying those salons that had operational problems.

That antiquated customer research was the first baby step leading to Great Clips' position as one of the most impressive companies in the world when it comes to knowing its customers and measuring each one's experience in any Great Clips salon he or she visits—anywhere. By simply having the salon make an entry of the customer's name or phone number, the home office will have an instantaneous, computerized record of the exact time of the visit, the length of wait time before being called to the chair, the details of the haircut, the time it took, products purchased, frequency of visits, number of days between visits, other Great Clips salons visited by that customer, and other relevant data that might later benefit the customer, the franchisee, or the franchisor. This and other technological breakthroughs at Great Clips will be discussed further in later chapters.

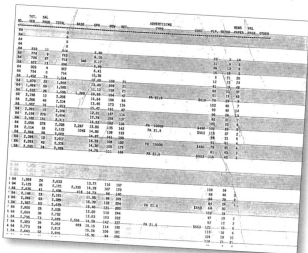

The Salon Performance Operating Tracking Report (SPOTR) from 1984.

CHAPTER 24

Franchisees Beyond Friends and Family

Franchisees are the fuel that drives growth in a franchise system. While growth is usually measured in terms of the number of locations, finding locations is worthless if there's no one to run them. So, finding and training the right franchisees is a top priority for any franchisor, and no one knew this better than Ray Barton, Steve Lemmon, and David Rubenzer.

For over a year after the first franchise was opened, every single one of the franchised salons was owned by a relative or friend of one of the three owners. They always knew that this would be a short-term, stop-gap strategy, but by late 1983 they were getting desperate to attract franchisees from a wider circle.

By one of those quirks of fate, it was during this same time that a man in Denver, Jim Hemak, was becoming disenchanted with his nomadic career. Jim was working with Junior Achievement, a national, nonprofit educational association, but was unhappy over his constant transfer from city to city. He was intent on being his own boss and finding a business that would provide more stability for him and his family.

As part of his search, Jim attended an investment seminar where he learned that only 20 percent of new businesses survive for five years, but franchise businesses had a 93 percent survival rate over the same five years. That was enough to re-direct his search toward buying a franchise. He then came across an anonymous ad in the *Wall Street Journal* comprising nothing more than a few cryptic bullet points:

- Everyone in America needs it
- A $10 billion a year industry
- Cash business—no receivables
- Minimal inventory
- Recession resistant
- Semi-absentee ownership

His interest aroused, Jim called the 800 number at the bottom of the ad to learn that it was posted by Hair Crafters, a full-service salon concept looking for franchisees. "Had I known it was haircare," he later recalled, "I probably wouldn't have called. What did I know about haircare?" Coincidently, it was during this time that Jim received a direct mail solicitation from a small Minnesota outfit called Great Clips. It was sent to names pulled from a magazine subscription list and solicited applications for franchises.

Jim, a man in search of a franchise and now having the haircare bug in his ear, followed up with a phone call. He was connected to Ray; they had a brief introductory chat and later a couple of productive follow-up conversations. Sniffing a sale, Ray wasted little time in flying to Colorado to meet personally with Jim.

If Jim harbored any suspicions that an outfit peddling franchises for cutrate haircuts was seedy or disreputable, they were dispelled when he met Ray Barton. First, Ray is genuinely friendly and outgoing, and it's hard not to like him from the start. Second, he showed up wearing an expensive-looking, tailor-made suit, a quiet tie for accent, shoes with a spit-polish glisten, and a handsome attaché case. "I had only one good suit, maybe two, at the time," Ray related, "but whenever I met with potential franchisees, realtors, bankers, or lawyers I made it a point to look successful and

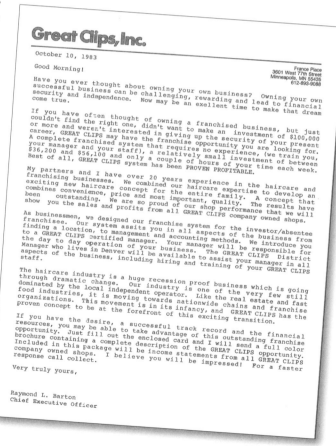

The original franchise solicitation letter, dated October 1983, that resulted in Jim Hemak and Norm Parsons becoming the first non-family franchisees.

respectable. Most people back then assumed that low-cost meant low quality, and I did whatever I could to convey the impression that we were a quality outfit. For the same reason, after every meeting I would follow up with a handwritten note to whomever was there to thank them for meeting with me."

When he tells this story, Ray will invariably smile and shake his head. "Today, my friends can't believe this. They hardly ever see me wear a necktie! I always try to act professional and be a gentleman, but I'm a lot more casual about it these days."

After a couple of hours over coffee at a Burger King, it was clear that the two men liked each other and wanted to continue their discussions. "I was impressed with him and with the concept," Jim said. "I followed up with a trip to Minneapolis—where I was from—and was likewise impressed with Steve and David."

Jim Hemak, the first non-family member franchisee, and Ray Barton in Augusta, Georgia, in 2000.

Jim signed up, and Great Clips finally issued its first franchise to someone who was outside of the "family-friend" circle! Jim Hemak went on to become a legend. For years, he owned more salons than anyone in the Great Clips system, and his counsel has been sought by franchisees and corporate executives alike. Jim's leadership and support have meant an enormous amount to the company and to Ray personally. He generously has spent countless hours talking with prospective franchisees, helping new franchisees learn the ropes, and being a leader among his peers. He has headed and even initiated franchisee committees and task forces. Even more important, Jim is Ray's sounding board; it's Jim to whom Ray will often turn when he wants to test an idea or bring up a potential problem.

To quote Ray: "Great Clips would not be where we are today without Jim Hemak."

Jim explains his commitment to the system this way: "Coming from a nonprofit background, it's my nature to go 'all in' when I find something I can believe in. After those first few meetings and conversations, I came to believe in Ray, and in his vision, leadership, and ability. Although there were highs and lows through the years, nothing has happened since to shake that trust. That might explain why I have been so active in supporting prospective and existing franchisees as well as participating on so many franchisee committees."

In short order, several other "strangers" followed the path to becoming Great Clips franchisees. Another, in Fort Collins, Colorado, was Norm Parsons who responded to the same direct mail solicitation that piqued Jim's interest. Dan Washburn, a young dentist, heard about Great Clips from a fellow dentist with whom he went to dental school. They partnered with a third person to buy a franchise in Tampa. A few months later Dan and his father, Bob Washburn, bought their first franchise in the Orlando market. Bob's accountant, Jerry Benik, liked the numbers he was seeing and bought a franchise for Atlanta.

Things were looking up!

CHAPTER 25

"Welcome! But Stay Away"

As more franchisees came on board, David and Steve grew even more insistent that the franchisees should be passive investors and leave management of the salons to Great Clips. To them it was a solid strategy. For one thing, the company could do it better, and for another, they reasoned that it would be easier to sell franchises if the franchisees understood that they didn't have to do anything. Then, too, there was the fear that they would just get in the way. They knew nothing about the business, and if they were involved they might start giving directions to the staff who knew more about haircare than they did.

While Ray was still uncomfortable with this approach, he acquiesced; he was—at least at that time—more interested in selling franchises than in operations, and if this made it easier to sell franchises, then why not? In fact, the strategy was working. Potential franchisees were told that Steve had managed The Barbers thirty-five corporate-owned salons, and that David was a seasoned stylist who had expertise in training and salon management, and even had been a Barbers franchisee himself. Why wouldn't the franchisees be glad to entrust their salons to these experts?

David succinctly sums up the rationale: "We were driven to open salons, and we needed their money to do it. For us, it was easy: Steve and I had been in the salon business for years, and we didn't think there was anything we couldn't handle. We even hired and fired their employees. Looking back, we probably broke every kind of law about employee-employer relations, but we never gave it a thought."

To Steve, there was no difference between a franchised salon and one owned by the company. He did inspections, rearranged furniture, gave orders to the employees—many of whom did not even know the franchisee and assumed that Steve was their boss. Jim Hemak recalls a time in Denver when he and Steve were out looking for sites, and they stopped in a salon franchised to Bill Divine. Without introducing himself, Steve embarked upon an inspection of the salon, checking out the furniture, fixtures, equipment, lighting, etc. The staff was looking around raising their eyebrows as if to ask, *Who is this guy?*

Suddenly, Steve barked, "Who's the manager?"

A young stylist said, "She's not here, but I'm the assistant manager."

"Look at that broken ceiling tile up there. Call somebody to get out here and fix it!"

When they walked out to the car, Jim asked, "Steve, did she know who you were?"

"Probably not."

While this logic made all the sense in the world to Steve and David, it started to grate on many franchisees after they made their investments. It was one thing to have Great Clips oversee salon operations, but quite another to be virtually locked out of your own business! Roger Ledebuhr, the first franchisee, put it this way: "If those guys had their way, they'd have a device to detect whenever a franchisee came through the front door. When it happened, a big net would drop down and grab him so he couldn't come in and interfere."

The understanding was that it would be okay for the franchisees to stop by to drop off the paychecks or bring in a box of doughnuts once in a while, but that should be about the extent of their presence in the salons. The franchisees dutifully obeyed. When Jim Hemak's first salon opened in June 1984, he was both excited and nervous. He, his wife Pat, and their five-year-old son stopped by at 8:30 in the morning and gave corsages to the staff, then left as instructed. They spent the next several hours sitting in Jim's Buick counting customers. "It was nerve racking," he vividly remembers. "We had just taken out a second mortgage and a personal line of credit to open the salon, and by 11:30 we still didn't have the fifty customers come in for their free haircuts. *Oh, my God*, my wife and I thought, *what did we get ourselves into? We can't even give them away!*"

Dee Tibbetts likewise had reason to question her judgment on the day she opened her first salon later that year, also in Denver. "I came in early, met the staff for the first time, and then went out to sit in my car—where I had a six-pack of beer if I needed it. *What have I done?* I kept asking myself."

It is well to remember that we are discussing a Great Clips practice in the early 1980s, when franchising was still a fairly new way to do business. Since then, franchising companies have learned the importance of franchisees being empowered to run their respective operations. The pendulum has swung back and forth on this issue and, generally speaking, has now settled at the point where the franchisor sets the standards and policies for the business and the franchisee carries them out. The franchisor does its job primarily from the corporate office, and the franchisees do theirs from inside the franchised units.

As we will see, Steve and David soon came around to accepting more franchisee involvement in the salons. In fact, they even insisted on it! But what they were doing in those early days was done in the good faith belief that it was in the best interest of all concerned.

CHAPTER 26

Career Paths

The company's growth during the first couple of years bodes well for the owners, but by early 1985, it presented David with a logistical nightmare. More salons meant more stylists to find and train, and the spread of salons into remote markets made both missions nearly impossible. His solution was to train *others* to train the stylists, then have these new trainers working in the respective markets. Furthermore, since training would not be a full-time job—at least not when the markets were just starting to be developed—each trainer in a remote market would serve the dual role of district manager to oversee salon operations.

The first group selected for this new role included several of the early stylists—Roxie Poliak, Pam Keller, Marybeth Callahan, Ruth Ann Grimsley, Carla Fryar, Cheryl Stensrud, Michelle Bates, and Bobbie Sylte-Kneeland. The easiest part of their new job, David explained, was to train other stylists to cut hair the Great Clips way. Far more challenging was to ensure that each salon "delivered the brand"—that is, showed the customer that low cost did not mean low quality. *From its earliest days, the Great Clips mantra was to give every single customer the same respect and comfort that he or she would get at a high-price, no-frills salon.* Each member of this new team learned her lesson well and later brought it with them to their new market when it was assigned.

Despite David's lessons, these new district managers were, in the beginning, ill equipped to handle all of the real-life problems they would confront in their markets. There was more to opening and running a salon than cutting hair. When Marybeth Callahan expressed apprehension, Steve Lemmon told her, "Don't worry. Just call me whenever you have a problem, and I'll tell you what to do."

Seeing the inadequacy of the initial training, David devised a more intensive five-day course for each new district manager in July 1985. Two of the first stylists to take the course were Michelle Bates and Bobbie Sylte-Kneeland. After they completed it, they were told about their new assignments: Michelle was to take Orlando and Bobbie would go to Atlanta.

Neither had ever been outside of Minnesota! On the following Friday afternoon, David took them out to celebrate with a boat ride on Lake Minnetonka. During the ride David unexpectedly announced, "I need you both in your new markets on Monday morning." They were stunned, but they somehow managed to get their affairs in order—Bobbie in record time. It took Michelle a few weeks to get to Orlando, but Bobbie was in Atlanta by Monday morning.

Even before this program was fully implemented, a new dimension was added. Steve, David, and Ray decided to offer franchises to a select few of these new district managers. Since owning a franchise at that time would not entail hands-on operational responsibilities, these district managers could enjoy the benefits of owning a salon while still doing their jobs for the company. At first, there was some concern that being both an employee and a franchisee would present a conflict of interest, but this was dispelled when the three owners realized that they already had crossed that bridge by issuing franchises to their own relatives and friends. Would it be any more of a conflict for Ray Barton's wife, sister, and mother to have franchises than for a well-trained employee to have one? And anyway, wouldn't this be a good way to open more salons?

The first of the new district managers to take advantage of this policy was Marybeth Callahan. Borrowing money from her father, she bought a franchise in Denver where she already was assigned to be the district manager. This worked out so well that the owners actively encouraged other employees to do the same. They eased the financial burden by offering them a credit toward the franchise fee based on years served. More important than enabling the opening of more salons, the policy reduced staff turnover, built loyalty, and provided opportunity—all creating a valuable sense of *esprit de corps*.

Providing these career paths was a source of pride to Great Clips, and it proved to be a financial success for some of those early stylists. Today, Marybeth Callahan owns eighteen Great Clips franchises; Ruth Ann Grimsley owns thirteen; Roxie Poliak, with her husband, Steve, own twelve; and Pam Keller owns six.

The Great Clips system continues to offer tremendous career opportunities for stylists. The above examples are dramatic, but they are not isolated. Throughout the system, former stylists are now managers, general managers, and executives for franchisees with multiple salons. And in some cases, stylists have become partners in franchisee organizations or even franchisees in their own right.

Michelle Bates, the stylist who was sent to Orlando in 1985, is a case in point. "I was only nineteen at the time, and I jumped at the chance to move to Florida. With the $100 in expense money provided by Great Clips, I moved to Orlando in September and we opened the first salon there the following month. It was owned by Dan Washburn and his dad, Bob. I was supposed to be in Orlando only long enough to help them get started, but after two years, the Washburns hired me. I have now been with them for twenty-five years, and today I'm the general manager of thirty-one very successful salons. My decision to move to Florida as a teenager changed my life in so many wonderful ways. Who could have known?"

Michelle Iacovetta provides another excellent illustration. Michelle started as a stylist for franchisee Bart Holtzman. Bart now owns thirty-eight salons in St. Louis and Denver, and Michelle's career advanced as his business grew. She went from stylist to salon manager, then to a district manager overseeing all of Bart's salons in Denver, and later to general manager for all of Bart's salons in both markets. Today, Michelle is the chief operating officer for the entire organization, and she has become a co-owner in a number of Bart's salons. This is the kind of success story that would be hard to find in other franchise systems.

The opportunities for Great Clips stylists are well known. As noted by John Halal of the Tricoci University of Beauty Culture, "Great Clips provides a comprehensive compensation package that includes health insurance, paid vacations, and excellent ongoing training. This encourages loyalty and job retention. I know of several of our graduates who have been able to advance rather quickly at Great Clips to positions of management and long-term careers."

CHAPTER 27

Trying to Keep Up with the Openings

Within two years after the first salon opened at the University of Minnesota, Great Clips salons were opening at a rate that the three owners couldn't have anticipated in their wildest dreams. The "passive investment" strategy made it easy to sell franchises for two reasons. First, the franchisees would not have to give up their existing jobs or careers. Second, since the franchisees did not have to live near their salons, the company could focus its recruitment efforts in the Twin Cities where management had contacts galore. *Together, these factors offered the unusual advantage of national expansion through local recruitment.* As a result, there were a growing number of Minnesota franchisees owning salons from Denver to Orlando. Absentee ownership was the order of the day.

The rate of salon openings was further accelerated by the company's ability to get them up and running very fast. For example, in the spring of 1983, Ray went to scout locations in his hometown of Des Moines, and within *two weeks* after he first saw a site in Westtown it was opened! Nancy Peyton signed an agreement to become a franchisee in the Twin Cities over Thanksgiving weekend in 1983, and three weeks later, on December 17, her salon opened successfully despite the subzero weather.

Opening salons that quickly was laudable, but it presented problems. For example, on one occasion, newspapers in Denver announced the opening of a salon for a certain Saturday, complete with the fifty free haircuts. But by Friday most of the fixtures and supplies had not yet arrived, and even the styling chairs were nowhere in sight! Marybeth Callahan, the district manager, and Ruth Ann Grimsley, the salon manager, could easily have panicked. Instead, they saved the day by energetic improvisation. They called other salons in the market, and cosmetology schools as well, to plead for everything they needed. "We were prepared to beg, borrow, or steal, but everyone really came through for us," Ruth Ann remembers. "Some of the people we called actually delivered the stuff to us!" The salon opened on time the next morning, albeit with twelve unmatched styling chairs, and with folding chairs and a card table in the customer waiting area. "It was hilarious," Ruth Ann remembers. "We were showing Great Clips brochures to customers so they could see what the salon was supposed to look like. It actually turned out to be a fun day for everyone."

Later that afternoon, Marybeth loaded up her car with a styling chair she had borrowed from a company salon and hurried to take it back so she could use it to cut hair during a later shift.

These helter-skelter experiences soon led to a change of strategy. Salons started having "soft openings"—something like dress rehearsals—to get things better organized and tested before publicizing an official grand opening with the fifty free haircuts. This method of opening avoided a host of problems.

CHAPTER 28

Reversal of Strategies

Steve Lemmon and David Rubenzer had underestimated the time and energy it would take to run all the franchised salons!

Both had developed their managerial talents at The Barbers where they excelled, and both assumed that they could seamlessly transport their skills to Great Clips. And Great Clips' initial success vindicated that confidence. However, they found that they simply couldn't keep up with the training and oversight demands of the expanding number of salons in multiple markets—*and this was only two years after they began franchising.*

For the first time they realized that they had hit a wall, and that perhaps Ray was right after all. Perhaps further growth *would* require that franchisees be more involved in salon operations. Until this time, Ray's was the only voice in favor of having the franchisees engaged in the operation of the salons. As Steve confirms, "Barton was the only one who really pressed that we had to get the franchisees involved."

Ray expresses his view in very basic terms: "There are only two reasons to franchise salons instead of owning them ourselves—capital and management. We were getting their capital, but we were missing out on the very important component of management. The salon requires leadership that no one can provide better than a franchisee who is protecting his investment and who has a *personal* interest in seeing how the salon is run and how the customer is treated."

Still frustrated when he looks back at those days, Ray adds, "I remember telling the franchisees how important their involvement was to the success of the salon. But Steve and David were telling them just the opposite! Maybe I should have been more forceful, but things were getting testier by the day and I had to pick my battles. There was only one of me!"

There is an age-old adage that tells how the mice will play when the cat's away. With the company not being able to oversee the growing number of salons, and the franchisees being absent, Great Clips found themselves precisely in that situation. A hair salon, like any other business, can't succeed when left in the hands of an unsupervised staff.

Things were breaking down fast, and the sting of absentee ownership was spreading throughout the system. Tom and Pete Schneider, David's brothers-in-law, had success with their franchises in Minneapolis where they lived and in Des Moines where they could easily drive. But things were drastically different when they opened salons in distant Omaha with David as a partner. "Omaha was a disaster for us," Pete painfully remembers. "We couldn't get there often enough because we'd have to fly, and our own employees took advantage of that. They would open late and leave early, and sometimes they didn't open at all. We took a bath and finally had to close the salons—even though we had long-term leases. It was cheaper to pay the rent than continue to pile up losses. I still call that my tuition to the School of Hard Knocks."

Omaha was not an isolated case. The same problems struck the Tampa market like a Florida hurricane! Dan Washburn, who with a couple of friends owned a Tampa franchise, put it this way: "We were in Minnesota, but they told us it wouldn't be a problem. They would find a manager, hire the staff, and take care of everything. All we had to do was open a bank account and make sure there was money in it. The salon was a total flop, and there we were in Minneapolis—helpless."

Other absentee owners of Tampa franchises experienced the same frustration of helplessly watching their investments crater. *In fact, all of the franchisees in Tampa closed their doors, and it was another fifteen years before Great Clips reappeared in that market.*

Even in the *successful* markets, franchisees who wanted to have a hand in the operation of their salons had growing concerns. Pat Stevens, for example, who had salons in the Minneapolis market—and who was Ray Barton's brother-in-law—was taken aback when he was told that the company was increasing the salaries for his stylists and managers. This led him into discussions with other Twin Cities' franchisees who shared his concern about having no say in the operations of their salons.

At about the same time, Denver franchisee Bill Divine had a conversation with Jim Hemak, also in the Denver market, about his desire to take a more active role in the salons. He discovered that Jim felt the same way. "We talked it over," Bill said, "and decided that we would take over our own operations. We didn't exactly kick them out. We simply told them that from then on all of the major decisions would be ours, not theirs." Great Clips had to accept it. It was, after all, the franchisees who owned the salons.

As previously noted, the franchisee "grapevine" is an efficient one, and in no time this issue became a major discussion point throughout the Denver market, with the franchisees generally in strong agreement with Bill and Jim.

This led to a very important event in the history of Great Clips. Jim called a meeting of the Denver franchisees in early fall 1984. This meeting, held at the Stapleton Inn near the Denver airport, was the first meeting of Great Clips franchisees anywhere in the country, and it was done without approval or input from the corporate office. Never before had franchisees come together on their own to get to know each other and talk over common issues. The group agreed that Jim would be the spokesperson if any messages were to be sent to the home office.

Many subjects were discussed, but the thrust centered on the company's failure at managing the salons. Once they got started, more and more voices were heard. The franchisees' frustration—and displeasure—was serious indeed, and it was duly conveyed back to the company. The message was received loud and clear, and it echoed what the owners themselves were beginning to realize. *It was a turning point—the company would thereafter step back, and the franchisees would be empowered and even encouraged to take a more active role in managing their salons.*

The transformation from a culture of absentee ownership to active involvement by the franchisees was a total one. The new policy required that all future franchisees—or someone with at least a 25 percent interest in the business—had to live in the market where they had their salons. (Existing franchisees in good standing were exempt from this policy.) This marked a 180-degree turn in the corporate attitude toward franchisee involvement— *what had been practically forbidden was now required.*

Great Clips franchisees have risen to the challenge. However, the *nature* of the franchisee's involvement changes as he or she acquires additional salons. For example, a franchisee with one or two salons will spend time recruiting stylists, keeping books, paying bills, scheduling staff, etc. But the franchisee who owns several salons will hire one or more managers or supervisors to do some or all of these tasks. Clara Osterhage, who owns twenty-eight salons in Ohio and Indiana, says, "I am active every day with our business, but not so much with the day-to-day operations. I have four excellent general managers who do that well, and they have come to look at the business as I do. That gives me the opportunity to devote time to two critical areas—real estate and human resource development. We will be opening twelve new locations in West Virginia—I already have leases for two of them—and there's no way I could expand like that without being able to focus on finding sites and developing people."

The historic meeting of the Denver franchisees became the forerunner of a new era of franchisee collaboration at Great Clips. The Denver group continued to meet three or four times a year to discuss best practices and projects they could work on cooperatively. And, of course, they compared notes on their experiences with the home office. The highlight of the year was the annual meeting when the franchisees would bring their families to a three-day retreat at a mountain resort. There was more fun than business on the agenda, and the golf, dinners, and cocktails built a strong camaraderie among the group. To top off the year, each December all of the franchisees in the market would bring their staffs together for a big holiday party.

This informal grassroots organization of Denver franchisees became the prototype for Great Clips market co-ops later formed throughout the country.

CHAPTER 29

Shopping for the Right Answer

As noted, Great Clips' rapid growth was outrunning its ability to manage the increasing number of salons. That same growth was also putting undue stress on the ability of the company to manage *itself*.

By 1984, the company's second year of business, there were no organizational charts to define and assign responsibilities, and each of the three owners took it upon himself to do whatever he thought needed to be done. That is never a good recipe for management, and it's even worse when the three parties were not always in agreement. Steve might consent to a site that Ray would reject, and David might hire someone who Steve wouldn't accept. Consequently, many important things happened—or didn't happen—only because pure chance dictated who made the decision.

This of course led franchisees and company employees to "shop" for opinions. The general understanding was *ask the right person and you'll have a better chance of getting the answer you wanted*. Most everyone liked and respected Ray, Steve, and David for their individual personalities and skills, but behind their backs there was head scratching over their well-known inability to see eye-to-eye on key issues. No company can succeed when management consistently gives mixed signals, and there was widespread concern that Great Clips was falling deeper into this trap.

The haphazard decision-making process wasn't limited to top management. The company had only eight employees at the time, each with a clear view of everything that was going on. And, without having well-defined responsibilities, each ventured opinions and made decisions in overlapping areas. In retrospect, this was frightening!

Ann Latendresse, for example, started as a receptionist in 1984, and remembers that soon after she was hired she was fielding calls from potential or actual franchisees on a wide variety of issues. "Just through conversation and observation," she said, "we all knew pretty much about what was going on, so I felt qualified to answer most questions. If I didn't, I'd just turn around and ask someone else—anyone who happened to be nearby."

But no one seemed to care about the mixed messages and lack of protocol. Salons were opening, and everything was moving forward. Why change?

The "home office" had since outgrown its space behind the Eagan salon, and had now rented office space on France Avenue. The premises were comfortable, and in spite of the growing tensions among the three owners—which were becoming more obvious—the overall atmosphere at the Great Clips offices was convivial. Steve had a liquor cabinet in his office, and Ray, in addition to having a few bottles of wine on hand, had a refrigerator stocked with beer. Fridays at 4:00 p.m. would find everyone gathered for a Happy Hour, and Ray would bring a glass of wine to anyone too busy to join in. This "family" atmosphere—but with plentiful kitchen treats instead of alcohol—prevails to this day, extending to franchisees and vendors as well as company personnel.

There was, obviously, a downside to this unstructured "seat of the pants" culture. *The necessary organization and discipline for sustained growth was just not there.* All policies and practices were transmitted orally from person to person; hardly anything was written down, and, as every youngster learns from the old game of "Telephone," verbal communications change drastically through repetition.

There was a screaming need for more structure. Simply put, Great Clips could not continue for long without getting its management act together. Something had to change, and that something appeared in the person of Rhoda Olsen.

What Henry Higgins did for Eliza Doolittle, Rhoda Olsen did for Great Clips!

CHAPTER 30

Rhoda to the Rescue

Great Clips began a metamorphosis in 1984. What had been a small seed of a company with no capital and little structure would soon blossom into a highly organized business that would go on to crush its competition and lead its industry. It didn't happen overnight, but that it was starting to happen was indisputable. The three owners who found much to disagree about were in complete accord when it came to the main reason for the transformation: Rhoda Olsen.

Rhoda Olsen, née Barton, is Ray's sister. Evidently, their parents liked the letter "R" since they named their six children Roxanne, Ray, Rebecca, Rhonda, Rhoda, and Regina. The five girls were always spoiling Ray, but it was Rhoda who was especially adept at keeping him out of trouble. Their mother, to make sure the kids came home at a reasonable hour, had a sheet listing their names, and each was to cross off his or her name when coming home. The last of the kids to cross off their name was

Rhoda Olsen, pictured in 2012.

to turn off all the lights. When Ray would be out past his curfew, it was Rhoda who protected him by crossing his name off the list and turning off the lights.

All of the Barton siblings were standouts with their own skills, and, while all had strong work ethics, Rhoda was recognized as the most extreme workaholic. Their mother, Alice, noted that "Roxanne, who ran for the United States Senate, works for power; Ray works for money; and Rhoda works just to work." Predictably, Ray majored in accounting where he thought he could prosper financially, and Rhoda, who didn't care a whit about money, studied social work and psychology at Mankato State University.

Rhoda was also a "take charge" person, which explains why her first counseling practice sessions didn't work out well. A counselor's job is to resist giving advice, but instead listen and encourage the client to come up with the answers. But not for Rhoda. "Why should I waste their time and mine? I know what they should do. They'll be just fine if they do nothing more than listen to me and do what I tell them to do!"

After her professor advised her that she wasn't cut out to be a counselor, she shifted to the area of assessment and diagnostics, which was a good fit for her statistical and analytical skills. She followed up with a master's degree in instructional design, which, she admits, is a fancy term for writing training programs. Upon graduation, she joined the human resources department at Land O'Lakes, where she wrote training programs for the agricultural and food sectors of the company.

After he left home to start a career, Ray saw Rhoda only about twice a year—at Christmas and in July for their mother's birthday. It was at that birthday, on July 10, 1984, when Ray casually asked Rhoda, "What are you doing these days?"

"I'm working for Land O'Lakes," she answered. "Right now I'm writing training programs for their HR and training people."

Ray's ears perked up. "Oh, we need some help with that kind of stuff. We have a franchisee orientation meeting coming up, and we don't have any materials to hand out. Is this the kind of thing you do?"

"Sure," Rhoda replied, "that's what I do. When would you need it?"

"The meeting's in two weeks."

"Two weeks! Do you have any idea what . . ."

"And by the way," Ray interrupted, "would you also be able to deliver the presentation. We don't have anyone who can do that."

Since the word "no" is not in Rhoda's vocabulary, she agreed to help out. That single conversation had a climactic impact on the history of Great Clips, far beyond what anyone could have foreseen. She hit the street running, and in just a few months she was preparing training programs, codifying policies, giving presentations, preparing job descriptions, and defining responsibilities.

She kept her job at Land O'Lakes while doing these assignments for Great Clips as a part-time consultant. As we will see, she later resigned from Land O'Lakes and joined the company as a vice president, and she is currently the chief executive officer. Whatever her title at a given moment, it is impossible to attach a job description to it. From her first day as a consultant, and ever since, one could find her presenting programs, settling disputes, keeping peace among the owners, working with franchisees, and doing anything else that needed to be done. When marketing needs to be tweaked, she tweaks it. When technology needs enhancing, she enhances it.

On the surface, that very first orientation meeting Rhoda had with the franchisees was short and uneventful. It took place only two weeks after Ray first talked to her, and she was a complete stranger to everyone there. She handed out her materials, covered some generalities about the franchise relationship, and asked for questions. "We didn't even know what to ask," Jim Hemak said. "But her empathy and sincerity showed through, and the franchisees, who until then had been virtually ignored once they signed up, felt that at last they had someone within the company looking out for them."

For the next year or two, while she served as a part-time consultant, Rhoda was getting the pulse of the company and learning the subtle dynamics of a franchise system. It was classic Rhoda: Take nothing for granted, understand everything, and do it better than anyone else.

She had the uncanny ability to navigate smoothly among the three owners and their perpetual differences, and she never gave the appearance of taking sides. "I just loved working with David," she said, as if unaware that he and her brother were increasingly at each other's throat. "David knew the basics better than anyone. This was, after all, the haircare business, and he was the only person in management who actually knew how to cut hair. He knew first-hand what customers wanted, and we could never lose sight of what he taught us about that."

When Rhoda did anything, she seemed always to add a little extra. The finishing touch for the stylist manual was provided by an uncle of her

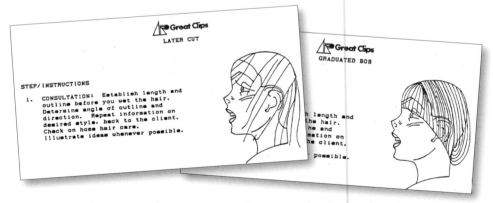

Instructions for designing the Layer Cut and the Graduated Bob taken from the 1984 stylist training manual.

husband, Greg, who had a flair for art. She had him draw schematics for the various hairstyles and cutting techniques, and, when used by trainers who worked in the markets, these became an important tool to ensure consistency throughout the system.

She followed up the stylist manual with a 416-page operations manual, a manager-training manual, a real estate manual, a marketing guidebook, and the company's first recruiting handbook.

By capturing everything in writing that had previously been taught by word of mouth, Rhoda replaced lore and instinct with clear instructions. This enabled the Great Clips system to be replicated from market to market and from salon to salon—an essential ingredient for any successful franchise system. But Rhoda describes this achievement in her customary self-effacing way: "I wasn't concerned about earning style points. I just figured that no one else was putting these things in writing, so whatever I did was an improvement. At least we were getting something tangible. Now we would all be on the same page."

PART FOUR

Fractures

CHAPTER 31

The Fissures Widen

By the summer of 1984, the three owners were beginning to feel added pressure from a variety of sources, and it intensified over the following months.

Now that the franchisees were becoming more involved in salon operations, they found their voice and were making constant demands on the company. Not only was this an added burden, but the owners nearly always disagreed as to how to respond—and that added to the frustration.

Money was also an issue. The revenues from franchise fees and royalties were inadequate to run the company *and* develop new markets. To give this a frame of reference: Assume that a salon had four stylists on a given day working full-time for eight hours, and it was a fairly busy day so that each averaged three haircuts per hour. This would total twenty-four haircuts for each, or a daily total of 96 haircuts at $6 each. The gross sales would be $576, and the 6 percent royalty or service fee due Great Clips would come to just under $35 for the day. Assuming further that there were 100 such salons in the system, *and that each was busy throughout each and every day,* the gross revenues to the company from royalties would be $3,500 per day, or roughly $1 million for an entire year. This amount would be totally inadequate for developing markets with corporate salons and training centers while sustaining the corporate office, paying rent, salaries, insurance and general overhead, servicing debt, and leaving anything for the owners. *In fact, these assumptions are optimistic. Not all salons are that busy every day, and Great Clips had nowhere close to 100 salons until 1986, four years after its first opening.*

An ongoing need for money is stressful. It causes fissures in relationships, and widens existing ones. This was all the more so at Great Clips where Steve and David blamed the money shortfall on the high cost of the ongoing development of new markets which was being driven by Ray. Those fissures were growing into chasms.

There was also frustration over the lack of success in finding franchisees to populate the new markets with enough salons to leverage the brand and make the markets—and the company—profitable. This had nothing to do with the viability of the concept. It was hard to attract prospects. As Jim Hemak explained, "People don't just wake up one day and decide they want to get into the haircare business. It was not the kind of opportunity that prospective franchisees dream about." Unlike burger franchises that were popping up all over, franchises for haircare at that time were new and relatively unknown and untested.

These pressures were taking a harder toll on Steve and David, who were focused on short-term profits, than on Ray who was more patient and willing to play the long-term game. Again and again, they confronted Ray, demanding a cutback on new market development so the owners could keep some of the revenues for themselves. And again and again, Ray fought back, insisting that they should just tighten their belts and wait for bigger paydays down the road. The issue remained unresolved—and the chasms spread.

Then there was a new point of contention. David sold Steve on the idea that revenues could be increased by adding services in the salons to build up the average ticket. At the top of their list were hair color services. Again, Ray resisted in his quiet but stubborn way. His philosophy was—and is—that if everything is kept as simple as possible, it will be easier to repli-cate in salon after salon. "Do one thing really well," he would say, "and do it better than anyone else, and success will follow. For us, that one thing is haircuts, period!"

Ray saw his position on each of these issues as sound business judgment; Steve and David saw it as bullheadedness. Reflecting back, nearly every point of contention was resolved in the way that Ray wanted it. That does not mean that he was right or that David and Steve were wrong. There is no way to know for sure what would have happened if Ray had relented on any or all of these issues. The fact is, Ray was more committed and more willing than the others to dig in his heels—which came across to them as bullheadedness.

In fairness to each of them, their differences—until now—did not dimin-ish their respect for one another. But things were starting to get personal, and the chasms were becoming impassable.

Although the three of them tried to keep their differences to themselves, their growing discord permeated the corporate office and the salons. The employees and franchisees couldn't miss it.

However, the three owners were in agreement on one thing; they all loved the company, and none of them wanted to leave. And they all openly acknowl-edged that something had to be done. With that as common ground, they set off to find a solution to what they now admitted was dysfunctional management.

The company's search for such a solution continued—in vain—for the next thirteen years!

CHAPTER 32

Plans A and B
to Stop the Bleeding

The first solution the owners pursued was to find someone who could bring them together and lead them in a single direction. Such a person, of course, would need the patience of Job, the diplomacy of Solomon, the wisdom of the Dali Lama, and the strength of Hercules.

Finding someone who met these criteria would be virtually impossible, but that didn't stop Ray from looking! In fact, he had someone in mind. Ray had once applied for a comptroller opening at North Central Food Systems, a $40 million company that operated thirty-three Hardee's fast food franchises in the Midwest. One of the officers of this company was Ken Miyamoto, and he had impressed Ray with his business accomplishments, good sense, and general manner. Ray invited Ken to Minneapolis to meet with him, Steve, and David.

The meeting went well, and, desperate to find a solution to their impasses, all agreed to offer Ken a job. The idea was to have Ken become the president of Great Clips, and the three owners would all be executive vice presidents—demotions for Steve (who had been president) and Ray (who had been CEO). Steve resisted. He liked being president and wasn't about to take orders from anyone else. Breaking the pattern of prior disagreements, David sided with Ray and they outvoted Steve. Ken Miyamoto became president of Great Clips.

Several people questioned how a burger flipper could be president of a haircare company. But Ray and Ken both knew that Hardee's and Great Clips faced the same problems and shared many of the same characteristics. Both companies franchised, and both, being in the low-cost range of their respective industries, catered essentially to the same type of customers.

Ken had an outgoing personality and was well liked and respected by the staff. But at the ownership level it was a different story. He may have had the title of president, but Steve, David, and Ray still owned the company and were beyond his control. They brought him in to unite them but then wouldn't let him do his job. Steve still refused to take direction, Ray continued to do basically what he had been doing, and David was a free spirit who liked to tinker and do things his own way. As Ken tells it, "If I asked David to take three steps to the right, he'd take two steps to the left and then jump five times to the right. He'd arrive at the right place, but he had to do it his own way."

Even Ray, who brought Ken to the company, refused to take directions from him. Ken agreed with Steve and David that the salons should add hair color services and other extras to increase revenues, but Ray wouldn't budge. Later, Ken came to agree with Ray, but by that time he was thoroughly frustrated with him.

Ken's executive function was soon reduced to being a go-between for the three executive vice presidents who often could not civilly discuss things among themselves. He found himself shuttling from office to office with messages from one owner to another: "Tell Ray this," or "Tell David that."

After it became evident to Ken and everyone else that he was not the answer to Great Clips' problems, Ray came up with a desperate attempt to break the perpetual deadlock: He offered to buy out his two co-owners, and he, Ken and Rhoda would thereafter run the company. This idea fell flat on its face. Ray couldn't raise the money, and even if he had been able to do so Steve and David would never accept what little Ray would be able to pay. In the end, they perceived Ray's plan as being a palace coup by an overly ambitious guy trying to take over *their* company that *they* founded.

As a result, the bad feelings were further intensified.

In March 1985, six months after Ken came to save Great Clips, the experiment ended and he gracefully left. He did, however, return a few years later to take charge of marketing at the company, a more suitable role for his talents.

Each of the three owners retained the title of executive vice president after Ken's departure, an awkward situation that lasted for about a year.

Desperate times make for desperate solutions. Ken Miyamoto was Plan A—the first attempt to make order from chaotic management. It failed within six months.

Plan B, hatched soon after Ken left in the spring of 1985, was even more desperate and was also doomed to eventual failure. Since the owners could no longer work together, they tried working apart. This ill-conceived plan involved dividing the existing markets into three groups, with each owner taking control of one of them. Amazingly, they readily agreed on the division; Ray took Minneapolis and Denver, both markets where his wife, Mary Lou, now had franchises; Des Moines worked for David since he now had family there with franchises. Steve was happy with the Florida markets and Indianapolis where he had friends and where he himself had invested in some franchises. Once those markets were divided, others easily fell into place, mostly through geography.

Anyone familiar with national franchising would know that such a "Hail Mary" idea was doomed to failure. First, with each owner focused on his respective markets, the company was left without a rudder at the home office. Second, and even more importantly, a national brand must have national uniformity. The customers don't care who owns and manages a salon; they just want to get the haircut and pay the price they expect when they come through the door. And with Great Clips there would be a stronger threat to uniformity if, for example, David introduced hair color services in his markets while Ray refused to do so in his.

If salon services differed greatly, so would prices—and so would the customer base. Marketing would then be different as well. Soon the national brand would be reduced to smaller, diverse regional brands, each meaning different things to different people—a crazy quilt. Finally, the already tough job of selling franchises would be all the more difficult; someone wanting the strength of a single, national image would find more appealing options elsewhere.

The bullet that mercifully killed this scheme was fired by the company's franchisees.

CHAPTER 33

The Franchisees Unite

It was mid-1985, and the franchisees were reaching the boiling point. They were now expected to take the lead in managing their own salons, but that presented big problems. Many lived in cities far from their salons, and many were busily engaged in their primary businesses or jobs. And even if they had the time and availability, they didn't have the experience. All of the company training had been designed for the stylists, not the franchisees. They needed direction in the details of running a salon, and this extended far beyond the cutting of hair.

On top of all this, there was dissatisfaction with marketing and, most important, a growing frustration with the owners' inability to provide unified management. Any one of these problems would be serious; taken together, they preordained malaise in the salons and the inevitable reduction in performance, customers, and profits.

Since the earlier meeting that Jim Hemak called for the Denver franchisees, there had been other market franchisee meetings. One of these was arranged in Minneapolis in the fall of 1984 by Pat Stevens, who was still bristling over the company's decision to raise the salaries of his staff, and fellow franchisee O. P. Portu, who had franchises in the Twin Cities and Tampa. Eventually, this led to Pat, Jim, and Jack Sell, a Wisconsin franchisee, proposing a system-wide advisory board to represent franchisees throughout the country with a view to consolidate their concerns and present them to the company. When contacted, the franchisees in all of the markets readily bought into the idea, and this led to the creation of the National Franchisee Advisory Board.

That board had its first meeting on June 22, 1985, three months after Ken Miyamoto left and just after the owners divided up the markets among themselves. Franchisees representing the respective markets convened and elected Pat Stevens as president. Although the group was collectively upset with management who, they were convinced, was not addressing their problems, the meeting was businesslike and civil.

The protocol adopted was for the Advisory Board members to meet among themselves. Then, after clarifying their concerns and positions, some members—usually Pat and Jim—would meet with Ray, Steve, and David. This gave them a unified voice and a means to express it. Many issues were brought to the owners, but the overriding theme was *get your act together!*

The confrontations with the owners were less adversarial than they might have been because of the leadership of Pat Stevens and Jim Hemak. Both were gentlemen—cool-headed and clear thinkers. And there were the personal relationships: Pat was Ray's brother-in-law, and Jim and Ray had been close since their first meeting at the Burger King in Denver. Nevertheless, they didn't pull any punches, and the National Franchisee Advisory Board definitely had a lasting impact on the future of Great Clips.

CHAPTER 34

If Plans A and B Both Fail . . .

In 1986, Steve and David played another card to resolve management conflict. They hired Michael Seid, a Supercuts veteran, ostensibly as a consultant; but Ray suspected that their real plan was to bring Seid in as a step toward diminishing Ray's role.

Seid's first assignment was to learn all he could about the company through interviews, and then compile a report of findings and suggestions. Ray put a simple, direct question to him: "Supercuts has an average unit volume that is significantly higher than Great Clips. Why? That's all I want to know, and I'd like the answer in just two pages."

When Seid met with the National Franchisee Advisory Board, he was not particularly well received, and by that point he himself realized that he had no future with Great Clips. The management conflicts were much deeper than he had realized and far beyond his power to fix. As he put it, "This was likely the most dysfunctional threesome I ever worked with. My recommendations were very well received, but it was impossible to get all three to agree to a plan. I could get one or two on board, but not all three. There was just no way forward as long as they were all there." The Seid experiment, like the Miyamoto and market division experiments before it, failed to bring unity to management.

Before Seid threw in the towel, he met with Ray to answer his question. "I don't need two pages to give you the answer," he said. "Supercuts has a higher unit volume because it is customer-centered. Great Clips, on the other hand, is a completely stylist-driven organization."

It was as if a bell rang for Ray! He immediately saw that Michael Seid was correct. David was a stylist, and because of his influence, many of the practices at Great Clips were designed more for the benefit of the stylist than the customer. It wasn't that David was choosing the stylist over the customer; rather, it was simply that he identified with the stylists and naturally saw things through their eyes.

Scheduling was a perfect example. Stylists were scheduled to work primarily during the daytime on weekdays because they preferred not to work evenings or weekends. Supercuts, however, booked many of their stylists on those same evenings and weekends *because that's when many customers preferred to get their haircuts.*

Even today, Ray looks at that conversation with Michael Seid as an epiphany. "This was a pivotal moment for me," he explains. "There was always something amiss—something not quite focused—about the way we were looking at the business. But in that one moment I saw with crystal clarity that we had to look at everything through the customers' eyes and do everything from *that* perspective. Everything else was secondary."

Ray often has an apt saying to summarize a business idea, and one of his favorites is that "organizing a business around your employees is a failed strategy." He now understood precisely that this is what had to change, but changing such a basic paradigm would be next to impossible—especially since David was a stylist at heart.

As 1986 was coming to an end, the situation at Great Clips was grim. The disagreements between Steve and David on the one hand, and Ray on the other, were nowhere near resolution. Franchisee profits were dwindling, and their investments were in jeopardy. And staff morale was declining by the day.

Worst of all, selling franchises and opening markets came almost to a halt. There had been an average of four new markets opened during each of the three previous years, *but only one market was opened in 1986, and no new markets would be opened during the next three years!*

Things were beyond depressing, and no solutions were in sight.

CHAPTER 35

A Light at the End of the Tunnel

All of the problems that weighed heavily on the company at the end of 1986 were, of course, still there at the beginning of 1987. In fact, Great Clips opened only eight salons throughout all of 1987—a record low for the entire history of the company after its first year. However, one thing happened that began to turn the ship slowly in the right direction and toward calmer waters.

David had been watching Rhoda and was impressed with the manuals and programs she had been writing as a consultant. He had seen enough to know that if she were there full-time she could bring badly needed order to the disorganized, struggling company. He floated the idea past Ray in late 1986. At the Barton family Christmas dinner in December, Ray put the idea squarely to Rhoda who said she'd give it thought.

In January, David began to press her to leave Land O'Lakes. He satisfied one of her concerns by assuring her that she'd be judged at Great Clips on her own merits and not as Ray's sister. She discussed it with her husband, Greg, who encouraged her to take the leap. He liked Ray and had confidence that he would make Great Clips a success and that having Rhoda at his side would assure it.

She accepted the offer, partly because Land O'Lakes was a male-dominated company in which opportunities for women were limited. "But at Great Clips," she said, "almost all the stylists and managers were women, and I thought I could help make a positive impact on their lives. That's always been important to me, and that's why I studied social work and psychology. I'd be able to do even more for people at Great Clips by providing jobs and opportunities."

On March 23, 1987, Rhoda joined Great Clips as a full-time employee. She was to report to David, and that was perfect—she really liked David and had enjoyed working with him when she was a part-time consultant.

Her first position was officially as vice president of human resources, but that designation didn't prevent her from being engaged in virtually every area of the company—not because she was *assigned* to do so, but because she felt *compelled* to do so!

Never one to stand on ceremony, when Rhoda saw something that needed attention, she rolled up her sleeves and went after it. She couldn't stop herself. To her, the carefully drawn lines on an organizational chart—which Great Clips did not even have at that time—were little more than speed bumps that might cause her to slow up for a moment, but they never stopped her from crossing to get where she thought she ought to be. Not only would she move *up* the chart to tell Steve, David, or Ray what they should be doing or *across* the chart to give direction to other officers, she would often move *down* the chart to assist the staff.

This behavior has not changed to this day. Dee Tabone, who was later to become her executive assistant, recalls, "If we had a staff or franchisee meeting coming up, Rhoda would be the first to lend a hand at packing boxes of materials or running out to get the microphones or projectors we'd need."

When a regional director in Texas left the company, Rhoda didn't hesitate to appoint herself as the "acting" regional director. She flew to Texas each week to visit salons and franchisees, to see the local staff, and then returned with stacks of notes and recommendations. "She wanted everything typed up and ready to go overnight," Dee remembers, "so she could get back to the field staff and franchisees the very next day. I had only been working for her for a few weeks, and I was frantic! I went home every night with her notes and dictation and, after putting my kids to bed, I worked until well after midnight. My husband and I didn't think I'd last a month at that pace, but it's now been over fifteen years and I'm loving every minute of it."

One can get a hint of Rhoda's energy and dizzying ability to multi-task simply by riding with her as she drives her van. Simultaneously she carries on a conversation, scribbles notes to herself, places and takes phone calls, and, when not flossing her teeth (honestly!), sips from a cup of coffee and eats cereal from a box. A Dictaphone is by her side—along with a backup— to record her endless stream of messages to corporate staff, her children, a franchisee in Phoenix, her insurance agent, or the cleaners. The floors and seats of the van are strewn with files, groceries, a few wrappers from trips through a McDonald's drive-thru where she takes her dog Annika for Quarter-Pounders, and, without fail, her workout gear, which is never more than an arm's length away.

Just as one can't describe a goatee without using your hands, one can't describe Rhoda Olsen without stopping to catch a breath!

She is of average height and in excellent condition after winning a bout with cancer. She has a full head of hair, which hopefully will never catch on fire, because she'd be too busy to put it out.

In her previous role as a consultant, Rhoda had been absorbed in writing programs and manuals, but now she had to see the company through a much wider lens. And she wasn't happy with what she saw. "Every time I lifted a rock," she recalled, "something ugly crawled out!"

The first thing that puzzled her was the difficulty of selling franchises. "Steve and Ray were both gifted salesmen," she said, "but they didn't have a defined product to sell. They were trying to sell an *idea*, but a potential franchisee wanted to see a *package*—something he could see and touch and show to his banker."

She was chomping at the bit to begin clarifying, refining, and documenting various parts of the organization, but she resisted until she could develop a better perspective of "the big picture." A franchisee meeting was scheduled for early June 1987, and she knew this could give her a great angle for seeing things through the eyes of the franchisees. Not only was this meeting a revelation for Rhoda, it gave the franchisees a welcome glimpse of a little light at the end of the tunnel.

Ordinarily, Steve or Ray ran these meetings, and their agenda was to list the things the franchisees had to do to be successful. But Rhoda ran this meeting, and she used an entirely different tactic. With a disciplined reserve that would have made her counseling professor proud, she didn't offer a word of advice to the franchisees. Instead, she went around the room and said, "Tell me what's wrong." Then she patiently listened and recorded the comments on a giant flip chart that everyone could see.

They told her they needed a better compensation program for the stylists, a consistent salon review program, better and timelier communications, better financial guidelines, sensible scheduling procedures, better marketing, etc., etc., etc. Whatever the issue, Rhoda wrote it down on her flip chart. By meeting's end she had filled thirteen oversized pages which kept her busy for the next two years. She methodically tackled every item on the pages and wouldn't cross it off until it was resolved.

More than merely solving franchisee problems, that one meeting began the redefinition of the relationship between the franchisees and the company. Until then, the franchisees were told what to do—at first to be only passive investors and later to be more active while staying obedient to the company and following directives. *But here was Rhoda, respectfully treating them as active partners whose input was sought and whose ideas were considered.* A bond was established on that day that forever strengthened the system by replacing conflict and suspicion with a sense of trust and camaraderie.

"I guess I grew up," Rhoda laughs. "As a student I was unable to sit quietly and listen, but that first franchisee meeting taught me how wrong I had been. I became a believer in the old proverb, '*You can't learn a thing while your mouth is open!*'"

In order to address the multitude of franchisee issues, Rhoda obviously had to be in and out of every department in the company. No one objected that the vice president of human resources was on his or her turf. It was, after all, Rhoda, and by now everyone understood her attitude toward the lines on organizational charts! She was all over the place, putting out fires, motivating people, tweaking the system. When Tim Lawless, a franchisee in Indiana, called Ray to say he was having some serious operational problems, Ray replied: "Call Rhoda, listen to her, and do whatever she says."

The more she worked addressing franchisee concerns, the more Rhoda identified with the franchisees; and the more she identified with the franchisees, the more she became frustrated with the three owners of the company. They discussed few issues among themselves, and they were hard to pin down as to common goals and policies. Worse, they were still focusing on the markets they had divided up among themselves back in 1985, and were therefore not sufficiently attentive to broad organizational issues.

Rhoda had no problems working with the three owners individually, but it was nerve-racking to work with them together. She remembers one meeting with the owners when she lost her temper with their bickering. "Quit messing with me!" she yelled. "You're playing games, and I don't want you putting me in the middle of them."

That's when Rhoda realized that her best contribution to the company would be to make sure the franchisees were successful. If she could do that, the company would succeed. She unwittingly figured out the two things that every successful franchising company in the country has come to learn: *(1) A franchisor can't succeed unless its franchisees succeed, and (2) it's mathematically impossible for the franchisor to outperform the franchisees.*

CHAPTER 36

Polishing Up the Act

As we saw, when Ray had his first meeting in Denver with Jim Hemak, he wanted to portray an image of success and respectability to belie any wrong impressions people might have about an outfit touting low-cost haircuts. Rhoda felt the same way, and while she and her brother were not in lockstep on all issues, they were in total accord on the need for a high level of professionalism at the corporate office.

One of Rhoda's first acts in this regard was to put a halt to the cherished Friday afternoon Happy Hours. A business was no place for alcohol, she reasoned, so she replaced the beer in Ray's refrigerator with soft drinks and emptied out Steve's liquor cabinet. Steve never forgave her for this. "It used to be just great when we all got together for Happy Hour," Steve said. "Then Rhoda showed up, and it wasn't as much fun around here anymore." Once the alcohol was removed, Happy Hours were less happy and eventually faded into oblivion.

Next, Rhoda keyed in on the sloppiness of the work product in the home office. Phone messages were either not taken or delivered inaccurately; letters and memos were sent out with typos and misspellings; and brochures were replete with grammatical errors.

She called the staff together and, in her typical no-nonsense directness, said, "We have to stop sending this crap out! How can we expect the stylists to deliver professional haircuts when we can't even write a decent letter?"

She was also unhappy with the way internal meetings were run. Agendas weren't prepared—or weren't followed—people interrupted, suggestions weren't recorded, and meetings ended without action plans or follow-up.

With Rhoda's prodding and tutoring, meetings were soon conducted more effectively, and everything that was sent out—letters, brochures, publications, and announcements—was written professionally. The staff saw the importance of doing things right.

Rhoda has a rare talent for motivating people, and her insistence on professionalism was contagious. Everyone in the office began to pay more attention to details, and they all took more pride in their work. From that point on, good wasn't good enough; nothing less than excellence was acceptable. The staff had often heard Ray say that his ultimate goal was for Great Clips to lead the industry. Now, because of Rhoda, everyone came to understand that Great Clips couldn't be the *biggest* until it was the *best*.

The drive for a higher level of professionalism was not limited to office processes. For some time, the franchisees had been openly complaining about the marketing. Jim Hemak, for example, voiced concern that "Great Clips had no ad agency, and the marketing they were doing was very elementary and ineffective." Marketing and advertising had been overseen by Tom Cook who had come over from The Barbers, but he had recently left. Rhoda and the three owners all agreed that a major overhaul was needed in this area and that perhaps it was time to hire an outside agency instead of trying to replace Tom.

Swinging for the fences, they hired Campbell Mithun, a Minneapolis-based firm that was the largest advertising agency west of the Mississippi at that time. The move was an instant hit with the franchisees. Pat Stevens, president of the National Franchisee Advisory Board, summed it up this way: "Until then, marketing at Great Clips was a 'ma and pa' kind of deal. The people at Campbell Mithun were pros, and they had credibility. They did research and developed a strategy for our marketing—something we never had before. Not all of us agreed with everything they did, but we saw the wisdom in their thinking and we supported their programs."

The agency produced several television commercials and print ads for the local markets, all based on research. As with any top-notch ad agency, their research went beyond customer preferences. In late 1987, for example, they researched the attitudes of stylists to learn how they felt about working conditions and job satisfaction. Of course, the stylists wanted higher compensation, but one of the findings was that they absolutely hated wearing uniforms. David, who still saw the business through the lens of a stylist, was quick to endorse the decision to get rid of the nautically-themed outfits. It was an illustration of how hard it was for management to adapt to Michael Seid's suggestion to view the business through the lens of the customer—not the stylist.

Great Clips would continue with Campbell Mithun for several more years, but it eventually became clear that it was a mismatch. The agency was growing and attracting major, high-paying clients, and at that point

Great Clips was pretty much standing still. The company didn't get—and wouldn't have been able to afford—the attention it needed. Nevertheless, the experience was a valuable one, and the people at Great Clips—like Ann Latendresse who was now in the marketing department—learned first-hand some of the intricacies of marketing from world-class professionals. That knowledge provided a foundation in the years to come.

Ray Barton holding the door open for the first customers at the Brookdale, Minnesota, franchised salon on July 16, 1983.

Mary Lou Barton and Ray Barton at the new Brookdale, Minnesota, salon on July 16, 1983.

Ruth Ann Grimsley, one of the early system stylists, participating in a training video shoot on location in Minneapolis in 1991.

Pioneer franchisee Tim Lawless and his wife, Kim, pictured in 1999.

Pioneer franchisee Dee Ann Tibbetts at the 1996 Great Clips Convention.

Great Clips' first non-family franchisee, Jim Hemak, with Ray Barton at Ray's induction into the Minnesota Business Hall of Fame, awarded by Twin Cities' Business Magazine in 2007.

Early stylist, corporate employee, and franchisee Roxie Poliak in the mid-1980s.

Pioneer franchisee Nancy Peyton receiving the Franchisee of the Year Award from David Rubenzer and Ray Barton at the Great Clips Convention in 1993.

Carla Fryar, a stylist from one of the original 1982 Super Clips concept salons, receiving the Franchisee of the Year Award from Rhoda Olsen at the Great Clips Convention in 2000.

Bobbie Sylte-Kneeland, one of the early system stylists, receiving a Franchisee of the Year Award from Charlie Simpson, Rhoda Olsen, and Ray Barton at the Great Clips 30th Birthday Convention in 2012.

Cheryl Stensrud, one of the early system stylists, receiving the Franchisee of the Year Award from Ray Barton and Rhoda Olsen at the Great Clips Convention in 2007.

Pioneer franchisees Dan and Bob Washburn receiving the Franchisee of the Year Award from David Rubenzer and Ray Barton at the Great Clips Convention in 1993. Also pictured, left to right, are the Washburns' long-time general manager Michelle Bates and Bob's wife Gretchen Washburn.

David Rubenzer, Steve Lemmon, and Ray Barton celebrating Great Clips' 5th anniversary in 1987.

David Rubenzer, Steve Lemmon, and Ray Barton celebrating Great Clips' 10th anniversary in 1992.

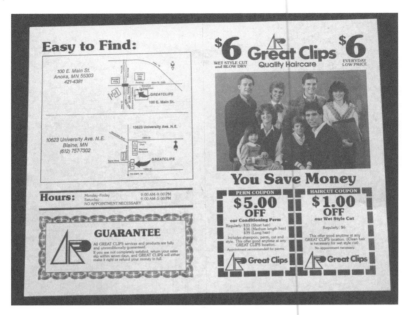

One of the first print advertisements ($6 haircut) in 1984, featuring pioneer franchisees Mary Lou Barton and Mike Testa (seated in front row) and promoting the Great Clips Guarantee that remains an integral part of the service today.

The GREAT New Look advertising introduced in 2012 featuring the innovative Online Check-In.

CAMPBELL-MITHUN
ADVERTISING

222 SOUTH NINTH STREET
MINNEAPOLIS-MINNESOTA 55402
612-347-1000

CLIENT: GREAT CLIPS, Inc.
PRODUCT: Haircutting Salons
CODE NO./TITLE: GCTV-01-84-A "Great Clips Quality Hair Care $7"
AGENCY: Tom Cook Studio DATE: Spring 1984   LENGTH: :30

1. (Music under) MAN: The next time you need a haircut,...

2. ...you could go to a barber shop or a beauty shop. Their haircuts may not cost much...

3. ...of course, they may not look like much, either.

4. Or you can go to a styling salon.

5. You know, one of those places where they cut and blow dry your hair...

6. ...at a price that blows you away.

7. Or you can come to...

8. ...Great Clips.

9. Great Clips is the place that gives you what you want.

10. A guaranteed style, cut and blow dry.

11. Both for one low price.

12. MAN (VO): Great Clips. $7. Open evenings. No appointment necessary.

Storyboards for the first Great Clips television advertising ($7 haircut) in 1984.

Great Clips, Inc.

France Place
3600 West 78th Street
Minneapolis, MN 55435
612-893-9088

The haircare industry is a huge recession proof business which is going through dramatic change. Our industry is one of the very few still dominated by the local independent operator. Like the real estate and fast food industries, it is moving towards nationwide chains and franchise organizations. This movement is in its infancy, and GREAT CLIPS has the proven concept to be at the forefront of this exciting transition.

If you have the desire, a successful track record and the financial resources, you may be able to take advantage of this outstanding franchise opportunity. Just fill out the enclosed card and I will send a full color brochure containing a complete description of the GREAT CLIPS opportunity. Included in this package will be income statements from all GREAT CLIPS company owned shops. I believe you will be impressed! For a faster response, call collect.

Very truly yours,

Raymond L. Barton

Raymond L. Barton
Chief Executive Officer

A Proven Concept

Every Great Clips Quality Haircare Shop is designed, located and managed by a success formula based upon years of experience.

Interior design is unique, colorful and functional yet requires a minimum investment.

Great Clips locations are chosen as the result of careful studies of population density and traffic flow.

Operations are designed for high volume/high quality hairstyling in a simple and direct manner.

Customers Will Be Lining Up ON Your Opening Day...

Great Clips success formula is based upon an intense marketing program aimed at the population located in the immediate vicinity around the shop.

Heavy saturation of this "local" market area coupled with Grand Opening promotion activity has the customers lining up on your opening day.

Extensive follow-on advertising continues to build the customer base.

BUSINESS REPLY MAIL

FIRST CLASS   PERMIT NO. 19872   MPLS., MN

POSTAGE WILL BE PAID BY ADDRESSEE

NO POSTAGE
NECESSARY
IF MAILED
IN THE
UNITED STATES

Great Clips, Inc.

France Place
3600 West 78th Street, #145
Minneapolis, MN 55435

Quality Control Keeps Customers Coming Back

Great Clips knows that to get customers in the shop once is not enough!

Quality haircuts are necessary for return business and positive word-of-mouth advertising.

Great Clips training program emphasizes the unique benefits of Great Clips' technical quality combined with excellent customer handling techniques.

Ongoing technical training assures consistent quality and service for the customer.

Great Clips Management Systems Keep You On Top Of Your Investment

Great Clips has refined the "paperwork systems" necessary to manage your shop to a minimum without sacrificing the necessary information needed for decision making.

Several hours a week are all of your time that is required to keep on top of your investment.

Action Reply Card

☐ Please contact me about the Great Clips Quality Haircare Franchise Opportunity

TELEX _____ BUSINESS PHONE _____ HOME PHONE _____

☐ I am interested in the following areas:

_____ _____ _____

NAME _____

ADDRESS _____

CITY/STATE/ZIP _____

HOME PHONE ( ) _____ WORK PHONE ( ) _____

Great Clips, Inc.

France Place
3600 West 78th Street
Minneapolis, MN 55435
612-893-9088

Good Morning!

Have you ever thought about owning your own business? Owning your own successful business can be challenging, rewarding and lead to financial security and independence. Now may be an excellent time to make that dream come true.

If you have often thought of owning a franchised business, but just couldn't find the right one, didn't want to make an investment of $100,000 or more and weren't interested in giving up the security of your present career, GREAT CLIPS may have the franchise opportunity you are looking for. A complete franchised system that requires no experience, (we train you, your manager and your staff), a relatively small investment of between $27,700 and $66,100 and only a couple hours of your time each week. Best of all GREAT CLIPS system has been PROVEN PROFITABLE.

My partners and I have over 20 years combined experience in the haircare and franchising business. We combined our haircare expertise to develop an exciting new haircare concept for the entire family. A concept that combines convenience, price and most important, quality. **The results have been outstanding. We are so proud of our shop performance that we will show you the sales and profits from all GREAT CLIPS company owned shops.**

As businessmen, we designed our franchise system for the investor/absentee franchisee. Our system assists you in all aspects of the business from finding a location to management and accounting methods. We introduce you to a GREAT CLIPS certified manager. Your manager will be responsible for the day to day operation of your business. The GREAT CLIPS District Manager who lives in your area will be available to assist your manager in all aspects of the business, including hiring and training of your GREAT CLIPS staff.

(continued on page 2)

Looking for franchisees—the first ADVO mailer from 1984 that caught Jim Hemak's eye.

1983

1987

Great Clips
for hair
Right for the times

1989

1990

Great Clips for hair
*Guaranteed Satisfaction.
Guaranteed Style.*

1994

Great Clips
Great Haircuts. Every Time. Everywhere.

2004

Great Clips
Relax. You're at Great Clips.

2006

Great Clips

2010

Great Clips IT'S GONNA BE GREAT

2012

Great Clips logos through the ages.

PRODUCT EVOLUTION

1983   **1988**   **1990**

1996   **2002**   **2003**   **2006**

Great Clips private label product lines through the ages.

CHAPTER 37

A Sudden Change in Leadership—and Vision

Another major event took place in late 1987—far more significant than hiring an ad agency. Steve, David, and Ray had all been executive vice presidents since Ken Miyamoto had left two years earlier. Now, after several years of interminable deadlock, Steve and David agreed to take a step back and give Ray the title of president.

This had little to do with any acknowledgement that Ray had been right on important issues—that would be an unimaginable concession. Instead, the promotion was more a surrender. All three of the owners were fed up with the bickering, and with three executive vice presidents they were like a ship without a rudder. Someone had to take the helm.

It isn't clear whether a single event triggered this shift in management, but Ray recalls David coming into his office angrily complaining about Steve. He said something like, "Do you know what our partner just did?" According to Ray, "I don't even remember what he was complaining about. I just stopped him right there and told him that I didn't care because there was nothing I could do about it. As long as we are all equals, each of us could do pretty much as we please. Steve must have done something that really got under David's skin, something really over the top, because that's when David started to push for me to be president." Steve went along with the change, either because he agreed that it was for the best or because he knew he would be outvoted if he disagreed.

At the same time, the owners finally discontinued the experiment of dividing the markets among them, much to the relief of the National Franchisee Advisory Board and Rhoda.

Alas, these moves did little to seal the fissures among the owners that would continue to widen in coming months.

When Ray first bought into the company in 1983, he carried the title of CEO, but that was really a "front" to strengthen his credentials with prospective franchisees, bankers, and the like. He never had the authority that went with the title.

Now, at last, Ray as president had a freer hand to lead the company with his own vision. His challenges were right out there in front of him and easy to see. Expansion had come to a virtual halt, franchisees were unhappy, and there was a lack of solid execution at the salon level. He was confident that he could overcome these challenges—a confidence that was inspired by an experience he had nearly ten years earlier.

Back in 1978, Ray had seen Art Bartlett, the founder of Century 21, give an impromptu pep talk at a cocktail party. He actually had stood on a chair to tell his franchisees how optimistic he was about the company's future, how they were going to lead the industry, and how vital the franchisees were to the success. It was like a halftime pep talk by Knute Rockne, the legendary Notre Dame football coach. Everyone was mesmerized and motivated, and the enthusiasm that spread through the room was awesome.

"He was captivating," recalled Ray. "He had the franchisees in the palm of his hand. They were nodding as he spoke. They *wanted* to believe what he was telling them."

Ray continued the story: "I hadn't met Art before that, but I wanted to congratulate him on his powerful talk. When I went up to shake his hand and we chatted for a few minutes, I realized that he was just an ordinary guy—but an *ordinary* guy who decided to do something *extraordinary*. He was smart and knew his business, but the thing that destined him for success was his dedication to be a leader and to lead people toward the vision that was clearly etched in his mind." With determination Ray added, *"Whenever I flash back to what Art did that day, I realize that I, too, can provide that same kind of leadership. I can provide a vision!"*

Now his time had come! Since he first had become an owner of the company four years earlier, he had a resolute goal to see Great Clips as the largest salon brand in the country. As ambitious as that was at the time, it was even more so in late 1987. There were now many more competitors and many of them had far more salons than Great Clips had been able to open. In fact, among the low-cost, salon chains at the end of 1988, Great Clips with 170 salons ranked eighth. The industry leader, Fantastic Sams, had 1,278! Sams was also the fastest growing brand at the time, thanks to its strategy of selling areas to regional developers who, in turn, sold local salon franchises. As mentioned earlier, this strategy allows for faster, less-expensive growth, but it can be problematic in that there are middlemen between the franchisor and the salon owners—and this can impede the consistency so necessary in franchising.

After a few years of stagnant growth, Ray was prepared to re-energize his expansion plans. He now had a better product to sell. Rhoda had lit the fires that led to better franchise materials and operating manuals, and she had been making great improvements in franchisee relations. She also had the staff, from top to bottom, doing their jobs better. *It was as if the company had intentionally suspended expansion in order to regroup and get its house in order, and now it was ready.*

Great Clips had planned its first convention for April 1988, and this would be the perfect opportunity for Ray to rally the troops—franchisees and staff alike. Recalling the Art Bartlett incident, he was determined to inspire them on the importance of working together to win the race to the top. Together, they would go after the competition, with industry leadership being the unwavering focus.

Ray demonstrated at that first convention, and at other meetings and conventions to follow, that he could exploit his low-key demeanor to deliver inspirational messages. At the 1994 convention, for example, Ray set out to motivate the franchisees to do a better job at recruiting stylists. He spoke convincingly of the career opportunities for stylists at Great Clips and encouraged the franchisees to "spread the word" to cosmetology schools and elsewhere. A few members of the American Association of Cosmetology Schools (AACS) attended that convention and, liking what they saw and heard, persuaded AACS to invite Ray to give the keynote speech at their upcoming convention in New Orleans—the first person to give that speech who wasn't affiliated with a school or didn't own a salon. After speaking at that convention, Ray was invited to sit on the association's board—again the first board member who did not own a cosmetology school or a salon. At one point, when the association was faced with a large legal bill it was unable to pay, Ray arranged for Great Clips to advance the money for later repayment.

The close relationship between Great Clips and that important association has endured to this day. The advantages have been mutual—Great Clips salons recruit students from the cosmetology schools, and many of the schools benefit from programs that Great Clips offers for specialized student

The Barton family at the 1998 Great Clips Convention: Rhoda, Ray, mother Alice, and sister Regina.

instruction. Further, many students at these schools, as well as students at non-AACS schools, are recipients of Alice Madden Barton scholarships created by Great Clips in honor of Ray and Rhoda's mother, Alice.

Ray realized that he needed a specific target when he addressed that first convention in 1988. Being "No. 1," or "The Best," or "The Most" sounds grand, but they are overused platitudes and none delivers the right message. "No. 1" doesn't necessarily mean "The Best," and being "The Best" doesn't necessarily mean "The Most." Ray wanted a target that was both *definite* and *measurable*. He liked the sound and feel of "billion dollar brand," so he worked backwards to figure out how to use that as a target. "It was kind of like coming up with a good punch line," Ray laughs, "and then trying to make up a joke to put in front of it." At the time, the average salon sales were under $300,000 per year, so it would take well over 3,000 salons to reach total annual sales of a billion dollars. No company was close to having 3,000 salons yet, but it was only a question of time. And if anyone would do it, why not Great Clips?

It was still more than a decade until the next century, and it was fairly common to use the year 2000 as a target for company goals. That led to the catch phrase "3000 by 2000," which Ray adopted as his rallying cry for the next several years.

As the convention approached, Ray was getting excited—but his excitement was outrunning his logic. There was no way they could open 3,000 salons within the next twelve years. It was a number they wouldn't reach for about *twenty-three* years. In the first six years, they had opened less than 200, and now they were looking for 2,800 more openings in record time with no money and no plan.

But he didn't let those details get in the way!

PART FIVE

Aiming High

CHAPTER 38

The First Great Clips Convention

In all, about eighty people attended the first Great Clips convention at the Marriott Hotel in downtown Minneapolis in April 1988. The franchisees had their *own* convention in 1986, but this would be the first time that franchisees and corporate staff met together for three days to learn, be inspired, bond, and have fun.

As one would expect, this important event had Rhoda's fingerprints all over it. She had helped produce such events while at Land O'Lakes, and she put that experience to good use. Having already eliminated many of the franchisees' misgivings about the company, she planned the convention to pave the way for even better relations going forward.

Fueled by a bottomless bag of her favorite M&M candies, she personally oversaw the setup of the audio-visual equipment, the organization of the slides, and even the writing of the speakers' scripts. And she saw to it that the entire office staff put their regular duties on the back burner to work on the big event.

She will be the first to credit the success of that convention to Mike McKinley. Mike is a motivational speaker and business consultant who not only gave a captivating speech but also coached the other convention speakers and fine-tuned their scripts. "I could not have done it without Mike," Rhoda readily admits. "There was nothing he wouldn't do to make the convention a success. He even climbed up and down scaffolds to adjust the lights. He had a lot of experience with those kinds of events, and knew what to do, and when and how to do it. It was as if he could see around corners!"

Actually, Mike's valuable assistance was evident in several of the early conventions, but his contributions were not limited to those events. As a consultant, he gave solid advice to the company and franchisees on the subtleties of customer care that are critical but easily overlooked. And, coming full circle, he played a major role in the recent 30th Birthday Convention in 2012; he was a keynote speaker and led a productive workshop for franchisees and their managers to elicit operational questions and provide feedback.

Mike McKinley is certainly one of the many heroes of the Great Clips story.

Only ten days before the first convention, one of the most beloved franchisees died. Judy Divine was only forty-two when she was struck with a sudden aneurism. She and her husband, Bill, were among the first franchisees in Denver, and she became known for her caring attitude toward her employees, her customers, and the corporate staff. Bill thought she was too motherly at times and tried to discourage her from trying to solve everyone's problems. Many of those at the convention had attended her funeral, and they were still in a somber mood when they arrived in Minneapolis.

As sad as Rhoda was over Judy's death, she was determined to have an upbeat convention. To that end, she created the Judy Divine Award for the franchisee who best exemplifies Judy's caring attitude toward her employees, and it was awarded for the first time at the next convention. Bill was touched by the gesture, but to Rhoda it was something more. She wanted that same attitude of care and compassion to be at the core of the culture at Great Clips. That was the chemistry she sought between the company and the franchisees, the franchisees and the stylists, and the stylists and the customers. With that chemistry for an anchor, the ship would not drift far. The Judy Divine Award continued for ten years; it was later renamed but never abandoned.

At that first convention, as with others in the future, meetings were serious, parties were fun, and friendships were forged. While the budgets at the early conventions were relatively modest, they always included a mix of motivational speakers, educational seminars, and award ceremonies.

Great Clips® for hair.

Great Clips Leads The Haircare Industry Into The 21 Century

Great Clips is a 3,000 salon haircare chain with operations coast-to-coast and annual sales in excess of

$1,000,000,000

"I was honored to be standing in front of all of our franchisees and employees to open that first convention," Ray remembers. Standing on the stage, he made public for the first time the slogan for his goal, "3000 by 2000." Behind him was a giant screen showing a mock 1999 newspaper headline that read: "GREAT CLIPS LEADS THE HAIRCARE INDUSTRY INTO THE 21ST CENTURY." The lead sentence of the made-up article below it read: "Great Clips is a 3,000-salon haircare chain with operations coast-to-coast and annual sales in excess of $1 billion."

Admitting that his twelve-year goal was farfetched, Ray spoke seriously to the audience, reminding the franchisees of a Denver meeting in 1986 when another prophesy of his had been ridiculed. At the time the average weekly volume of the Denver salons was about $3,000, with the highest being around $7,000. Ray told the group, "Someday we will have a salon doing $10,000 per week." After the meeting, he was asked what he had smoked for breakfast, but his words came true. Within two years a salon in Boulder, Colorado, was *averaging* nearly $11,000 in weekly sales.

In his talk, Ray drew an analogy between the fast food and the low-cost haircare industries. He reminded the audience that in the early years of both industries—the 1950s for fast food and the 1980s for haircare—there were no dominant players. But in a Darwinian way, the best fit survived while

3,000 at last! Great Clips' first franchisees Roger and Marylu Ledebuhr, who also opened the very first franchised salon in 1983 with partner Mary Lou Barton, opened the landmark 3,000th Great Clips salon on July 15, 2011, in Albert Lea, Minnesota.

others either stagnated or fell by the wayside. The same was true in other industries. In time, a clear leader emerged. It was McDonald's in fast food; why shouldn't Great Clips be the one in haircare?

Ray himself knew that he was overly ambitious, but he stuck with his goal and kept it front and center. He liked the enthusiasm it generated, and if it was over the top, well, it kept people talking about it.

In fact, he wasn't all that far off. True, Great Clips did not reach 3,000 salons until 2011, eleven years late, *but by the end of 1999, Great Clips did indeed live up to that make-believe headline—it led the haircare industry into the 21st century by becoming the world's largest and fastest-growing salon brand.*

CHAPTER 39

More Power to the Franchisees

The importance of the National Franchisee Advisory Board can't be overstated. It was a vehicle to consolidate the concerns of the franchisees, which were then conveyed to the company in an orderly and civilized manner. The company listened, and problems were solved or avoided.

However, from the perspective of the company, the Advisory Board was not a well-suited forum for ongoing or continuous dialogue because there were no company representatives on the board. The board met on its own and *later* communicated what it wished to the company. No one had given this any thought until 1987 when Ken Miyamoto was rehired by Great Clips to take over marketing for the system.

As he began work on a marketing plan, he asked about the franchisee marketing council: Who was on it, and when did they meet? Marketing council? Great Clips had no such thing. "Then how do you get the franchisees' input on the marketing plan?" Ken asked. When told that there was no process for franchisees to participate in marketing, Ken was dismayed. "How can you get away with that?" he asked. "The franchisees are the ones paying money into the advertising fund, and not giving them a say in how it's spent is usually the major complaint in any franchise business. That's why it's a standard practice for companies to have a marketing council."

He explained that at Hardee's, as at some other companies, it was called the MARC—for Marketing and Advertising Review Council. After spending twenty years at Hardee's, Ken knew what a MARC should look like, and he proceeded to create one for Great Clips. As soon as he had a rough outline of the concept, it was presented to Jim Hemak, who was president of the National Franchisee Advisory Board. Jim liked the idea of the franchisees having input on the way the advertising fund would be spent, and the franchisees followed with their endorsement of the program.

Franchisee input on marketing comes in many forms, depending on the franchise system. In some systems, the franchisees have no involvement whatsoever; in some they have advisory roles; and in a few cases they have a role so strong that it amounts to a virtual right of approval. At Great Clips, the MARC does not have an actual approval right over marketing, but it has been so collaborative between the company and the franchisees that no program has been launched since its creation over the MARC's objection.

As willing as Jim Hemak was to embrace the MARC program, he wasn't willing to abandon the existing National Franchisee Advisory Board, which addressed a wide variety of *non-marketing* issues. As he explained it, "First, I assumed the MARC meetings would be run by the company, but we had other issues to discuss and I didn't want them getting lost. Second, I wanted to keep the board alive in case the company ever changed hands and we had to deal with new people."

His view changed after the MARC was organized and became the main forum for interaction between the company and the franchisees, even on non-marketing issues. Like the Advisory Board, it was representative in that franchisees were elected and met regularly with the company. Jim and the other franchisees soon agreed that the Advisory Board could become a less active organization, focusing on issues not addressed by the MARC. Also, it would be available to represent franchisees if there were a change in owner-ship of the company or any other major upheaval. The logical next step was to replace "Advertising" with "Advisory" so that MARC would stand for Marketing and Advisory Review Council.

The creation of the MARC was a giant step forward in many respects. From the company's point of view, franchisee issues were more out in the open. "Those earlier Advisory Board meetings made me nervous," Ray confessed. "I never knew what they were talking about, and I was always bugging Jim about it."

Rhoda also embraced the change, saying, "If the franchisees have a prob-lem, I want to hear about it." The franchisees were likewise happy. Becoming a part of the marketing process made them feel that now, more than ever, they had a genuine role in system-wide decisions. And to have company personnel present when non-marketing issues came up proved helpful.

A powerful politician once proclaimed, perhaps ungrammatically, that "all politics is local." The same can be said, and more accurately, for fran-chise marketing. Knowing that, Ken Miyamoto's next step was to develop a plan to create local marketing co-ops for the separate markets along the lines that Jim had already established in Denver. No matter how sophisticated the marketing talent back at the home office, the franchisees in the local markets have the better handle on their customers' needs and preferences.

Each market now has a co-op that is an association of the franchisees in that market. The co-op has two primary functions: (1) To collaborate with Great Clips on the best way to spend marketing dollars in the market, and (2) to agree among themselves on *additional* initiatives which they underwrite by separate contributions to the co-op. These initiatives might take many forms—running commercials and ads within the market, promotions (which may involve tie-ins with other companies), sponsorships of local teams or events, charitable initiatives, public relations initiatives, and so forth.

Co-op boundaries are determined by the Designated Market Area (DMA). This has nothing to do with lines on a map, but instead is mostly a function of TV and radio signals. Thus, salons within the reach of Chicago television and radio may be within the Chicago co-op even if located in northern Indiana, and some markets in New Jersey might be in the Philadelphia co-op.

Self-governance is an important element of co-ops. Each elects its own president and other officers, and establishes its own budget. However, meetings are attended by one or more corporate representatives, generally from the marketing or operations departments, but in an advisory capacity only.

As vital as the co-ops are to marketing, they serve an equally crucial role as a forum for franchisees to get better acquainted. Here, they can discuss mutual issues that go far beyond marketing, such as staffing and compensation. Mike DiCarlo is a case in point. Mike is still grateful to the franchisees in his first co-op for helping him learn the ropes when he was starting out in the Denver market. While working as a manager at the Copper Mountain ski resort he met Dee Tibbetts. Dee was a ski instructor at the resort, but also a Great Clips franchisee at the time when franchisees were passive investors. Mike, Dee, and two others formed a partnership that opened salons in Denver. Mike eventually went out his own and had as many as twenty-nine salons in Denver and Phoenix. He later consolidated in the Phoenix market where today he has sixteen salons.

"When I started," Mike recalls, "several of the franchisees in Denver were either based in Minneapolis or previously had been with the company in Minneapolis. In addition to Dee Tibbetts, these included Bill Divine and even Mary Lou Barton. And, of course, we had Jim Hemak, who was very involved with Ray and the people in the home office. Being that close to the core of the company, these people were fountains of information on how to run the business, and they were very generous in sharing with newcomers. They certainly accelerated my learning curve and helped me get to where I am today." Attesting to Mike's success as a franchisee, in 1999 he received the Great Clips Franchisee of the Year Award.

The MARC brought the franchisees and the company closer together, and the local co-ops brought the franchisees themselves closer. The exchange of ideas and concerns were now institutionalized for the first time, and all of the stakeholders felt they were part of a single interdependent system. The MARC and the co-ops were truly milestones for the entire Great Clips family.

However, as more franchisees began to acquire still more salons, issues arose that could not be resolved through the MARC and the co-ops alone. New forums were needed.

Mike DiCarlo points out that, "Our system was primarily geared to helping the new franchisee and those with one or two salons. And that was the way it needed to be in order to protect the brand. But when some of us got up to ten or twenty salons, a whole new range of management and organizational challenges were presented—compensation structures, divisions of authority, job descriptions for different levels of management, and so on."

Mike explains that, during the MARC meetings, franchisees who owned several salons would find time to get together for breakfast at a nearby Perkins restaurant to discuss issues common to the size of their organizations. "We would ask one another questions like, 'How much do you pay your general manager? What is your bonus plan? How do you share responsibilities among you, your general manager, your salon managers, and your assistant managers? How do you leverage your size to reduce expenses?'"

According to Mike, "Rhoda could see that there would be more and more large franchisee organizations in the system and that it was something that had to be dealt with." Since 1993, Rhoda had harbored ideas about developing training and processes for franchisees with more than a couple of salons and for the exchange of information among them, but it wasn't until 1996 that the ideas began to materialize into action.

With her support, Great Clips transformed those informal breakfast gatherings into a body called "Grow Your Organization" (GYO) to deal with the problems unique to the franchisees with eight or more salons. GYO and its committees continue to meet regularly with carefully prepared agendas, and it has become a precious resource for multiple franchisees. Mike DiCarlo fully endorses this program: "I've been with Great Clips for nearly twenty-five years, and I still learn so much from GYO. Being able to communicate with franchisees having the same problems is invaluable."

In franchising, it can be a fatal error to assume that one size fits all. GYO is one more illustration of how Great Clips avoids that trap by providing a forum for franchisees to deal with issues unique to them.

Building upon this new level of unity, Great Clips began to arrange annual regional and marketing retreats (known as Spring Seminars) that were open to all franchisees. These gatherings were held at resorts that provided fine dining as well as recreation such as golf. Rhoda, the quintessential workaholic, was in charge of the Spring Seminars. As one might suspect, the working meetings were scheduled back-to-back, morning, noon, and night, with brief breaks for lunch and dinner.

The franchisees, however, wanted to mix pleasure with business and have a little fun. Bill Divine, a veteran of the legendary mountain retreats that Jim Hemak had organized for the Denver franchisees, spoke up. "People wear out after three days of meeting all day and then coming back at night for more," Bill said. "We made a little fuss and were able to get the schedule changed so we'd meet from eight in the morning until noon. Then we played golf or relaxed in the afternoon and later went out to dinner in groups. So we learned a lot and we still had a lot of fun, and because of that we started to get better attendance at the retreats." Bill added, "This was

Rhoda Olsen showing off her hoola hoop skills at the Spring Seminar in 1998.

a great group of people, and we were all starting a new chapter in our lives at the same time. And so many of us are still close friends today."

It soon became evident to everyone (including even Rhoda) that the time spent socializing was incredibly important to the health of the company. It contributed to the sense of family and led to lasting friendships. And, not to be overlooked, during the downtime a lot of helpful information was exchanged on everything from nitty-gritty problems to best practices.

Rhoda fully endorsed the inclusion of more socializing and relaxation, but she didn't allow such an alien concept to alter her own schedule at the retreats!

By 2007, there were over 2,000 attendees at the convention, and bringing everyone together each year was not cost-effective in terms of the benefits achieved. These conventions were so packed with speeches, awards, breakout sessions, planned meals, and entertainment that there was little down time for the socializing and casual exchanges of ideas that are so important. Accordingly, beginning in 2008, the company began holding its conventions every other year instead of annually, and in the off years they now hold four zone meetings strategically located across the United States. These zone meetings are both valuable and popular, and are even better attended than the biennial convention.

CHAPTER 40

If Three's a Crowd, What's Four?

The new sense of togetherness among the franchisees, and between the franchisees and the company, did not extend to the executive suite.

In 1989, about a year after Ken Miyamoto came back to take over marketing, Steve and David walked into Ray's office. Ray took one look at their faces. *Uh-oh!*

The two of them announced a plan: Ken would pay the three of them a total of $500,000 to buy enough of their shares to own 51 percent of the company. They made it clear that there was nothing Ray could do about it. If he would not agree to sell Ken any part of his one-third stake, Steve and David would each sell Ken enough of theirs to give him the 51 percent. Either way, Ray would remain a minority shareholder, and he would no longer be lead officer. It was like handing Ray a blindfold and offering him either the bullet or the rope.

Knowing that he'd never be able to change their minds, he reluctantly went along. At least he would get some cash out of the deal. Ken was told to draw up the formal contract. Curiously, months went by without Ken producing an agreement. When Ray asked about it, Ken would reply, "Still working on it."

It was inevitable that word of the plan would get out—and it did. It was the main backroom conversation at a franchisee seminar that spring in Phoenix, and Jim Hemak decided to confront Ken. "Ken," he said without beating around the bush, "there's a rumor that you're going to take over the company. What's the story?"

Ken ducked the question, asking one of his own: "I'd really like to keep Ray around. What role do you think he should play in the company?"

Jim was flabbergasted. "Here I was trying to deal with a rumor that didn't make a lot of sense, and now Ken's answer indicated that it was already a done deal!" After pausing to reflect, Jim went on to say, "Ray sold me on becoming a franchisee. There's a saying in the nonprofit world: People give to people, not to causes. When I joined Great Clips, I was investing in what Ray Barton represented, and not just in a hair salon."

And then, adding to all of the other intrigue in the Great Clips saga, nothing happened! Ken never produced an agreement and never bought the shares. Why not? The entire episode just faded away without further discussion. Ray still isn't sure if it was because Ken couldn't raise the money, or if he was worried about having an uphill battle with the franchisees, or if he was afraid about being entangled with the three owners.

Whatever the reason behind the ill-fated plan, it is offered here to illustrate one more desperate effort to bring some order to the chaos that was plaguing top management—either as a *bona fide* attempt to have a new president or as a bluff to get Ray to leave.

CHAPTER 41

The Founder Says So Long— But Not Goodbye

A shift in the ownership of Great Clips did occur in 1989, but it had nothing to do with Ken Miyamoto.

Steve Lemmon was losing interest in the business for both professional and personal reasons. The state of management was such that his control was compromised, and that had been a tough pill for him to swallow. He had enjoyed the helter-skelter of the early days when everything was foot-loose and he could make decisions without much interference. Starting a business had energized him, but as the business grew far beyond the salons and new issues piled on top of old ones, it was less fun. And the three-way power struggle was wearing him out.

As his discontent grew, so did an itch to start a new venture. His dream to buy a sailboat and start a charter business in the Caribbean had been gnawing at him for several years, and it was getting stronger. In fact, during trips to the Florida market, he would take the time for sailing lessons, and he'd poke around the boat shops to find that perfect boat.

Adding to all of this was a new romance! Steve and Kay Kivo had fallen madly in love with each other, plus Kay shared his interest in sailing. There was only one downside to this perfect match—Steve was still married to Adrienne. They had previously started divorce proceedings, but had not yet reached a settlement. Adrienne found a very good lawyer who somehow convinced Steve to give her a promissory note pending the final settlement —*and collateralize it with his Great Clips stock.* This meant that he couldn't sell any of his shares without Adrienne's consent.

So when Steve decided to leave Great Clips in 1989, he had a dilemma: He had to sell his shares to Ray and David in order to raise the money he needed to buy a boat, but he couldn't do it without Adrienne's consent. And even if the shares were worth enough to buy the boat *and* pay off Adrienne, Ray and David didn't have that kind of money on hand. David diplomatically resolved the quandary by persuading Adrienne to accept payments for her settlement over an extended time, with the payments coming from him and Ray instead of from Steve. Those payments would then be credited against the amount they agreed to pay for Steve's shares. There was enough upfront cash to enable Steve to buy his boat. In the end, Steve retained a 10 percent non-voting interest in the company. This entire arrangement was made part of the final divorce settlement.

At one point, there was some talk of Adrienne taking some of Steve's stock instead of cash, but she rejected the idea. "As it turned out, the stock would have been worth more in the long run," she acknowledged, "but I was afraid those guys would run the company down the drain. I didn't want any part of it."

Ray was relieved. As he put it, "Things were chaotic enough as it was without bringing in a new owner. But we are certainly grateful to Adrienne. By agreeing to extended payments she made it possible for David and me to buy Steve's shares."

By the time the transaction was completed, Steve and Kay had already picked out the 75-foot ketch rig sailboat they planned to buy for their charter business. But before leaving for Florida, Steve wanted to say goodbye to the company he had founded. That opportunity came at Great Clips' second convention in October 1989. Arrangements were made for him to address the convention with a supporting slide show.

The speech turned out to be a comedy of errors! First, there was a twenty-minute delay because the light bulb in the slide projector had burned out. Rhoda, who was in charge of everything (of course), felt terrible, and she was the one who scurried around to find a replacement bulb, Ray in the meantime was sure that Steve suspected it was a deliberate act of sabotage. Then once Steve finally began his farewell address, he apparently lost track of time and went well beyond his allotted ten minutes. Much of the extra time was devoted to showing slides of his new sailboat and a pitch for his charter business. The franchisees liked Steve and they enjoyed his speech, even though some in the audience joked that the talk had morphed into a commercial.

Subsequently, Steve and Kay took possession of their new boat, *The Serene*, and set up a charter business on the island of St. Thomas where every day was 85 degrees and sunny. Steve was happy to be removed from the day-to-day affairs at Great Clips, but was kept abreast of the latest goings on by David. He and David remained good friends and even made some investments together.

No one had any idea that Steve's status as a non-voting minority shareholder would last only a few years, and that he would later find himself back on the Board of Directors—*and right back in the middle of the ongoing battles for control of the company.*

CHAPTER 42

Franchisee Innovations

The improved relations with the franchisees produced an unexpected bonus. The franchisees brought a wealth of skills and experience to the system, the improved communications encouraged them to pass on their ideas, and everyone benefitted.

Franchisee input can be traced back to when Jim Hemak brought the Denver franchisees together so they could speak to the company with one voice, and it was taken to the next level when Jim and Pat Stevens launched the National Franchisee Advisory Board.

As the franchisees became more engaged in the management of their salons, Ray continuously prodded them for ideas. As an observer of McDonald's, the role model for many franchise companies, Ray had seen that some of that system's greatest innovations came from the franchisees. The Big Mac, the Egg McMuffin, and the Filet-O-Fish sandwiches were all the creation of franchisees, and more than one McDonald's franchisee has taken credit for adding breakfast to its menu.

Franchisee ideas went beyond salon management and extended, for example, to bringing enormous improvement in the build-out process. Ordinarily, franchisees begin to pay rent when they take possession of the premises—or perhaps after a short grace period—but they don't start to make money until the build-out is complete, everything is in place, and the salon is open for business. Thus, speeding up the build-out and installation of furniture and fixtures is an ongoing goal.

Great Clips was adept at quick build-outs when it was a small chain, and Steve Lemmon was personally involved with each new salon. But as the system expanded and a greater number of people were involved, slow build-outs became a bottleneck to opening salons. Something had to be done! The answer to the problem was found in the experience of a new franchisee, John Marcotte. Knowing that John had a background building out stores for Best

Franchisee John Marcotte, creator of the Salon-in-a-Box concept (late 1980s).

Buy, Ray asked him to find a way to speed up the build-out process at Great Clips.

"After studying the situation," John said, "I realized that the major snag had been in the complexities of getting the furniture, fixtures, equipment, and supplies to the salons. Surprisingly, the delivery problems were holding us up more than the internal work such as plumbing, wiring, and painting. After meeting with the vendors, I created a system where shipments from all of the vendors could be sent to one place and then consolidated onto one truck and brought to the salon at the right time with a single delivery. That also made it easy to know at any moment where everything was."

As part of the process, John also made some changes in the selection of vendors, with the dual benefit of increasing product reliability and quality while reducing costs. He completed the mission in about nine months, after which the company hired staff to oversee the process. This effort became known as "Salon-in-a-Box," and it worked wonders. It made for earlier openings and avoided the snafus of having to open with missing furniture, fixtures, equipment, or supplies. It was one more milestone in Great Clips' success story.

Jim Hemak found an ingenious way to solve an unusual staffing problem. In 1991, Jim agreed to expand into the struggling Milwaukee market with multiple salons. Beginning in 1992 and going full bore, he opened eight salons in the next twelve months and later grew the total number to nineteen. Staffing a large number of salons is always a challenge, but Jim encountered an unexpected hurdle. When he opened his first salon in the market there were eleven local cosmetology schools providing licensed stylists, but eight of them closed in the next eighteen months! These closures, which happened for a variety of reasons, left Jim with a critical shortage of stylists. This was a crippling situation, and it went on for six long years. Finally, in 1998, his new general manager, Laura Nehmer, suggested that Jim invest in an apprenticeship program, complete with a full-time director. There, under supervision, *trainees* would be permitted to cut hair and serve customers. These trainees would later be qualified to take the Wisconsin cosmetology license exam. The program was approved and regulated by the Wisconsin Division of Workforce Development. In a matter of months, this unique idea—which had never been tried before in the Great Clips system, if anywhere—turned Jim's Milwaukee operation around with better staffing and higher profits.

As previously noted, Great Clips today is unquestionably on the leading edge of high-tech data-gathering among all retail chain operations—haircare or otherwise. This, too, had its genesis with a franchisee. Bob Urich had worked at IBM and had a strong background in computers. Ruth Ann Grimsley managed one of Bob's Colorado salons at the time, and she remembers the early "technology." "All data in the salon was still handwritten in those days," she said, "like keeping track of customer counts with hash marks on a sheet of paper."

Bob thought this was archaic, so he started to develop programs to replace handwritten reports covering bookkeeping, customer counts, scheduling, and a variety of other functions. He trained the staff to use the computer for these purposes, and he kept tweaking the programs to improve them, always careful to keep them user friendly. There were some other programs for salons available on the market, but they were weak; moreover, Bob's programs were specially adapted to the Great Clips model. It was a giant step forward. Eventually, Bob formed a company to serve the computer needs of all the Great Clips salons, and he was clearly responsible for putting the company on the road to becoming the technology leader in the industry.

As the system grew, Bob's small company was unable to handle and support the increasing technological demands of the growing number of salons. Great Clips explored alternatives, and in 1992 settled on Innovative Computer Software (ICS) as its point-of-sale vendor. ("Point-of-sale" refers to the point where the sale is made and consummated—where the customers are greeted and where they pay for their haircuts.) ICS continues to be the system provider for all point-of-sale data collection, and has kept the system far ahead of its competitors in the use of this critical customer data. A sampling of the valuable innovations attributable to ICS will be reviewed in a later chapter.

As important as technological advances have been to Great Clips, one can only wonder how they were adopted in the first place at a company of which Ray Barton was president! It's true that today Ray is fairly adept when it comes to e-mail and a few of the more basic electronic tasks. However, back in the 1980s, when he was planning to take Great Clips to number one in the haircare industry, he was a virtual Neanderthal when it came to office technology.

Carolyn Bastick, who has filled a number of roles at Great Clips over the years, was the franchise coordinator in those days. She was constantly swamped with mail. There were letters, leases, contracts, and other documents to be received, revised, signed, and sent out. In addition she was responsible for all the state and federal offering circular filings. By then, nearly every office in the Western Hemisphere had at least one fax machine; *but not Great Clips.*

Frustrated with being the log that caused the jam in transaction after transaction, Carolyn went to Ray to plead for a fax machine. She mentioned that it would cost $1,400.

"What?" exclaimed Ray. "Why do we need a fax machine? What's wrong with using the mail?"

All of her arguments fell on deaf ears until she hit the magic button. "Ray," she said, "what if you needed your lawyer, Jeff Keyes, to see an important document right away? It would take two days to get it to him by mail and two more days to get it back, but with a fax machine he could read it and reply instantly."

That Ray could understand. He reluctantly agreed to the purchase, and once he saw the machine in operation and how it sped up transactions, he fell in love with it. Later, he was much more willing to accept other technologies, even when their use and capabilities baffled him. According to Dianna Anderson, his executive assistant, "I sometimes have to help him at the copy machine."

Chapter 43

"I'll Keep Saying It Until They Believe Me!"

Ray had never abandoned his goal of "3000 by 2000," but he couldn't get others to embrace his vision. And with all the trouble they were having in recruiting new franchisees, the goal became even less realistic. Not one to give up, Ray re-focused his strategy: *If we can't do it with new franchisees, then we'll do it by having our existing franchisees expand with new salons of their own. Either way, we're going to get to 3,000!*

To that end, he arranged an invitation-only meeting in January 1990 for franchisees with multiple salons. The two-day event had the theme "5 to 50," so named to encourage the idea that franchisees with five salons should start thinking about expanding to fifty. Of course, Ray knew that those numbers were arbitrary and overly ambitious, but he wanted the group to start thinking big and he wanted growth to be a constant topic.

About thirty franchisees from the Twin Cities and elsewhere attended the meeting. A professional speaker led most of the meeting, but Ray didn't miss his chance to deliver his vision in his own words: "Someday, some company will be able to reach 3,000 salons. It's not a matter of whether it will happen—it *will* happen! The question is who will do it. Why not us?"

The franchisees in the room were raising their eyebrows at one another, but their skepticism didn't stop Ray. At one point, each franchisee was asked to pick a number of salons that he or she would ultimately like to have. Simply by imagining that growth the idea started to become real in their minds. After all, these were people who had already invested in Great Clips and were enjoying success, some more than others, so it was preaching to the choir. Some, like Bill Divine, didn't need any encouragement. "I was fine with the whole idea," he said. "I was already opening as many salons as I could."

The franchisees were finally coming up with numbers to represent their potential growth, but it was all verbal and intangible. Rhoda came up with an idea to memorialize these "commitments" in a way that would make it more real. She had Carolyn Bastick take the mock "3,000 salon" head-line from Ray's 1988 convention speech and then, with careful cutting and pasting, create an imaginary *Wall Street Journal* front page featuring Ray's ambitious goal. As the "5 to 50" meeting reached its climax, Rhoda asked

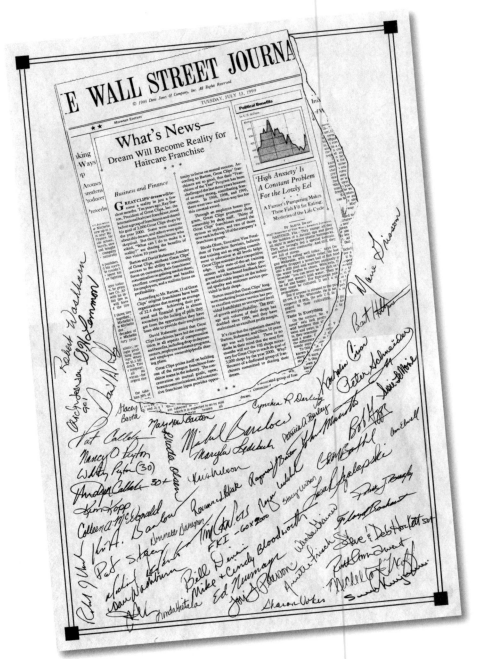

Wall Street Journal faux article created at the January 1990 "5 to 50" meeting and signed by corporate staff and participating Great Clips franchisees, many of whom set opening goals for the future.

every franchisee in the room to sign that make-believe front page and insert the number of salons that he or she aimed to open. This simple ritual reinforced the franchisees' commitment to growth and created a tangible reminder of their lofty goals.

"I still have the framed 'article' hanging on my wall," says Ed Neumayr, one of the franchisees at the meeting. "At the time, I didn't think it was possible, but we all walked out of that meeting more inspired and with higher ambitions than we had when we walked in. In fact, very few of us hit the numbers we wrote down, but we did achieve enough growth after that to blow away the competition."

Ray, for his part, kept the motivation alive by repeating the goal of 3,000 salons by the year 2000 at every opportunity, and he was quoted on the claim in several newspapers. He made sure the goal was included in all company publications. Even his letters closed with the words, "Looking forward to working with you as we grow to 3,000 salons."

One night, his wife, Mary Lou, said to him, "Ray, you've got to stop talking about those 3,000 salons."

"Why?"

"Because people are starting to believe you!"

CHAPTER 44

Franchises! Franchises! Come and Get 'em While They Last!

Despite all of Ray's grandiose predictions and the enthusiasm of some of the franchisees, expansion had come to a near standstill by 1990. A lack of money prevented the opening of *new* markets and, even more troublesome, the lack of franchisees prevented the development of *existing* markets. There were not enough existing franchisees to fuel the needed growth, and *new* franchisees were almost impossible to find.

Ray was struggling to find a way around this roadblock when, out of the blue, his prayers were answered. A friend referred him to Jeff Elgin who had recent success in selling franchises, first for National Video and later for Figaro's Pizza. Jeff was living on the West Coast when Ray called him and invited him to Minneapolis to consider a job with Great Clips.

Ray was so impressed with Jeff that at that first meeting he offered Jeff a job to take charge of franchise sales. After getting to know Ray and taking the time needed to learn all he could about Great Clips, Jeff was persuaded to accept the offer. The only obstacle was that he and his wife were in the process of buying a home in Vancouver, Washington, where they had their hearts set on living. Knowing he'd have to get Jeff over this emotional hurdle, Ray upped his offer. Jeff immediately called his wife: "Cancel the house in Vancouver. We're moving to Minneapolis."

The way Jeff put it, "Great Clips was one of the best franchise companies I've seen before or since. They were stellar in every area: Concept, attention to operational details, franchisee support, and commitment to marketing. The only thing they didn't know was how to sell franchises."

Jeff spent considerable time digging through company manuals and brochures, viewing training and convention videos, and interviewing employees and franchisees—all with the goal of finding the right fuel to light the fire. "When I first joined the company," Jeff recalls, "I regarded Ray's slogans of 3,000 by 2000 and 5 to 50 as little more than 'puff pieces,' but within a month or two I actually came to believe it was possible. However, these were goals—not viable tactics or strategies." Jeff needed much more; he needed a definite plan to get things moving—and fast! And then it came to him.

"In the 1970s, I sold life insurance," said Jeff, "and selling franchises is not all that different. In either case, you're selling something intangible—people can't wear it, eat it, or drive it home. So you have to put it in more of an emotional package. People buy a salon in order to have a better life, not because of a lifelong ambition to cut hair. So we sell a salon by selling a dream, but we wrap it in a way that a banker or investor will understand."

Building on the idea that people will pay more to achieve a dream, Jeff came up with a unique plan to spark momentum. "We start by raising the franchise fee," Jeff told Ray. "It's at $12,500 now, so let's make it $30,000."

Ray nearly had a coronary! "We can't even sell them at $12,500! How in the hell are we going to sell them for $30,000?"

"The price is irrelevant," Jeff calmly explained. "The prospective franchisees have to perceive *value* because it is *value* that people want." He then went on to show how he intended to implement the value idea. "Okay, we'll compromise and say the franchise fee is $22,500—but we don't stop there. We offer the franchisee the opportunity to sign up to open *four* franchises within two years, and if he does, that the total fee will be only $30,000—or only $7,500 apiece. That's $5,000 less than your current fee, and $20,000 less than if he buys four of them one at a time. We'll call that the Market Buster program. And to add to that, if he does get all four opened in two years, then we'll give him two more for free. In that case, his average fee is only $5,000. Those are values he'll understand."

Now Ray was starting to nod his head. He and Jeff both understood that the real money in franchising is in the service fees, or royalties, that keep coming in month after month. Only the short-sighted franchisor will try to make money on the initial fee. "I see where you're going," he replied, "but I'm worried about our existing franchisees. I've been begging them to open more salons at $12,500 each, and they'll be upset to hear the price to buy another franchise is $22,500."

"No problem. We'll tell them that the old price still applies to them for five years—provided that they give us a $1,500 deposit now for each one they commit to open within that time."

Ray wasn't so sure about this. "We've never asked them for a non-refundable deposit before. They won't like this."

Jeff smiled and said, "Let me worry about that."

Relying on his knowledge of human nature—and on how the franchisee's mind works—Jeff initiated a sense of competition among the existing franchisees. He reasoned that any franchisee who thought others would get ahead of him would not want to be left behind. And he was right. *Within one month of announcing his plan, he had 330 deposits for future salons! Nearly $500,000!*

This remarkable program produced an added benefit: Once a franchisee paid a deposit for a future salon, he was offered the chance to pay an *additional* deposit to get on the real estate priority list for his market. The same competitive motive prompted him to sign up for this as well, lest others get ahead of him and block him from getting a site for a future salon. It worked so well that, in Denver for example, the real estate priority list jumped from two or three names to over thirty!

As well as the $1,500 deposit plan was working out, Jeff couldn't get any traction for his more ambitious Market Buster program. No one was interested in paying $30,000 to commit to four or more salons within two years. However, after the program was in place for six months, Indiana franchisee Tim Lawless broke the ice and signed up. In the next ten months, thirteen more franchisees bought Market Buster deals—another $390,000!

When Jeff Elgin joined the company in 1990, there were about eighty signed franchises waiting to open. Within one year, there were hundreds! The fire was lit, and the momentum fanned its own flames. Now Jeff could say with all seriousness to prospective franchisees, "Don't be left behind! We already have hundreds on the list!"

The good news was that Jeff Elgin opened the floodgates for the sale of franchises. The bad news was that now there weren't enough sites for all of the new salons waiting to be opened.

Finding the right locations at the right rent is always a challenge, but more so for Great Clips in the 1980s and early 1990s. Landlords want reliable tenants who they know can pay the rent. In most of the country at that time, no one had ever heard of Great Clips. Furthermore, Great Clips neither signed nor guaranteed the leases, and the credit of the franchisees was not all that reassuring. So, when a landlord could choose between a well-known, creditworthy tenant and a franchisee of an unknown chain of low-cost, beauty salons, it wasn't much of a contest.

To make matters worse, there was a shortage of sites. Great Clips salons did better in shopping centers, but the country was experiencing a real estate slowdown during some of those years, and new shopping center construction was down.

Between the shortage of sites and the cool reception from landlords, the company faced an uphill battle to find "homes" for all the salons that franchisees, thanks to Jeff Elgin, were now eager to open.

It would be impossible to overstate the importance of nailing down good real estate sites for the salons. Indeed, when William Dillard, the founder of Dillard's department store chain, was asked to name the three most important elements of a retail business, he replied with the famous quote: "Location, location, location!"

No one at Great Clips ever challenged that axiom. Even though it is the franchisee who signs a salon lease, the company will occasionally sign a lease rather than let an exceptional site get away if it's likely that a franchisee will soon be available to take it. That the little-known company was able to find decent sites at all during those days was a remarkable achievement. According to Ray, "We just hung in there. We were persistent and relentless—but always polite—and it paid off." During the first nine years of the business, Steve, Ray, and even David handled real estate duties to some extent, but with Steve now gone and David fully occupied with training, it had all fallen on Ray's shoulders. Ray felt that he understood the real estate side of the business, but with all of his other responsibilities he knew he couldn't do it alone and it was too important to let slide. It was time to hire a full-time director of real estate. The position was filled in June 1991 by Dean Wieber, who had worked in commercial real estate for eleven years representing large corporate tenants.

To quote Dean, "Ray and I learned from each other. He taught me a ton about salesmanship, and I enhanced his knowledge of real estate. Even though Great Clips was not well known to commercial landlords at the time, Ray could click off all of the reasons why we would be a preferable tenant to others. I used this information to develop our talking points to landlords, and this is what allowed us to position ourselves over other prospective tenants who were larger and better financed. At the same time, I helped Ray better understand the merits of various types of shopping centers, anchor tenants, and trade areas. We made a great team."

Reflecting on his early days with Great Clips, Dean added: "Ray was optimistic and always saw the positive side of things. Consequently, I often had to quiet his enthusiasm for mediocre sites when I knew that we could find better alternatives."

Dean did an outstanding job. When he went into new markets to find sites, he made it a point to know the area—everything from the local politics to the hometown sports teams. He could tell landlords everything they wanted to know about Great Clips, and he did his homework on any companies competing for the site. Soon, the landlords were more willing to sign leases for Great Clips salons than they had in the past.

The progress in franchise sales and lease signings once again got Ray to thinking about his goal of 3,000 salons. Great Clips remained about seventh in the field of single-brand hair salons, with Fantastic Sams still being the leader by far.

Ray started to wonder, *Should we adopt the Fantastic Sams strategy of finding regional franchisors that can help us develop markets and sell franchises all over the country?*

CHAPTER 45

The Master Franchise Experiment

Ray Barton's eternal quest for 3,000 salons was not motivated by greed or grandeur—it was for the *betterment of the individual franchisees.* Since his days at Century 21, he had been a keen observer of franchising. One of his observations, formulated in his mind after studying McDonald's, and confirmed time after time, was this: The greater the number of *total* outlets in a given market, the better each *individual* franchisee performs in that market.

Of course, this point could be carried to extremes. No one would seriously argue, for example, that every Kentucky Fried Chicken (KFC) franchisee in a market would survive, let alone thrive, if there were a KFC *on every corner.* But except for the theoretical case of over-saturation, the importance of market dominance to the individual franchisee is no longer disputed. There are several explanations for this, but the most obvious is that marketing dollars spent by each franchisee *tend to benefit all franchisees flying the same flag.* This is how "brand awareness" is enhanced. And marketers will contend that every incremental dollar spent will produce more than the preceding dollar. That is, the results of spending $2 will be *more* than twice the results of spending only $1. As observed earlier, this is often referred to as leveraging the brand.

Based on this reasoning, having twenty salons in each of *five* markets will produce higher individual salon sales and profits than having the same number of salons spread over *ten* markets. This explains why Ray naturally focused first on developing *existing* markets before concentrating on new markets. But when he did the arithmetic he realized that, even if he fully saturated the existing Great Clips markets, he would have only about 600 salons. *Not good enough,* he thought. *We need those 3,000 salons.*

There was one self-imposed factor that impeded growth in certain markets. Great Clips did not want to give any one franchisee such dominance in a market that it would decrease market-wide cooperation among all of the franchisees. So while it was important to have the *brand* dominate the market, it could be counter-productive for one franchisee to be able to overpower his fellow franchisees when it came to local marketing and promotions. An early policy dictated that no franchisee could own more than five salons in a market. Jim Hemak suspected that the policy was aimed at him and his growing number of salons, and he dubbed it the "Hemak Rule." As more and more franchisees were growing, that rule proved too limiting. Still, even today the company strives to ensure that no one franchisee has such a disproportionate number of salons that he or she could take over the market.

Two of the old issues combined to hamper the opening of new markets. First, it was very expensive to prime a new market with offices, employees, a corporate salon, and training center. Second, David renewed his earlier objection to widespread expansion. As he had maintained for years, it was time to start enjoying the profits and not pour them into reinvestment. The "race to the top" was simply not that important to him.

All of this brought Ray back to an idea that had been haunting him on and off—an idea that might bridge the gap between him and David on the expansion issue.

The idea was to find investors who would put up two or three million dollars to "buy" a region. In Ray's mind, this would be strictly an investment, with Great Clips finding the franchisees and locations, developing the region's infrastructure, and overseeing all operations. The investors would simply be paid a percentage of the fees collected by the company. This process would be repeated with other investors in other regions, thus facilitating much faster growth (as Ray wanted) without overtaxing the company's limited resources (as David wanted).

Even though the idea was still sketchy, Ray began to put out feelers looking for potential investors.

It wasn't long before Ray made a connection with Michael Connolly who was also based in the Twin Cities. Michael's credentials were impeccable: An MBA degree from Harvard, work experience with major retail chains such as Blockbuster and franchise chains such as Wendy's, and a stint with the financial side of American Express. And he also had ample access to the capital he would need for the investment. In fact, he had the resources to develop more than one region.

Ray was impressed, and the feeling was mutual. "I liked Ray, and I liked all the numbers I saw," Michael said. "Great Clips was one of the finest examples of how to support and nurture franchisees while using a disciplined system." It seemed like the perfect match, but there was one glitch: Michael wanted to run the regions himself. "I wasn't interested in being a passive investor," he recalls telling Ray. "I wanted to get back to operations." He had been a successful executive in other businesses but, he explains, "This was my chance to build a business on my own."

Ray was wary about giving up control of development in the regions selected, but Michael would not be deterred. He was willing, of course, to follow the Great Clips concept in terms of the training, the haircut, and the services offered to the customer, but beyond that, he wanted no interference. He wanted the right to select the franchisees and the sites in his regions, and he would provide the training.

This put the ball squarely in Ray's court. This was contrary to his plan of having only passive investors who would finance regional development. Further, he knew it was risky to put an independent-thinking entrepreneur like Michael in charge of the Great Clips brand in large parts of the country. He'd be difficult to control. Ray's sense of danger, however, was overcome by his urge to grow. On balance, he concluded that "Michael was my best option to jump start the national expansion that the brand needed—and that was worth the risk."

Once they had a meeting of the minds over the general parameters, with Great Clips having certain approval rights, they got into details. They began by agreeing on four regions that Michael would develop. This took a little imagination because, until then, Great Clips thought in terms of single markets, not in terms of multi-market regions. The four designated regions were:

1. Pacific Northwest (generally from Portland to Vancouver, British Columbia)

2. Northern California (generally from San Francisco to Sacramento)

3. Mid-Atlantic (generally from Washington, D.C. to Philadelphia)

4. Chicago (the city could support enough salons to be treated like a region)

Ray insisted—and Michael agreed—that development of these regions would not begin simultaneously, but in the order listed above. Ray had already learned the importance of highly focused market-by-market development, and the same would surely hold true for region-by-region development. Only after development in a given area was well under way with training centers and staff would development elsewhere be undertaken. Equally important, Ray exacted a timeline whereby Michael would have a development schedule, and if he didn't meet it he would be in breach of contract and forfeit rights.

Finally, Ray reserved the right for Great Clips to take back any one of those regions without a payment provided there had not yet been any development in that region. If development had begun, Great Clips could still take the region back on terms yet to be agreed upon.

Ray set up a meeting to discuss the plan with Jeff Keyes, the company lawyer, and with Jeff Elgin. Never one to hold back, Jeff Elgin said, "The Pacific Northwest is my old stomping grounds. Why don't you let me develop it?"

"You don't have that kind of money," Ray replied. "Who would back you?"

"I would," Jeff Keyes volunteered.

This interchange didn't alter Ray's plans. Jeff Elgin was doing a Herculean job selling franchises, and Ray couldn't afford to lose him. And Elgin, after giving it more thought, realized that his niche was sales and that he might not do so well wrestling with all the other details required to develop an entire region.

Michael organized Great Clips Regional Companies (GCRC) while he and Ray were still ironing out the details of the arrangement. They both agreed that the ultimate objective was to protect the brand by ensuring that GCRC delivered the same customer experience as offered at all other Great Clips salons, whether in Portland or Tampa. As Ray put it, "No matter how many master franchisors we ended up with, a customer traveling across the country should see Great Clips as one seamless enterprise."

To that end, it was finally agreed upon that Michael's GCRC would be responsible for regional training, finding sites, finding franchisees, and providing franchisee support. Great Clips, on the other hand, was firm in maintaining approval rights over salon décor and training materials as well as the final approval of any franchisee selected by GCRC. All advertising fund contributions from the franchisees (5 percent of salon sales) would be paid to Great Clips, for which the company would be responsible for all system marketing and advertising in the region. Initial franchise fees and royalties (6 percent of salon sales) would be paid to GCRC as the master franchisor, and from these resources GCRC would pay Great Clips 15 percent.

All of the legal filings required by the states, provinces, and the Federal Trade Commission were handled by Carolyn Bastick at Great Clips. A franchisee in one of the GCRC regions would sign his franchise agreement with

GCRC—not with Great Clips—but the agreement would be prepared by Carolyn who would then send it to the franchisee and GCRC for signatures.

To gear up for the regional development, GCRC had to hire a staff of regional directors, trainers, real estate managers, and franchise recruiters. Most of the GCRC employees were out in the field, but those in the home office worked out of the Great Clips offices in Minneapolis. Michael insisted on that, and it suited Ray just fine. It made it easier for him to see what was going on.

Michael Connolly's plan to develop his regions was an ambitious one. "I was on the road 220 to 250 days a year," he lamented. "I'd get up in the morning, go to the office, catch a noon flight to one of the regions, check out real estate and visit salons during the days I was out there, and meet with franchisees in the evenings."

In many respects, Michael faced the same obstacles the Great Clips owners faced when opening new markets. Because the brand was unknown in these new areas, he had little sway with landlords and had difficulty attracting franchisees. Furthermore, all of his early franchisees were new to the system and required extra support to run their salons. He was reliving the same challenges that had been confronting Ray, David, and Steve over the past ten years.

With the carefully crafted division of responsibilities between the two organizations, cooperation and experience-sharing were common. Ray and Dean Wieber spent time in the new regions to provide real estate guidance, and Jeff Elgin assisted with franchise sales. David Rubenzer would occasionally visit the regions to guide training efforts and help impart the "feel" of a Great Clips salon. And, of course, whenever Michael ran into serious issues with franchisees, he knew he could call upon Rhoda, the "great mediator," to come out and smooth things over.

GCRC was fortunate to sell some franchises to a few existing Great Clips franchisees who wished to expand into the new regions. These were early franchisees that were exempt from the policy barring franchisees from having salons in remote markets. John Marcotte, the franchisee in St. Louis who had perfected the single-delivery system for build-outs, opened salons in Seattle under a multi-unit package developed by Jeff Elgin, and then for a time had some salons in Portland. And Jim Hemak, from Denver, opened three salons in Seattle in partnership with several friends, one of whom, Gil Fulleher, lived in Seattle.

Despite all of his precautions, Ray began to see storm clouds building on the GCRC horizon. According to him, "We had a system that required doing things a certain way, but Michael was an entrepreneur and wanted to do things *his* way. True entrepreneurs don't always like being confined to a given system. Additionally, Michael was 'all business' while we were a little more like a big family."

One problem arising out of this different culture style can be illustrated by the case of Jerry Sullivan. Jerry, a good friend and former business associate of Jeff Elgin who had extensive franchise experience, had flown out to Minneapolis to be interviewed by Rhoda for a job in operations.

He was virtually bowled over when he met Rhoda and David, and was impressed how everyone was treated as equals. It was clear to him from all the conversation how deeply Great Clips cared for its franchisees. "Everybody loved everybody!" Jerry exclaimed. "The staff loved Rhoda and David, Rhoda and David loved the franchisees, and every franchisee I met loved the company. I felt like I'd be joining a great family. When I got home and told my wife about the people, she agreed that I should become a part of Great Clips."

However, instead of taking the operations job, Jerry and his wife decided to sign up for a four-salon package in Portland where GCRC was just starting development. By the time they had opened their first salon, they felt betrayed. "There was no Rhoda or David, and there was little of the support I had heard about. Michael and his people were on the fly, and we didn't get a lot of attention. Worse," Jerry recalled, "Michael was not following the Great Clips model in several respects, and he was not about to have someone with my franchise experience challenging him on this. At one point, he took out his checkbook and offered to buy us out on the spot. I finally took him up on his offer shortly after we opened our second salon. I was only too happy to sell out and leave."

Although GCRC's organization lacked the charisma that franchisees found at Great Clips, they did have one thing going for them that kept them in the game—money! "They brought a lot of money to the party!" David shook his head as he watched how much GCRC spent on development, explaining that "money can carry you only so far in this business. You need a strong people component, and without it, you just can't get past a certain point—no matter how much money you have." David's point was confirmed by the challenges that later confronted GCRC.

By 1994, as the Pacific Northwest Region began to stabilize, Michael decided it was time to move on to the Northern California Region in order to keep up with his development schedule. "This turned out to be a big mistake," he now says, "and we compounded that mistake by starting to develop the Mid-Atlantic Region the following year. The demands on our capital, on our time, and on our people were endless. If I had to do it all over again," he said," I would not have gone into those other regions, but our contract had a development schedule. Ray was holding me to that schedule, and I didn't want to breach it."

There were two other problems in developing the Northern California and Mid-Atlantic Regions—competition and high rents. Competition spelled lower customer counts, and high rents spelled lower profits. Other low-cost brands had already established solid footing before GCRC entered those regions. Supercuts was the primary competitor in California, and Hair Cuttery was the culprit on the East Coast.

The story of Scott and Melissa Simon is illustrative. The Simons bought the first GCRC franchise in the Mid-Atlantic Region, opening a salon in Baltimore in October of 1995. Because GCRC was slow to get their development plans moving, the Simons had to fend for themselves to find vendors and train stylists. To make matters worse, their primary competitor was armed and waiting for them!

According to the Simons, Hair Cuttery employees later told them that they were shown a video which falsely depicted Great Clips timing each haircut, and that any Great Clips stylist exceeding the allotted time could be fired! The sense of intrigue intensified when the Simons discovered, a few days after the grand opening, that they had somehow lost phone service at their salon. Scott Simon then thought about the potted plant that Hair Cuttery sent them for the grand opening, and jokingly asking if it was bugged.

Notwithstanding the rocky start, the Simons definitely got retribution when they opened their second Great Clips salon six months later—*and very close to a Hair Cuttery salon*. It was an immediate success and remains one of the top performing sites in the entire Great Clips system.

Michael Connolly and Ray both saw that GCRC was getting out over the tips of its skis and could not possibly keep up the development pace established in the contract. It was agreed that GCRC would continue with the three regions already started, but that the Chicago Region would be relinquished to Great Clips. It wasn't long before Michael, becoming more disenchanted, stepped back and turned the day-to-day management of GCRC over to others.

CHAPTER 46

Great Clips Develops Its Own Regions

The regional expansion by GCRC may have been painful, messy, and cash-intensive, but it was productive in terms of salon openings. And Great Clips, as a company, was not standing still while this was going on. Jeff Elgin was doing a tremendous job of finding new franchisees for other markets and convincing existing franchisees to open more salons. These combined efforts, coupled with Rhoda Olsen's continuous fine-tuning of the franchisee support system and Dean Wieber's real estate accomplishments, all led to another milestone: *By 1994, Great Clips had become the fastest growing salon brand in North America—only two years after being at a virtual standstill!*

Everyone in the company recognized the synergies that were making this happen, and the credit was happily shared. People were attributing the growth to Jeff's phenomenal success in selling franchises. Jeff was giving credit to Ray, Rhoda, and David for supporting the franchisees he was bringing on board and to Dean Wieber for finding the sites for these new salons. Jeff, in a self-deprecating way, shrugs his shoulders and says, "I shouldn't get that much credit. Our franchisees are our best salespeople. They are the ones who can testify to the success of the system. Prospective franchisees listen to them. If they don't get the support I promise them, they will not validate the system, and without that validation I'll have nothing to sell. That's when everything falls apart. I see this often in franchising, but Great Clips won't let that happen. Everyone worked hard to make sure that my promises are kept."

It was time for Ray to go back to the drawing board. *Can we handle all of this growth with our existing organizational structure?* He had been watching how Michael Connolly was developing his multi-market regions and concluded that—if done right—this was a strategy that should work for *all* expansion. And Great Clips could do it alone. Regional intermediaries like Michael Connolly would not be needed. With the careful configuration of new regions, *each with multiple markets,* the relocation of staff would be minimized and franchisee support would be fully maintained. Further, by considering the pattern of television, radio, and newspaper coverage, a regional plan would make for much more efficient marketing.

The key, Ray knew, would be to install a strong regional director in each of the new regions—a director familiar with real estate, franchise sales, marketing, operations, franchisee support, and training, and who, above all else, could deliver the brand. In fact, the concept was not new. "We had regional directors back at Century 21 when I was there," Ray explains. "And McDonald's has had regional managers overseeing multiple markets forever."

The first region chosen was Chicago after it was given up by GCRC. (Chicago was actually one big market, but due to its size it could support so many salons that it was treated like a region.) The choice for the first regional director for Chicago was an inspired one—Jerry Sullivan. Jerry had been a GCRC franchisee with multiple salons in Portland, but became disenchanted with the GCRC operation. He sold his Portland salons back to GCRC and moved to Chicago.

"By this time," Jerry relates, "Great Clips was becoming a much better-known brand and was starting to attract more sophisticated franchisees—like former corporate presidents or vice presidents who were prepared to open ten or twelve salons. They expected to deal with someone with solid business experience—someone who had walked the same walk as they had. *Gone were the days when the top Great Clips representative in the market was a trainer or former stylist with no business experience.*"

Jerry did an excellent job developing Chicago, but the entrepreneurial itch never left him. Today he is once again a Great Clips franchisee with nine salons in Boise, Idaho.

The story of Steve Hockett, the regional director selected to bring Great Clips into the major markets in Ohio and Kentucky, makes for great water-cooler chitchat. Earlier, in 1988, when he was twenty-seven, Steve and his wife Deb bought a Great Clips salon that had been open for five months. Steve, who had an MBA degree, admits unabashedly that "I failed as a franchisee."

After later closing his salon, Steve went to work for the company in the marketing department and then moved over to operations. He later left for six years, but then returned and has been with the company ever since.

"I had a passion," he says with intensity, "and I was determined that my failure was going to help other franchisees succeed. After becoming the regional director in Ohio, I told my staff, 'We're going to open salons, we are going to have people be successful, we are going to be aggressive, and we're going to keep pounding away.'" It's this spirit that epitomizes the caring but competitive culture of Great Clips. "Today," Steve says with pride, "there are more Great Clips salons operating in Ohio than in any other state or province in the entire system."

Steve Hockett, currently executive vice president and chief operations officer, speaking at the 2000 Great Clips Convention.

Steve Hockett is now the chief operations officer at Great Clips and one of the top executives in the entire organization! But it isn't his title that allows him to perform so well; by his own admission it was his failed experience as a franchisee that gave him the empathy and insight to understand what it takes to run a salon.

CHAPTER 47

Going to Court over Prices

There is one area where sound franchising practice can unwittingly run afoul of the law.

Every student of franchising knows the importance of consistency, a point made throughout these pages. Outlets flying the same flag must deliver the same experience to the customer. There should be a similarity of appearance, products, services, and treatment of the customer. That is what creates the brand, and assures the customer traveling through Nebraska that she will get the same haircut in Omaha that she gets back home in Dallas. Every franchisor insists that the franchisees follow the manuals down to the last detail, lest their salons or restaurants start to look and act differently from one another. Indeed, failure to follow the standards can lead to a forfeiture of the franchise.

One would think that this need for standardization would certainly include the charging of a standard price in every outlet. However, in the United States, federal and state laws prohibiting "price-fixing" agreements, dating back to the nineteenth century, have been construed to apply to franchisor-franchisee agreements that control pricing. Specifically, at least until the mid-1990s, courts have ruled that there are severe limitations on the rights of a franchisor to set the prices that franchisees must charge their customers. There are similar limitations on the right of franchisees to agree among themselves as to the prices they will charge. In theory, these restrictions are designed to give the ultimate consumer the benefit of a free and competitive marketplace.

It was against this backdrop that Ray, in the 1980s, took a bold risk by converting an informal, voluntary pricing practice into a new pricing policy that franchisees were *required* to follow. As before, the franchisees could choose their own prices, but haircuts were required to be priced in "even dollars." Thus, the franchisee could charge $6, $7, or any other even dollar price he wished, but he could not charge $6.99 or $7.50. Further, the practice was that the price charged seniors and children must be the same as for all other customers.

This change was made because one of the early franchisees in the Twin Cities, Bob Levine, decided to ignore the earlier "even dollar" practice. Bob's motives are a little unclear. Like many retailers, he may have believed that $7.99 would sound to the customer like a real bargain compared to $8, and that someday it would surely be easier to charge $9.99 than $10. Furthermore, he had been Steve Lemmon's lawyer and good friend, and that could have made him even less willing to march to Ray's pricing policies. Whatever the real reason, Bob Levine disregarded the new directive by continuing to charge "off-dollar" prices and having separate prices for seniors and children.

Ray, Rhoda, and other company personnel did their best to persuade him to adhere to the new policy, but he'd have none of it. In fact, he tried to enlist other franchisees to follow his lead. Ray then had a series of meetings with Jeff Keyes who did legal work for Great Clips and who was a seasoned litigator. Any lawyer familiar with the antitrust laws knows the risks of trying to defend anything that smacks of franchisor-dictated pricing, and would have followed the traditional "safe" course by counseling Ray to back off. But this policy did not sound to Jeff like a traditional "price-fixing" plan. Moreover, backing off on this issue would weaken the company's ability to enforce *other* policies, and if that happened, Ray knew he could lose control of the brand. The Great Clips franchisee community was watching and waiting to see what he would do.

While Ray and Jeff were soft spoken, they were not "safe players." They decided on a radical, audacious strategy that challenged the conventional wisdom of the day. To press the issue with a frontal attack, *they had Great Clips file suit against Bob Levine in the United States District Court!*

Great Clips asked the court to enjoin Levine from charging the off-dollar prices, and the case was fought strenuously on both sides. After hearing testimony and reviewing the legal arguments, the federal judge entered a final decree upholding Great Clips' pricing policies and ordering Levine to comply with them. The court evidently decided that requiring even-dollar pricing did not amount to price fixing since the franchisee could charge any even-dollar price he or she chose.

To say that this court victory was important would be a colossal understatement. Bob Levine was a practicing lawyer and was well-known throughout the Great Clips franchisee community. All eyes within that community had followed the case. If Ray had backed off, or if the company had lost the case, the credibility of Ray and the company would have been severely damaged. The pricing policies, which are so essential to the brand, would have been nullified, and all salon pricing would have been up for grabs. Even worse, franchisees would be more prone to ignore other policies and recommendations, and the harm from that would be incalculable. But by pursuing—and then winning—the case, Ray sent a message to his franchisees: *Our policies are sound, and I will do whatever I have to do to defend and enforce them for the benefit of our franchisees and our brand!*

Attorneys familiar with the antitrust laws took note of Great Clips' bold strategy and the court's decision. Because of the way price-fixing laws were interpreted in the 1980s, few defenses were available to franchisors who tried to control franchisee prices, and most franchisors stayed far away from any legal controversy on that issue. Alan Silberman, an esteemed lawyer who is a former chair of the American Bar Section of Antitrust Law, and also recognized as one of the "senior statesmen" in franchising in the United States, confirms the conventional wisdom of that time. In his own words, "Franchisors were advised by their lawyers that they could *recommend, suggest,* and even *urge* that certain pricing guidelines be followed, but they were told never to *dictate* prices to their franchisees. And nearly every pricing communication to the franchisees ended with something like this: 'Of course, pricing decisions are ultimately yours to make; our suggestions are based on our assessment of the market, and we think they make sense, but the ultimate decision is yours.'" But Silberman (who has taught the Practicing Law Institute's course on antitrust pricing rules for nearly three decades and has defended major American franchisors in landmark litigation) leaves no doubt that the strategy followed by Ray and Jeff was bold, creative, and well-founded.

"*All* franchisor policies essentially control a franchisee," Silberman notes. "That's what franchising is all about. But here the Great Clips policy rested on a marketing strategy that defined brand attributes, made Great Clips and its franchisees more competitive, and on balance was a consumer benefit. So, rather than being an example of 'rigging prices,' it was consistent with basic antitrust objectives because it was consumer oriented." The bottom line, Silberman states, is crystal clear: "*Challenging conventional wisdom with common sense, and then taking a risk to present it affirmatively, was legal skill and business judgment at its finest.*"

PART SIX

Ready–Aim–Fire!

CHAPTER 48

Oil and Water

After Steve Lemmon left Great Clips for the seven seas, everyone assumed that the pressure in the executive suite would subside. Sure, David and Ray had issues with one another, but they were both gentlemen, and neither was nearly as outspoken or volatile as Steve had been. Two gentlemen should be able to resolve their differences easily, right? Wrong! The fault lines continued to send troubling seismic waves.

The temptation to psychoanalyze is dangerous, but irresistible. Both men had a passion for Great Clips, but each saw it through a different lens. Ray envisioned a national enterprise with 3,000 salons, 30,000 stylists, and hundreds of corporate employees, all fitting nicely into their respective boxes on a giant organizational chart. David's vista was much smaller. He saw a person sitting in a chair, covered with an apron, getting a haircut by a stylist who he had trained to perform in a professional and friendly way. Ray appreciated the importance of delivering the right haircut, but he did not let that obscure his view of the big picture. And David appreciated the importance of a sound business structure, but he didn't let that distract him from the haircut.

Ray's business card showed him as "president" of the company; David's read "barber." Ray's office had the standard décor of a corporate executive; David's office furniture included a barber's chair.

Whenever David suggested a change in the salon—for example, how the customer was logged in, how the stylist clocked in, or how the payment was handled—Ray spontaneously tried to figure out if such a change could be implemented in 3,000 salons and taught to 30,000 stylists. If not, it had to be shelved, and that was anathema to David. Ray believed deeply that there could not be a strong brand without consistency, there could not be consistency without simplicity, and there could not be simplicity if there was constant tinkering. This is a point that he still preaches at every opportunity—as did Steve Jobs, the founder of Apple, who was often quoted as saying, "Simplicity is the ultimate sophistication."

But David loved to tinker! To him, styling was artistry, and artistry was creating. It was his need to create, to revise, that was so frustrating to

Ray! He was continuously coming up with new ideas and, out of a pride of ownership, kept pushing to make them part of the system. An example was his ongoing drive to introduce hair color services; another was his idea to initiate a "call ahead" program that would rub up against the no-appointment policy.

Ray was still president, and he rejected these proposals as unnecessary, difficult to implement, and counterproductive, and David resented being overruled. He never stopped berating Steve Lemmon for bringing Ray into the business in the first place: "What does this *accountant* know about haircare?"

Also hanging over the relationship was the old gratification timetable. David still wanted to enjoy the profits of their labors here and now, and Ray still wanted to reinvest the profits to fuel growth for later rewards.

The tension was becoming more and more obvious to the staff and even the franchisees, and it was threatening the flow of business. In the past, it had been Steve and David who tried to squeeze Ray, but now it was Ray who began to do his own squeezing.

His first ploy was to offer to buy out David using the same price formula that they had used to buy out Steve Lemmon five years earlier. "Are you out of your mind?" David replied. "This offer is a joke." He didn't even bother asking for a higher price.

In desperation, Ray resorted to a more drastic strategy in the early spring of 1994. As president of the company, he told David that *he wanted him to leave!!* Even though the by-laws gave broad powers to Ray as president, the idea of firing David was filled with problems. David was popular with the staff and many of the franchisees, and such a move could have serious repercussions. Furthermore, David's termination would require board approval, and Rhoda's vote was not assured; she loved her brother but had deep respect for David, and she had shown time and time again that being Ray's sister was secondary to her concern for the business.

If Ray's strategy was to bring things to a head, once and for all, it was a rousing success—*even if not as he had intended!*

CHAPTER 49

War and Peace (Well, at Least War)

David did not react lightly to Ray's attempt to oust him from management of the company! In the spring of 1994, shortly after Ray asked him to leave, two nearly identical events took place. They may have been accidental or they might have been staged, but they set the groundwork for a major change of ownership and, once and for all, determined the future of the company.

Steve Hockett and David were flying back to Minneapolis from a meeting in Des Moines that spring, with David sitting just ahead and across the aisle from Steve. David had some paperwork in front of him, and, either by accident or design (accident, according to David), he was holding a document in such a way that Steve, when he happened to glance in that direction, saw it. It was a legal-looking document with a large caption in capital letters:

DAVID RUBENZER, *Plaintiff*

v.

RAYMOND L. BARTON, *Defendant*

Oh, my God, thought Steve, *it's a lawsuit! David is planning to sue Ray!*

He did not say a thing to David, but back in Minneapolis he related the incident to Rhoda, his supervisor. She simply said, "Well, I'm not surprised." In the spirit of honesty, Steve then told David what he saw and that he had reported it to Rhoda. "I hope you won't hold it against me that I did that," he said.

"No, I won't," David replied.

The entire incident evaded further discussion until a couple of weeks later when Jeff Elgin and David were on a flight back to Minneapolis. As was the case with Steve, David was holding the same legal document in such a way that Jeff could not help but see it. Jeff, too, saw that it had to do with a lawsuit.

CHAPTER 50

Same Battle—New Battlefield

Contrary to what many believe, a business is not run by its president or CEO. It's run by a shareholder-elected Board of Directors, and the officers—including the president and the CEO—serve at the pleasure of the board. The board appoints the officers, and it can fire them. That said, most privately owned companies regard their boards as ceremonial, signing the minutes of an "annual meeting" that never takes place and leaving the president to run the show as he or she sees fit. (Generally, none of that makes any difference because it's usually the president who owns all or most of the stock and therefore controls the board, but that clearly wasn't the case at Great Clips.)

Until Ray and David signed their settlement agreement, the Great Clips Board of Directors was essentially inactive. Ray as president pretty much had his say in spite of his differences with David. But now, by effectively reactivating the Board of Directors, David and Ray did little more than move their disagreements from their offices to a new battlefield—the boardroom.

The new board consisted of the five shareholders whose shares now fell into two distinct voting blocs—49 percent for David and Steve and 49 percent for Ray and Rhoda (who, on governance issues, was expected to vote with Ray). Jeff Elgin, who held the remaining 2 percent and was the fifth person on the board, was expected to be the swing vote. In reality, that didn't make the tensions disappear. When he voted with Ray and Rhoda, David and Steve were upset with him, and the opposite was true when he sided with David and Steve. Jeff stood up to the pressure and he did his best, but giving him a vote at infrequent board meetings did little to ease the day-to-day dysfunction at the top.

David, as the new chairman of the board, kept his promise to "conduct a board meeting every few months to make Ray's life miserable." These meetings only served to highlight the conflicts. The day-to-day angst was getting worse.

Despite all of Jeff's efforts, he could see that things were getting further out of hand. "No matter what we did," he said, "it was obvious that we'd never have peace as long as Ray and David were under the same roof. Therefore, my *new* goal was to get one of those guys to trigger the buy-sell agreement so that only one of them would be left."

Jeff really didn't care who was left to run the company, Ray or David, but he knew that one of them would have to go. His thinking was not purely out of loyalty to the company; he figured it was the only way to keep his Great Clips stock from going up in flames.

A few months earlier, Jeff had arranged for franchisees to put pressure on Ray to consider a settlement with David. Now he came up with a truly Machiavellian strategy to get Ray to trigger the buy-sell. "The settlement agreement called for five new outside directors," Jeff explained. "With my swing vote, I was able to get Pat Bradley on the board, *and I knew that would drive Ray crazy—maybe enough to offer to buy out David.*"

Pat was a lawyer in the Twin Cities, and back in the 1980s Steve had hired Pat to do some legal work for Great Clips franchisees. Later, Pat became a franchisee himself by buying a Great Clips salon from Steve's parents. More recently, David had consulted Pat when Ray tried to oust him from the company. Even more to the point, David, Steve, and Pat were good friends. With all of these connections to David and Steve, it was painfully obvious to Ray how Pat would vote as a board member.

But Ray didn't react as Jeff had anticipated. Instead of triggering the buy-sell, Ray came up with a plan of his own. Sensing that Jeff was uncomfortable with the burden of having the swing vote on the board, he set out to find a new board member who would be acceptable to Jeff—so much so that Jeff would be willing (and relieved) to step aside and give the new director his vote, a vote that might offset Pat's. Now all Ray had to do was find the right person.

In early 1996, Ray had attended a national meeting of the Young Presidents' Organization in Williamsburg, Virginia, and he recalled meeting one of the speakers who just might fill the bill. It was Shelby Yastrow, the general counsel and a senior executive at McDonald's. Not only did Shelby have the business credentials for the board seat, his franchising experience with McDonald's, the granddaddy of all franchisors, would be a definite plus. Moreover, and as already noted, Ray had always looked at

McDonald's as the gold standard of franchising, and he assumed that Steve and David would likewise see the potential of having someone from that company on the team. Ray called Shelby, who was in Chicago, and invited him to Minneapolis to discuss joining the Great Clips Board of Directors.

Ray figured it was a long shot. Why would an executive of a Fortune 100 company, a "Dow 30" company that dwarfed all other franchisors, want to sit on the board of a small, privately owned company in Minneapolis? At the time, Shelby's only familiarity with Great Clips was from being a customer at a Great Clips salon near his home in Chicago's northern suburbs.

"I'm still not sure why I flew up there," Shelby said, "but in that phone call Ray kind of played me like a fiddle. He told me how much he enjoyed my talk in Williamsburg, how much I could help Great Clips, and how personally grateful he'd be if I came up to visit with him." Chuckling, Shelby added, "Of course, he conveniently forgot to mention that I'd be walking into a war zone, and that if I joined the board I'd be risking my life with every vote!"

Shelby spent an entire day in Minneapolis meeting with the key executives—Ray, Rhoda, David, Jeff, and Steve Overholser, who had been recently hired as controller and later became the company's chief financial officer in 1997. Even Jim Hemak and a couple of other franchisees were invited to have lunch with him, underscoring that the Great Clips franchisees were part of the team. By the end of the day, David assented to Shelby joining the board.

"They did a real number on me," Shelby recalls. "I've always prided myself in being able to dig deep and get to the bottom of things, but after a day of asking penetrating questions, I came away without a clue that there were any tensions. Jim Hemak did allude to some 'issues' among the owners, but he said my presence would help smooth them over. In any event, the depth of these issues went over my head. The four owners I met that day certainly seemed to be in sync. When I got home, I told my wife how well everyone got along—a big, happy family!"

Shelby called Ray a few days later to accept his offer to join the board. He liked everything he saw during his visit, but the clincher was the opportunity to use his franchising experience to help Great Clips achieve its goals. "As successful as McDonald's was," he explained, "we did a lot of things wrong in the early years and, because of our size, they were hard to correct. I could help Great Clips avoid many of those same mistakes before they got ingrained. McDonald's was about twenty-five years older than Great Clips.

For me it would be like turning back the clock and doing things right the first time around. Golfers call it a Mulligan."

In later chapters we will see examples of how this "Mulligan" helped Great Clips avoid land mines, two of which could have caused franchisee revolts: One was where (and whether) to have company-owned salons, and another was how to deal with franchisees objecting to other salons being placed close to their own locations.

Shelby's first inklings of internal conflict occurred a week or two later. Ray came to Chicago where Shelby gave him a tour of McDonald's headquarters. The next day, David called Shelby to ask what he and Ray talked about, and he asked for equal time. That strange scenario was repeated after many phone calls between Ray and Shelby. But the inklings turned into stark reality at the first board meeting Shelby attended—and where he met Steve Lemmon for the first time.

All of the old points of contention were brought out—maybe to test Shelby's thinking. David and Steve contended that profits should be distributed to the shareholders, but Ray maintained that they should be reinvested for growth. David and Steve thought the salons should add additional services such as hair color, but Ray wanted to stay focused on a no-frills haircut. David and Steve wanted to take the company public, but Ray wanted to keep it private.

"This was the first time I met Steve Lemmon," Shelby recalled. "Wow! He sure had a way with words. He'd never say, 'I don't believe I agree with you' if he could say, 'You're full of crap.' It was amazing. Ray, David, and Rhoda were all conducting themselves like professionals, even on contentious issues, but Steve was behaving like a thug, hurling non-stop invective and insults—always at Ray."

Today, Shelby laughs about it, but he didn't see it as a laughing matter at the time. "I sat there thinking, *what in the hell did I get myself into?* I wasn't a director—I was a *referee*! All I needed was a black-and-white-striped shirt and a whistle. I didn't need this stuff, but I liked Ray and Rhoda, and I couldn't turn my back on them." He added, "And to be honest, I really liked the Great Clips concept and wanted to be a part of it."

A short time later, the company invited Charlie Kanan to join the board. Charlie had great credentials—ten years with Burger King, CEO of Play It Again Sports, and a General Mills executive. Like Shelby, Charlie had no investment or other interest in Great Clips and was likewise considered to be an "outside" director without a bias toward any owner.

Michael Connolly had already observed what Shelby discovered at his first board meeting. "All the while I was trying to develop my regions," he said, "Great Clips' management was at war. Here we had a business with a solid concept, an effective delivery system, and a great staff, and it was in danger of crumbling from the top down." Then Michael made an interesting point: "Jeff Elgin figured that the best way to save the business was for either Ray or David to leave, so he kept stirring the pot to get one of them to buy out the other, and that only added to the chaos at the top."

Things were on the verge of exploding, and only one more spark was needed to light the fuse.

CHAPTER 51

The Spark That Lit the Fuse

Things were about to come to a head, and the tipping point seemed to be an issue brought up at that first board meeting that Shelby Yastrow attended—the issue of going public.

In the discussions leading up to the settlement agreement, Ray had grudgingly assured David and Steve that he'd start grooming Great Clips for an IPO, an initial public offering. David wanted the assurance of an IPO to be part of the agreement, but Ray refused to make a binding commitment. The final agreement compromised their views by providing that Ray and David "intended" to have an IPO within five years.

Ray admits that he gave lip service to that intent just to hold David and Steve at bay. Down deep he was opposed to taking the company public. He had two reasons: One, in order to sell shares to the public, he'd have to fatten up the company's short-term profits because the offering price is a multiple of earnings. To do that, he'd have to suspend growth during a crucial time, and this would derail his plans to become the largest haircare brand.

Ray's second objection was that he didn't believe Great Clips could survive as a public company—at least not until some date far in the future. "Wall Street likes to see a balance sheet with a lot of hard assets, and we didn't have them. Our main asset was receivables, and our income was only from franchise fees and royalties. Also, we weren't nearly large enough to sustain the kind of growth and profits—year after year—demanded by public shareholders." In more simple terms, Great Clips was just too small to attract any attention in the arena of public companies, and that would not change in the foreseeable future.

David, however, could not let the subject alone. When it was clear that he could not change Ray's mind, he brought the discussions into the boardroom where Steve picked up the cudgel, mostly out of loyalty to David. "I was already gone," Steve explained, "and all of a sudden I'm back on the Board of Directors. So now I have to fly up from the Caribbean for board meetings in the middle of winter. We're looking out of the window in Minneapolis and looking at the freaking flag pointing straight out. The wind chill is like minus-20, and my body is adjusted to 85 and sunny every day."

It was in this frame of mind that Steve jumped on the IPO issue—*at that very first board meeting that Shelby attended.* He went after Ray relentlessly, accusing him in colorful language of everything from bad faith to lousy management, even presented an open letter to the board berating Ray for sitting on the IPO issue. It was a notable performance.

Still reflecting on that meeting, Shelby says, "As wild as Steve was, I was even more struck by Ray's manner. He sat there as if Steve were throwing daffodils instead of daggers. No reaction at all! He didn't say a word. He must have been terribly embarrassed to have me hearing all this slop, but he never looked at me and he never interrupted Steve's diatribe. I wanted to run over and hug the poor guy."

Although no longer a member of the board, Jeff Elgin weighed in on the IPO issue and came down on the side of David and Steve. This wasn't necessarily because he thought it made good business sense; rather, he explains, "I was fed up with the contentious management, and was in favor of any idea that would give me an opportunity to sell my shares in the company." He even presented a plan to slow down expansion for the purpose of building up profits to enhance the share value. The plan included the audacious element that Jeff would be the CEO of the company. Not surprisingly, the plan never got off the ground.

Jeff's plan also called for opening more corporate-owned salons, ostensibly to create equity for the balance sheet. This, too, was an old bone of contention. David had always liked the idea of more corporate-owned salons, especially because they would provide "laboratories" where the company could test new ideas before implementing them throughout the system. Ray, on the other hand, was queasy about the idea. He was committed to franchising and saw that as the best way to grow. Furthermore, developing company-owned salons would require the use of scarce capital that could better be used to develop more markets for franchised salons.

The board's most outspoken opponent of corporate salons was Shelby Yastrow, who put it this way: "If Great Clips started down that path, we'd be competing head-to-head with our franchisees for customers, managers, stylists, and locations. There is no faster way to lose the trust of your franchisees. And without that trust we'd be doomed to failure. Anyway," he added, "a franchisee protecting his own investment will typically run an outlet better than a corporate employee with no money at risk."

Shelby had dealt with all of these issues at McDonald's where a sizable percentage of its restaurants were company-owned. "Based on everything I've seen," he said, "if Great Clips does decide to own and operate salons, they should be limited to isolated markets in which there are no franchised salons. The only exception is if we have to take over a salon because the franchisee dies or otherwise leaves the business, and in that case we should sell or "spin" it to another franchisee as soon as possible."

There was still another problem with having company-owned outlets in a franchise-based organization, he pointed out. It requires a separate division with its own department heads, staffing, budgets, and oversight, and this can turn out to be an expensive distraction.

These points bolstered Ray's own thinking, and he held firm against opening company-owned salons. This widened further the gulf between Ray and David, and, from David's perspective, put Shelby squarely in the enemy camp.

Whatever issue was on the table, it seemed to drive the main players deeper into a whirlpool of controversy.

The year 1996 was drawing to an end, and so was Ray's stamina. He had endured fourteen years of sniping and bickering, and he was nearing the end of his rope. *He didn't blame only David or Steve; he knew that he was as intransigent as they were, but that didn't make him less miserable.*

And now he had an epiphany. "Until then," he said, "I was so committed to growing the company that I was willing to live with all of the fighting. It got a little better when we bought out Steve, but when Steve marched back into the boardroom I was pushed to my limit."

He went on to say, "I was always afraid to trigger the buy-sell agreement because it might backfire on me and I'd be the one who was bought out. And that's when it hit me. I'd rather get bought out and leave than put up with this misery for the rest of my life."

Ray described it as a "freeing moment," as if a weight had been taken off his chest. *"I'll try to raise the money to trigger the buy-sell, and if it backfires and I'm out of the company, well, it'll be better than this."*

CHAPTER 52

Putting the Finger on the Trigger

Once Ray crossed the Rubicon, his mindset changed. Before, the question in his mind was *whether* to trigger the buy-sell agreement. Now it was *when* to trigger it.

His first task was to figure out how much money he'd need. As he saw it, he had to buy out Steve and Jeff Elgin as well as David to make his control complete. (Obviously, having Rhoda remain as a shareholder would not be a problem.) He calculated that it would take $15 million; a lower number would encourage them to turn the gun around and *buy him out* under the terms of the shotgun buy-sell. Since there was no way that he could personally pay back a loan of that size, his aim was to have the company borrow the money and use it to buy and then retire the shares that David, Steve, and Jeff owned; the net effect would be the same: Ray and Rhoda would be the only shareholders.

His second task was to find the money! Ray was only too aware of how hard it was to raise that kind of money for these purposes. "Most lenders or investors put money into companies to help them grow," Ray explained, "but here the money would come in one day and go out the next to pay off the other shareholders. Nothing changes except that the company that had a weak balance sheet to begin with now has a weaker one with a giant debt. What lender or investor would accept *that?*"

Ray's first step was to meet with Jeff Rosenfeld and Hans Solon who brokered loans for various businesses in the Twin Cities and who had experience with franchising companies. He also had meetings with Jim D'Aquila who was with Dain Bosworth, a large brokerage firm. After consulting with his personal lawyer, Morris Sherman, Ray decided he'd be better off with a bigger outfit, so he chose Dain Bosworth. He paid them a deposit, signed a contract, and sent a thank you note to Rosenfeld and Solon along with a restaurant gift card.

Steve Overholser, who had served as the corporate controller since 1995, and would later become Great Clips' chief financial officer, developed various financial models required by Dain Bosworth. Steve prev had worked at Burger King and was familiar with the fiscal intricacies of franchising. "Using these models as a base," Steve explained, "we could project income statements, cash flow, and balance sheets to interrelate with each other. Building from there and using different assumptions—such as the number of new salons in a given year—we could make intelligent and variable projections for, say, five years into the future. This is the kind of information that lenders and investors demand."

The amount of required information, with backup and supporting data, was mountainous, and every item had to be checked and double-checked. The burden on Steve Overholser was a heavy one. And to make it heavier, Steve was fairly new on the job. Moreover, when he joined the company in 1995 the state of the books was a mess owing to the absence of a controller for several months. Annual reports had not been filed, financial statements were several months behind, and reconciliations of accounts had been lagging. "When I first walked in the door," Steve remembered, "I could see that it would take several months to get caught up, and there was no way to do it with my two-person team. I was able to convince Ray to let me increase my staff, and that's what enabled us to pull together all the data that we later had to assemble for the investors."

As so often happens in the world of high finance, Dain Bosworth balked *because the amount Ray needed was too small!* Ray recalls that Jim D'Aquila of Dain had a novel solution: "What if we loan you $35 million instead of $15 million? That way you could buy out the other guys for the $15 million, and you can have the $20 million for the business."

That spooked Ray. "I don't want to do that," he said. "I couldn't handle that much debt."

After a few more conversations, Ray heard nothing more from Jim or anyone else at Dain Bosworth. Then he called them, and the calls weren't returned. He finally reached Jim and said, "Look, I don't know what's going on, but when people don't return my phone calls it's not a good sign."

Jim's response was short. "What if I just return your deposit and we tear up the contract."

"Fine." Ray then called Jeff Rosenfeld again and asked, "How badly will you rake me over the coals if I crawl back to you guys?"

"Don't worry," Jeff replied, "we won't be too hard on you."

So Ray paid another deposit—and then learned that Jeff and Hans Solon were splitting up. "So what happens to me?" Ray asked, fearing that this would be another dead end. "I just gave you a check!"

"You can work with me," Jeff answered.

So instead of working with a major company, as he had intended, Ray would now be with a one-man shop.

Working with Jeff Rosenfeld turned out to be a stroke of good luck. He held Ray's hand and led him through the bewildering process of finding an investor, preparing a comprehensive business plan, addressing a myriad of contingencies, and then making a persuasive presentation. First, they had to prepare a "book"—a business plan that told the Great Clips success story, explained the nature of the competitive marketplace, laid out a growth strategy, and showed how the investor would be repaid. The "book" had to address every aspect of the business—the staff, customer demographics, pricing, marketing, and everything else, including contingencies, that could possibly be relevant information to someone sinking millions of dollars into the operation.

Ray wrote the narrative, Steve Overholser provided the numbers, and Morris Sherman covered the legal angles involving the rights of the shareholders and other creditors, as well as the complications surrounding the employees who had been granted options for non-voting shares.

Jeff Rosenfeld remembers an obstacle that had to be overcome: "Investors don't like franchise deals," he said. "All the equity lies with the franchisees, and the only real asset is an expectation of royalties. If things go south, there isn't a lot of liquidation value." Then Jeff continued, "And as if that weren't enough, investors put barber shops and restaurants, with their high failure rate, at the bottom of the list."

Rays mission was clear: Show the investors that Great Clips was the exception to these rules. He thought back to the early 1980s when he had to persuade Cindy Darling at Park National Bank to give the company a $20,000 line of credit. Now he had to use the same optimistic pitch to get $15 million!

The first three meetings with investors were disasters. The first was with J. P. Morgan in New York in early 1997. Jeff Rosenfeld remembered it well. "Morgan's main guy at our meeting was named Simon, and it was clear from the moment we walked in that he wanted no part of us. They're a huge financial institution, and to them we were small potatoes. We were out of our league, and they didn't do anything to convince us otherwise."

There were subsequent investor meetings in Boston and New York, but they were likewise dead ends. Ray didn't think this would be easy, but he thought there would be *some* interest in the company that he had been nurturing for the past fifteen years. "These guys looked at us like we were on a street corner begging for handouts," Ray recalls. "I learned why East Coast bankers aren't known for their warm and ingratiating personalities."

Dianna Anderson, who had been Ray's executive assistant since 1993, remembers those gut-wrenching meetings well. "It had to be very stressful for Ray," she said. "He would call me from the meetings to give me a list of documents and information he had to have ASAP. I'd drop everything and scurry around the office gathering up whatever he needed, and then fax or overnight it to him. Sometimes he'd have two meetings in one day, and I'd never leave the phone even for a minute except when I'd dash off to get something he asked for."

It was then that Jeff Rosenfeld called RFE Partners, a private equity group in Connecticut. He was connected to Peter Reiter who, at the time, was an analyst near the bottom of the totem pole. Peter was not the least bit interested, explaining that RFE had never invested in a franchise business, and, in any event, they were phasing out of retail investments and concentrating instead on service businesses. Not to be deterred, Jeff outlined that Great Clips *was* in the service business; it was their *franchisees* that were in the retail business. Peter eventually relented and agreed to arrange a meeting, and Jeff immediately sent out a batch of the business plan books.

When Ray and Jeff Rosenfeld arrived in Connecticut for the meeting, Peter was still dashing around searching for partners willing to sit in. Most of them demurred, coming up with excuses not to waste time with a small, low-cost salon chain. One of them, however, had taken the time to read the entire business plan, and it provoked enough interest that he agreed to join the meeting. His name was Mike Foster.

"To be honest," recalled Mike, "I went in thinking that we'd never pursue this deal. But Peter and I walked out of the meeting being very, *very* impressed with Ray. We really picked up on his passion and on his ability to make this work."

Peter echoed Mike's thoughts, saying, "It was a good fit, but it was not a normal situation for us. Usually we go through the entire investigatory process—it's called 'due diligence'—and then we either invest the money or we don't, and that's that. But here we had that convoluted shotgun buy-sell agreement, so we had to spend a ton of time and money up front on due diligence and then maybe find out we didn't have a deal because David gets his own loan and he buys out Ray."

As the meeting was winding down, and after answering question after question, Ray had two of his own questions for Mike and Peter. "First," he said, "I asked if they ever invested in a franchise business. They said no. Then I asked if they ever invested in a retail business, even though it was technically the franchisees and not us who were in retail. They said yes, but it didn't work out and they were no longer strong on retail. I thought it was a lost cause."

Nonetheless, RFE decided to move forward, and on May 1, 1997, they began their due diligence. They went over the Great Clips books with a magnifying glass, visited the corporate offices, talked to staff, toured salons, and questioned franchisees. Everything came back positive.

"I was particularly impressed after talking to franchisees," Mike Foster remembers. "Their enthusiasm for the concept and the prospects of having a major national brand were very compelling. That was really unusual. In most franchise concepts, there's a lot of tension between franchisee and franchisor. They're not always best buddies. But here there was a strong feeling of togetherness; everyone was on the same team. This feeling of partnership can be traced back to Ray who always said, 'The better our franchisees do, the better we do.'"

Shelby Yastrow recalls getting a conference call from Mike and some others at RFE during the due diligence period. "First," Shelby said, "Mike seemed to have a lot of comfort from my being on the Great Clips Board of Directors. He said to me, 'Okay, being with McDonald's you must know everything there is to know about franchising.' Then he grilled me for an hour or so about everything under the sun: What did I think of Great Clips management? Was the concept viable? Were their franchise documents in order? Did they have strong franchisees? What problems did I see for the future? Was there any litigation on the horizon? And of course they questioned me about Ray and if I thought he was able to run the company for the foreseeable future.

"Then Mike asked the kicker question: 'If we make the deal, would you commit to remain on the board until we're repaid?' I said that I would, as long as Ray wanted me to stay."

Shelby makes another point about his role in this process. "I really wanted to help Ray get this financing so he could buy out the other guys, and I definitely wanted to have a role in the negotiations and the due diligence meetings. However, as a board member I had a fiduciary duty to *all* of the shareholders—even Steve Lemmon—so I felt I had to stay out of all these negotiations and not take sides. But that didn't mean that I couldn't honestly answer all questions put to me by RFE."

RFE liked everything they were learning about Great Clips, but they needed even more reassurance. Not having made franchise deals before, RFE invited Merchants Capital, a firm with considerable franchise experience, to be a co-lender. Richard Goff of Merchants Capital then contacted Francorp, a consulting firm with a global reputation for evaluating franchising companies. Francorp was commissioned to review all of the data in detail and then report back on the viability of Great Clips as a franchisor—and borrower.

On June 6, 1997, Francorp issued its overwhelmingly positive report:

"After careful review, Francorp believes Great Clips, Inc. and the Great Clips franchise network have a lot to be proud of currently and to look forward to in the future . . . Francorp believes Great Clips has what it takes to successfully reach its goals as outlined in the Great Clips Business Plan."

The document went on to praise Ray's leadership, Rhoda's pragmatism and devotion, the "rifle approach" to expansion, and everything else down to the selection of franchisees and the quality and training of the salon stylists.

Mike Foster of RFE was relieved to read the report. "It gave us a lot of confidence. Consultants aren't generally very complimentary since they think they can do things better than anyone else, and they go out of their way to look for problems. But here they came back with the highest possible grades for Ray, Rhoda, and the entire Great Clips organization. They even said, 'We would like to work with them in the future, but we think they know as much as anyone in the industry.'"

Before the end of the month, the RFE investment committee approved the Great Clips transaction which, including expenses, totaled about $15.5 million. In fact, there were other investment firms who participated in the deal, but since RFE had the lead role and the largest stake, the transaction will be called the RFE loan for our purposes.

A further word of explanation is in order. Investments of this nature can be very complicated and consist of many components such as loans, equity participation, conversion rights, collateralization, escape clauses, and endless restrictions and covenants. In fact, the RFE-Great Clips deal included all of these elements—for example, a preferred stock component with a conversion right that would entitle RFE to common stock with a "put," that is, a right to sell it back to the company at fair market value. That's why the financing usually comes from private investment firms instead of from the corner bank. Although the transaction proposed by RFE had many elements that make the transaction difficult to characterize in a word, we will refer to the transaction as a "loan" in the interest of clarity and brevity.

Jeff Rosenfeld deserves tremendous credit for his persistence in getting RFE to consider the deal, but he acknowledges it was Ray who convinced RFE to say "yes." "Ray actually choreographed the process from our end," Jeff said. "As a former CPA, he had a total grasp of all of the numbers, and he presented everything in a persuasive way. Plus, it was clear to RFE that Ray was playing it straight and hid nothing."

Chief Financial Officer Steve Overholser has an interesting observation along these same lines. "Having been a practicing CPA," Steve explained, "Ray has a good handle on all the figures. He doesn't really need all the sophisticated data that most executives need in order to know the numbers and run a company. Nonetheless, he insists that we meet the highest accounting standards. His familiarity with all the accounting concepts and requirements has been very beneficial to the company, and to me personally because we can communicate at a level we both understand."

Steve made another point that explains the company's effectiveness with investors dating back to the first loan from Cindy Darling at Park National Bank: "Ray's philosophy has been to create a reasonable financial forecast and then deliver more than he promised. Over the past fifteen years, we have not only delivered our annual budget every time, but we have exceeded it each year by about 3 percent. A few times we've had to cut some discretionary expenses to do that, but we won't hesitate if that's what it takes to exceed what we promise."

CHAPTER 53

Aiming the Shotgun

The RFE commitment to finance the buy-out came just in time. At the Great Clips Board of Directors meeting in June, just days before the commitment came through, David and Steve proposed still another plan that would have cut into Ray's authority—and they planned to put the proposal to a vote at the August meeting. The proposal was a clever one, and it reflected their growing frustration with Ray; however, it flew in the face of traditional corporate governance.

The plan was that only the *outside* board members, Pat Bradley, Charlie Kanan, and Shelby Yastrow, could vote on board matters. Since a board of directors has the ultimate control over a corporation's affairs, this plan effectively would put total control of Great Clips in the hands of three men who had no ownership, who knew virtually nothing about haircare, and who had other jobs. And the people who collectively owned the entire company and had all the experience would be giving up all control!

The reason behind the plan was transparent. Pat Bradley was clearly in David's camp, and by now it was fairly apparent that Shelby shared Ray's views on most franchising and governance issues. But what about Charlie Kanan? David and Steve would never have made the proposal if they were not confident that Charlie would be on their side. So this latest plan would, for all practical purposes, give David full control of the company; Ray's title as president—which could not be taken away from him under the settlement agreement—would mean absolutely nothing.

What would happen if this proposal was put to a board vote in August? By all odds, David, Steve, Pat, and Charlie would vote "aye," and Ray, Rhoda, and Shelby would vote "nay." Four to three. The only way to block the vote would be to call a special meeting of the *shareholders* to elect a new board, but the shareholders would be deadlocked because the shares were now evenly divided between the two camps—gridlock. Jeff Elgin's 2 percent could tip the scale, but it was unlikely how—or if—he would vote on such an extraordinary question.

This nightmare was exacerbated for another reason. The law imposes limitations on the extent to which a director may abandon his right to vote, so it wasn't clear that the board even had the right to deprive the inside directors of their right to vote. *This whole thing could end up in a protracted fight in the courts!*

As Ray saw it, the only way to fend off the vote was to break the news that he was prepared to trigger the buy-sell to buy out not only David's shares but Steve's and Jeff's as well. Once he had the shares, the new proposal would be moot.

Ray also reasoned that Steve and Jeff would be relieved to see the buy-sell triggered and cash out.

In July, representatives of RFE sat down with David, Steve, and Jeff to explain that they were backing Ray. They were hoping to bypass the process outlined in the buy-sell agreement. Peter Reiter of RFE was part of the meeting, and he recalls saying, "'Look, we analyzed the business, and we're prepared to come up with the money for a generous offer. We can structure this any number of ways—such as a long-term payout that might be better for you tax-wise.' They heard us out," Peter said, "and then politely said 'no,' so we had to go through all the mechanics established in the buy-sell agreement."

It's to the credit of RFE and other lenders, and Mike Foster in particular, that they didn't use any of their "escape clauses" to walk away from the deal after seeing the depth of the discord among the owners. Even knowing that two of them would be gone after the buy-out, the attitudes and emotions could wreak havoc with all of the details yet to be worked out.

Obviously, all of this alerted David, Steve, and Jeff that the buy-sell was about to be triggered, but they still didn't know how much Ray would be offering. David decided to jump the gun and start to line up his own investors who would back him if he wanted to turn the shotgun around and buy out Ray and, by extension, Rhoda. One of the people he contacted was Bob Levine—a franchisee and no friend of Ray after the earlier pricing lawsuit. Other potential backers included friends, family, and other business people with whom David had made strong connections over the years. Not only was he well liked, he was respected *and trusted* by all who knew and worked with him. The prospects of raising the money were positive.

As part of the process, David also went to commercial investors who asked for the same kind of data and projections that Ray himself had to produce for investors. To do this, David enlisted the help of Steve Overholser, the company controller at the time, but Steve couldn't simply give him the same information he had given to Ray. David's business model and future development plans differed from Ray's, and therefore all the assumptions and projections were different. So, in effect, Steve had to do most of the work a second time.

While David was scurrying around to line up investors, Ray was beginning to realize how close to the brink things were being pushed. There were now three distinct outcomes that were possible, *and each had a dark side*: (1) He could buy the others' shares per the buy-sell agreement, and end up being crushed with a $15.5 million debt; (2) he could pull the trigger but the shotgun could backfire, and David, acting alone or with the others, could buy his shares and would put him out on the street; or (3) he could pull back and do nothing, in which event he would be in the same rocky boat he'd been in for the past fifteen years, and possibly be emasculated by David's plan to give control to the three outside directors.

An added concern had been nagging at him. If he ended up making the deal, then RFE, to protect its investment, would insist on having representatives on the board of directors. They may even demand other controls, such as reinvestment limitations, that could stifle his ambitious growth plans for the company.

Ray discussed these reservations with his lawyer, Morris Sherman. "I've been involved with many partnership breakups," Morris said, "and I know that these are emotionally packed situations. People who are driven by emotions often make bad decisions, so I had to make sure that Ray was being objective throughout the process, that he was thinking with his head and not his heart. I always tell my clients that they have to reach a point of indifference about the outcome, a point where they'll walk away before making any further concessions."

Ray also talked with Jeff Rosenfeld who helped him prepare what was needed to get the RFE commitment. Thinking along the lines suggested by Morris Sherman, Ray told Jeff, "You know, if I do get bought out I could pay the taxes, invest the money in tax-free bonds, and still have more money than I could spend. How bad is that?"

In the course of all these ruminations, David surprised Ray by approaching him to see if there was a way they could mend things over and stay together.

Ray discussed all of this with Mike Dougherty, his wife's brother-in-law. Mike was both a good friend and astute businessman, and had several breakfasts with Ray during this entire ordeal. As Ray put it, "Mike was my 'rock' and really kept me in the game whenever I was thinking about throwing in the towel." After listening intently to all that was going through Ray's head, including David's most recent stab at mending things over, Mike succinctly offered the following: "Continuing with David and Steve under any scenario is not a solution. Give it two hours, or two weeks, or two months, and then you'll be right back where you started." He then looked Ray squarely in the eye and said, *"You're holding the gun and it's loaded. Now pull the trigger!"*

With that one statement, and in that one instant, everything was suddenly crystal clear to Ray.

CHAPTER 54

Bang!

Ray pulled the trigger on the day of the next board meeting, August 14, 1997, *and Rhoda pulled it with him.* They both presented David, Steve, and Jeff Elgin with a signed offer to buy their collective shares for $15 million. The buy-sell agreement gave them sixty days to respond, and the clock began to tick. They could either accept the offer and take the money, or they (or any of them) could buy out Ray and Rhoda for the same price per share. Doing nothing would constitute an acceptance of the offer.

David decided that he would try to raise the money to turn the tables and buy out Ray and Rhoda. But, if successful, his plan was to ask Rhoda to stay on as an executive. *The battle was on!*

Earlier, when David was trying to round up investors, he didn't have a gun to his head, and no clock was ticking. Now he had to reinvigorate his efforts, and he had the additional challenge of having to do in sixty days what it took Ray six or seven months to accomplish. But that wasn't his only disadvantage. Ray had gone to investors with a vision, an aggressive growth strategy, and a management team that were appealing to investors and experts in franchising. David, on the other hand, envisioned slower growth with the profits redirected to the shareholders, a plan that hardly excited investors. Also, David said he'd have a broader array of salon offerings, such as hair color services, which would raise prices and extend haircut times. This likewise could turn off any investors who might get gun shy when they see tampering with a proven concept.

Mike Foster said, "I can't imagine how any investment firm would fund the company unless both Ray and Rhoda were running it. Nevertheless, with help from Steve Overholser, David put together a business plan to present to professional as well as private investors. It surprised Ray and Jeff Rosenfeld that David would reach out to institutional investors with a plan that called for modest growth and a change in the successful no-frills concept.

"I was prepared to get a call from one or more of the professional lenders David approached," Shelby Yastrow said. "I figured that they'd ask me the same kind of questions that RFE asked several weeks earlier. But I never got such a call—probably because experienced investors never got that far into their due diligence before taking a hike."

In any event, David was soon re-directing his efforts back toward people he knew. His popularity and trustworthiness would be solid assets for attracting non-institutional investors. And instead of trying to find one investor who would put up $15 million plus expenses, he approached friends and even Great Clips franchisees and vendors. The minimum investment would be $150,000, but those lending at least $2 million would be given seats on the Board of Directors with David and Steve. One of the first franchisees to join his camp was Bob Levine, Steve's lawyer, who was still bristling over losing the pricing lawsuit filed by Ray.

David's approach had a certain grassroots allure in that the franchisees could own a part of the company and, with a large enough investment, could even sit on the board. Of course, this could also lead to problems. Even in the happiest franchise systems the franchisor and the franchisees had different agendas, and both groups represented on the company board could be ineffectual at best—and explosive at worst.

By approaching franchisees for his financing, David unwittingly spread the divisiveness between him and Ray into the entire franchisee community. The franchisees were effectively being forced to choose between the two of them. It even risked becoming a popularity contest. If you liked David better than Ray, you'd invest with David; if you liked Ray better, you didn't. In fact, the great majority of the franchisees liked both of them, so for them it was strictly a business decision—*if they thought Ray could run the company better than David, then they would put up money to get Ray out of the company.* Curiously, everyone at this point was focusing on Ray and David as if not aware that Rhoda had joined Ray in triggering the buy-sell.

Ray was deeply concerned with the discordance that David's campaign could cause among the franchisees, and he decided he couldn't sit on the sidelines and watch. He appealed to one of his dear friends and trusted franchisees, someone who had the respect of the entire system—Jim Hemak. "We met for lunch at the old Flagship Athletic Club in Eden Prairie, a Minneapolis suburb," Jim remembers, "and Ray was asking for my help. It was the first time that we franchisees had any input at all on the management of the company. I respected Ray's ability, vision, and commitment, and I assured him that I'd work to persuade other franchisees to support him. I wanted him to lead the company in the future and believed that he and Rhoda were the best option for the majority of the franchisees."

For better or worse, the franchisees had the perfect opportunity to hash things out at the 1997 Great Clips convention. It took place in September—right in the middle of the sixty-day window during which David had to act on Ray's offer. It turned out to be one of the most interesting conventions in the company's history, but with the most *intriguing* action taking place behind the scenes. The corridors, elevators, eating areas, and private rooms were abuzz with whispers: *Who's going to end up in charge? Which is better for us? Whose side are you on? Can the system survive all of this? What happens to us if it doesn't?*

Rhoda was in charge of running the convention, and it was a nightmare for her. She was determined to have a normal, businesslike convention, with all of the infighting left outside. The convention theme was "Straight from the Heart," but neither Ray nor David could speak from the heart while on stage. If they had, Rhoda would have turned their microphones off. She had literally forbidden them from trying to sway the franchisees from the stage. While they gave their presentations, she was backstage with the script in one hand while the other hand was prepared to pull the plug.

"The worst part," Rhoda recalls, "was trying to ignore the elephant in the room. Everyone there knew what was going on, and we had to pretend that everything was wonderful. Conventions are forums to discuss the future, but how could we do that without knowing for sure who would be leading the company? So instead I changed the focus to the competition out in the marketplace, keeping everything external, to take the attention off the internal machinations."

The offstage highlight of the convention was when Jim Hemak convened a special session of the National Franchisee Advisory Board for an open discussion on the buy-sell issue. Ordinarily, the Advisory Board had about twelve members show up, but this time more than fifty franchisees crowded into the room.

David and Ray were both invited to present their pitches. Ray came and delivered a well-rehearsed presentation—not unlike those he had been using for nearly a year with investment firms. David, however, didn't show up, but he did have a number of vocal advocates in the room.

Jim Hemak, true to the promise he made at the athletic club, delivered the bacon for Ray. He circulated a petition in favor of Ray and his management team, and it was signed by nearly ninety franchisees who together owned more than 350 salons. This was a significant reflection of the overall franchisee sentiment. The petition, which would be shown to anyone who asked, read in part:

> "We have great respect for David Rubenzer and his associates, and appreciate the contributions made by them toward the success of the enterprise. However, we strongly believe that our future is best served if Ray and Rhoda and their team remain to provide the direction of the company."

David did make another appearance at the convention's final session. He read a humorous poem while dressed as a 1960s beatnik. The poem, which may have been inspired by the days when David stood behind a barber's chair, caricatured Great Clips franchisees through the eyes of their stylists and focused on traits that were hardly flattering. A large screen behind David projected cartoons that further lampooned the franchisees described in the poem. The stylists and managers in the audience thought this was hysterical, but many of the franchisees found it to be off the mark. To be fair, David has a keen sense of humor, and at any other time his poem would have been well received, but the tensions in the air that week filtered out—at least to the franchisees—much of the comedy.

If David had hopes that the convention was an opportunity to bring franchisees into his camp, they were all but dashed by his presentation and by the many signatures on Jim Hemak's petition. Ray and David were both popular, but it was becoming obvious that the franchisees believed that their future would be brighter if Great Clips was run by Ray, whom they saw as an all-around businessman. Furthermore, Ray had worked hard to develop a strong relationship with the franchisees; he made himself accessible to them and constantly reminded them that they were the backbone of the system. This led to a trust that trumped their admiration for David.

CHAPTER 55

Rhoda Delivers the *Coup de Grace*

In his campaign to encourage the franchisees to stick with him, Ray had a secret weapon, a weapon so powerful that it rendered David's case hopeless: Rhoda!

Rhoda had adroitly stayed out of the David-Ray skirmishes, and she was careful not to imply that she was taking either side. Ray was her brother, but she adored David. When she did express her views on some of the most contentious issues, she did so diplomatically while recognizing that both views had merit. As she put it, "My job wouldn't let me leave the field of battle, but I did my best to stay out of the line of fire."

However, now that the fight was out in the open and the future of the company would depend on the outcome, Rhoda no longer had the luxury of neutrality. The franchisees knew how critical she was to the success of the business, so she was increasingly asked whether she would stay if David ended up with the company. Clearly, she was a linchpin in their thinking.

"For the longest time," she remembers, "I resisted making any commitment about staying, one way or the other, even though I put my shares in with Ray's for the buy-sell. But in reality, my allegiance was not to either of them—it was to the franchisees and to the system as a whole. I just wished there were a way for both of them to stay and work together. Bart Holtzman, a franchisee who was all set to invest with David, asked me directly whether I'd stay if David owned the company, and I wouldn't give him a straight answer. I know that I sounded evasive, but at that point I really didn't know what I'd do if David ended up on top."

Rhoda's impartiality began to fade as she learned more about David's intended Board of Directors, some of whom were outspoken franchisees who had opinions that might not be in sync with the system as she saw it. As it happened, most are still in the system and are supportive of company policies, but in the heat of the moment, Rhoda was concerned that she might have trouble working with them. Reluctantly, she finally told David that she would not stay if he ended up running the company with them on the board.

He continued to pursue her, and they met at a Perkins Restaurant a week before the sixty-day deadline expired. "You think Ray's tough?" she asked. "These guys will cut you off at the knees. They'll complain, they'll make demands, and they'll be in your way at every turn." She also told him that he was putting too much of his net worth on the line, and that he could very well end up broke.

David didn't respond, but he left the meeting with more doubts than at any time since the buy-sell was triggered nearly two months earlier.

In the waning hours before he had to announce his decision, David had received the final commitments for the $15 million he'd need to buy out Ray and Rhoda. *He had actually been able to raise the money he needed to counter the buy-sell!* But he had this constant thought running through his head since that last conversation with Rhoda: *Is this really what I want to do?*

Just as Rhoda had predicted, in the previous several days, his designated board members were making more and more demands, and the pressure on David was getting intense. One wanted "his man" to be made vice president of marketing; another wanted "his man" to head up operations; and another wanted the entire marketing department jettisoned in favor of having all marketing handled by an outside agency. To ensure a return on their investment, they wanted people laid off and payroll slashed in every corner of the company. Ray and Rhoda would never take that route regardless of how badly they needed financing; they trusted the existing business model and believed in the staff that made it work.

David was shaking his head. *Can I really fire all of these great people just to fatten the return for the investors?*

Then his thoughts turned to his proposed board of directors. *The only way I can control this pack of wolves is with Steve Lemmon's vote,* he recalls thinking, *but in six months Steve might be asking, "Where's my return? What's in it for me? If I had sold to Ray, I'd have a couple of million bucks in my pocket and I'd be back on my boat. And all of the other guys who put in two million dollars for their board seats will be hounding me for returns."*

David now did his own form of due diligence, anticipating all of the decisions he'd have to make, the demands he'd have to deal with, the employees he'd have to fire, the pressure he'd have to endure every day, and the sleep he'd lose every night.

His final decision lightened his heart: *To hell with it! I'll take Ray's money and live happily ever after!*

The sixty-day period to make a counter-offer ended on October 13, 1997, and David waited until the last minute. On that very final day, he announced his decision to accept Ray's offer and sell out. Since neither Steve nor Jeff made a counter offer within the allotted time, they too were obligated to sell their shares.

As a purely technical matter, Ray and Rhoda did not actually offer to buy the shares of David, Steve, and Jeff Elgin. Instead, they pursued a slightly different procedure permitted in the buy-sell agreement: They set up a new company and had that company make the offer to buy everyone's shares. Since they would control the new company, this method would give them total ownership of Great Clips. The only fly in the ointment (there is *always* a fly in the ointment!) was that the buy-sell agreement allowed Steve Lemmon to refuse to sell if the offer came from someone other than an existing shareholder. Nevertheless, Ray and Rhoda banked on the conviction that Steve would prefer to take the cash and sell if David left. They were right. Steve joined David and Jeff in selling his shares.

At 9:00 a.m. on the closing day—the day the shares and cash were to be exchanged—Steve Lemmon was calling for his money. "What's holding things up?" he demanded. It seemed there was a little glitch. RFE was still awaiting a written agreement from Ray that he would *personally* guarantee all of the warranties and representations in the buy-sell documents.

"What?" Ray was dumfounded. His lawyer had assured him that he wouldn't personally have to guaranty any of the company's obligations, even though personal guaranties were common in these transactions. "But," he now admits, "I was so desperate to close the deal that I would have signed anything RFE wanted. I quickly put in a call to Mike Foster, and he called me right back to say, 'I took a look at the agreement and saw that we never asked for a personal guaranty. So forget about it.'" Ray continues, "There is no way to describe my appreciation to Mike. Even if they had forgotten to include the personal guaranty, he knew darn well that I'd sign one to get the deal done. But he didn't ask me to do it. Our relationship has been outstanding ever since, and I've never given him any reason at all to regret the trust he showed in me."

CHAPTER 56

A Time for Healing

Later that afternoon, after the closing, Ray summoned the staff at the corporate office in Minneapolis and broke the news. There was a lot of relief that it was all over, but it would be terribly unfair to both Ray and David to call it a celebration.

Ray was well aware how much David was liked and respected by the staff, and that many throughout the system would be truly sorry to see him leave. Even Ray had mixed emotions. He had a deep personal respect for David, and for the past fifteen years they spent much more time working together as a team than they had working against each other. Not then—or ever since—would anyone see Ray gloat over the outcome of this long struggle.

Dianna Anderson has been Ray's executive assistant for over twenty years, and is obviously very close to him. Thinking back on that day, she still feels a certain sadness. "It was like watching your parents get divorced," she said. "You can't say that you love one more than the other. You love them both, and you hate to see one of them leave." Then Dianna added, "But Ray got custody of the kids—us!"

The office administrator at the time, Sunu Cheeran, knew there would be a change in atmosphere at the home office. "David had a light side to him," she says, "and he had a wonderful sense of humor. Ray, who is an outstanding businessman and really cares for the staff, also has a fun side but doesn't show it as often."

Ray made a special point to reach out to those staff members who were especially close to David. For example, he said to Ann Latendresse, a close friend of David, that he understood how badly she must feel. She replied, "Ray, I've never really taken sides. I value my friendship with David and his contribution to the company, especially as it relates to the artistic side of the business and to engaging the stylists. But I understand your direction and growth plans for the company, and I support them."

Pam Keller had been hired and trained by David years before and had been close to him ever since. She still appreciates the sensitivity that Ray showed that day, saying, "After he made the announcement he made a point to seek me out and ask, 'How are you doing?' He cared about my feelings, and that meant the world to me." As with Dianna Anderson, Pam also likened the situation to a parental divorce: "You're concerned that any favoritism you show one will be construed as disloyalty by the other, but Ray's manner that day showed that he empathized with me and he understood perfectly how I felt. My loyalty to the company and its success has never wavered prior to or after that day."

Shortly after the announcement, Ray hosted a dinner that included a number of franchisees. Jim Hemak proposed a toast to Ray and Rhoda, and remembers saying: "I've never come across anyone as focused and as diligent as Ray, and no one more competent and compassionate than Rhoda."

Another franchisee at the dinner was Pat Stevens. "Ray is my brother-in-law," Pat said, "but that had nothing to do with my relief over the way things turned out. I have a lot of money tied up in this business, and I'm for whatever will make it grow and succeed. That's the bottom line, and that's why I was happy with the outcome."

Bill Divine echoed what many other franchisees said: "It's hard to say what direction David would have taken the company, but I can't believe that the company would have succeeded as it has without Ray and Rhoda."

Even those franchisees who were in David's camp during the buy-sell negotiations accepted the final outcome, and many are still in the system and fully support it. One is Pat Bradley who, the reader may recall, Jeff Elgin managed to get on the board "to drive Ray crazy." Another good example is Tim Lawless who has salons in Indiana. Tim was a strong backer of David, but he remained in the system and continued to grow. Today he has thirty-nine salons, and Ray describes him as "an aggressive, growth-oriented franchisee who is totally supportive of all we are doing. Tim has great operations, and he's always willing to reinvest his profits into upgrading his salons."

Ken Miyamoto, who had earlier held key positions at Great Clips, offers this perspective: "I liked both Steve Lemmon and David Rubenzer. I thought they were great guys and still do. They had lots of strengths, but would they fit into a large franchise operation fighting for brand dominance in markets all over the country? Absolutely not. That required a rare talent, and Ray had it. David and Steve were good guys, but the company they founded just outgrew them."

Any ill feelings or divisions within the company or among the franchisees healed quickly; everyone again focused on the success of the system. Even David showed his faith in the future of the system by using some of his buy-out money to expand his portfolio of Great Clips salons. He formed numerous partnerships with family members, in-laws, and several stylists he had mentored, and he currently has ownership in forty-eight salons, making him the largest franchisee in the system as of this writing.

Despite being such a significant stakeholder in the system, David chose not to attend Great Clips conventions or other meetings after the buy-out. Many franchisees and corporate staff regretted his absence and, without success, encouraged him to attend. Rhoda even planned for an impromptu award for him should he ever show up at one of the conventions. She and Ray understood that, regardless of the disputes over control, David deserved to be honored for developing the core salon concept on which the company's stunning success was built. Then, to the delight of everyone, David *did* attend the 2012 Great Clips convention where the thirtieth birthday of the company was celebrated. This "homecoming" and the special recognition David received will be discussed in the final chapter of this book.

Reflecting back, Ray believes that the years of discord made him a better executive and a better leader of the company. "Because we disagreed on many key issues," he says, "I learned that I couldn't sell an idea without having all the facts buttoned up and without considering all the alternatives. I now do that as a matter of course, and it's helped me to make better and more considered decisions."

Although Ray displayed a calm, sober attitude during the squabbles with Steve and David, the daily bickering had to take a toll. For fifteen years there was tension, and it was all the more stressful because Ray knew that the staff and the franchisees were aware of it. One would think, therefore, that the buy-out would have removed that heavy burden and that Ray could at last find some peace of mind.

And he did—*for all of four months!* In early March 1998, barely four months after the buy-out, Ray saw his doctor because of chest pains and, after tests, learned that he needed triple bypass heart surgery. This was totally out of the blue. He had always enjoyed good health, watched his weight and diet, and had been a runner for the previous twenty years. In fact, he had run three marathons. "When Rhoda called to tell me," Shelby Yastrow remembers, "I was floored. This guy had been fighting wars for years and had just gone through a tortuous transaction without knowing until the last minute how it would turn out. At last, the seas calmed for him. And then—bang—he gets blindsided by this! It just wasn't fair."

Happily, Ray recovered from the surgery beautifully and has never had a problem since. He takes great care of himself and seems to be in perfect health. "Right after the surgery," Ray says, "I was convalescing at home and really came to enjoy it. However, my wife, Mary Lou, and my daughter, Annie, finally decided I was in their way and they chased me back to work! I've cut down on the travel a bit, but beyond that nothing's changed. And I feel wonderful!" Ray continued to run for years after the surgery and is still an enthusiastic water skier. In fact, in the summer of 2010 he and his water skiing partner, Louie Tilton, logged over 300 miles on the lake near his home.

Mary Lou recalls Ray's surgery and convalescence in a more reflective way: "It sounds strange to say, but in a way it changed things for the better. Up until a few months before, Ray was always tied up in knots with David and Steve, and then, after they were gone, he felt smothered by the debt to finance their buy-out. The heart scare was the jolt he needed to put things back in perspective. It gave him the chance to stand back and see that he and the business were finally on the course he wanted, and the terrible infighting was behind him. Now he saw that he could start to enjoy life again!"

Mary Lou continued: "Ray is really a great guy—fun, ambitious, and caring, and he's a wonderful partner and father. These traits never left, but they again rose to the surface after his surgery. It was so nice to have him relaxed and at home, especially since this was Annie's last year before going away to college, but he's correct about our chasing him back to the office when he was feeling better. I could see that he was getting antsy—even if he didn't—and he needed to get back."

Great Clips' all staff photo taken in 1996.

Here we grow! Great Clips' all staff photo on the company's 25th anniversary in 2007.

Great Clips, Inc. Executive Team in 2012: Back row, left to right: Steve Overholser, Terri Miller, Rob Goggins, Sandra Anderson, Nancy Uden, Steve Hockett, and Michelle Sack. Front row, left to right: Kathy Wetzel, Charlie Simpson, Rhoda Olsen, Ray Barton, and Yvonne Mercer.

AUGUST 2002

THE BUSINESS JOURNAL

GREAT PLACES TO ★ WORK

SPONSORED BY

Watson Wyatt
Worldwide

WELLS FARGO

Great Clips, Inc. was named as one of the Great Places to Work by the Minneapolis/St. Paul Business Journal in 2002.

Ray Barton serves as Receptionist of the Day as part of a fund-raising event in 1999.

Great Clips, Inc. employees volunteering during the annual Great Needs. Great Deeds.® fund-raising week in 2002.

The July 2005 Great Clips Charity Golf Classic event brochure featuring Ray Barton's grandsons, Eddie and Nick Graczyk. First started in 1997, this event has raised nearly $3 million to benefit programs at Children's Hospital in Minneapolis, Minnesota.

'Quality, Convenience, Price'

By Doug Hennes '77
Photo by Mike Ekern '02

Ray Barton's steadfast vision has Great Clips approaching 3,000 stores and $1 billion in revenue

You almost think Ray Barton is joking when he talks about how he built Great Clips into the largest hair-care brand in the world.

No high-powered marketing campaigns backed by million-dollar budgets from wealthy investors. No simultaneous openings of dozens of shops in multiple markets around the country. No acquisitions of rival hair salon chains.

Barton succeeded the old-fashioned way: one store and one market at a time. That was his strategy nearly 30 years ago as a start-up, and it remains his strategy today.

"We just plodded along," he said. "We never were a star. We put one foot ahead of the other, just like a horse. Then we woke up one day and we were the biggest."

He shrugs, not in an immodest way, but to suggest that was the only way he felt comfortable doing business. He knew from the beginning that he wanted to build Great Clips into a national brand because he felt one was bound to emerge in the industry.

"When we started franchising, there was this idea of building a national brand," he said. "We may not have used that term, but was it possible? Yes. Some chains had 400-500 salons, but no national presence. We figured, 'Why not us?'"

Why not, indeed. Great Clips has become that national brand, with 2,900 stores in 43 states and Canada and annual revenues of $800 million. Barton expects to hit a long-envisioned 3,000-store milestone this year and $1 billion in revenue by 2013.

Not bad for a guy who went to five colleges, left two jobs in a six-month period and lost money in his first franchise venture before landing with Great Clips.

Barton was born in South Dakota, the only boy in a family of six kids and the son of an engineer dad who built grain elevators and a mom who ran a restaurant and a cheese shop. They moved around the Midwest during his childhood and settled in the Twin Cities, where he graduated from Minnetonka High School in 1967.

He served in the Navy Reserves, got an accounting degree from San Diego State University and spent

Ray Barton being interviewed for an article in the Winter 2011 edition of the St. Thomas University alumni magazine in his role as a member of their Board of Trustees.

FRANCHISEE AWARDS

Year*	Franchisee of the Year Award	Judy Divine/Caring Heart Award
1989	N/A	Mary Lou Barton
1990	Bob & Billie Urich	Nathalia Ciresi
1991	Pat Stevens	Oj Wolski
1992	Jim Hemak	Marybeth Callahan
1993	Dan & Bob Washburn	Nancy Peyton
1994	Mike, Cindy, Jim & Nancy Bloodworth	Frank Wedcle
1995	Ed Neumayr	Bob & Carol Peterson
1996	Bob & Dianne Douthitt	Dianne Hickman
1997	Dick & Patty Dayton	Kent Houston, Steve Harding & Bob Tuholske
1998	Mary Lou Barton	Ruth Saylor
1999	Mike DiCarlo	Clara Osterhage
2000	Carla Fryar	Sue Petrowich
2001	Clara Osterhage	Denise Bradfield
2002	Pete Schneider	Kim Vosika
2003	Dennis & Sandy Rymers	Mike Dixon
2004	David Oliverio	Lee Vescelius
2005	Pat Stevens	Jean Hamilton
2006	Keith Chalmers	Nick & Denise Schiera
2007	Cheryl Stensrud	Renae Newport
2009	Leonard Robinett, Jr	
2012	Bobbie Sylte-Kneeland; Carrie Langan; Kim Vosika	

Franchisee Hall of Fame

- ❖ Pat Stevens
- ❖ Jim Hemak
- ❖ Tim Lawless
- ❖ Ed Neumayr
- ❖ Pete & Tom Schneider
- ❖ Mary Lou Barton
- ❖ Marylu & Roger Ledebuhr
- ❖ Dan & Bob Washburn
- ❖ Ruth Saylor
- ❖ David Rubenzer
- ❖ Clara Osterhage
- ❖ Mark Tucker

*Awards only presented those years when the Great Clips Convention is held

Franchisee awards 1989 to 2012:

- *Franchisee of the Year Award recipients are outstanding representatives of the franchisee community who exemplify excellence overall.*

- *Franchisees inducted into the Great Clips Franchisee Hall of Fame are long-term franchisees who have made significant contributions to the Great Clips system and community, and have achieved business milestones by building a successful Great Clips business.*

- *The Judy Divine Award was presented to those franchisees who best exemplified Judy's caring attitude towards her employees.*

Pioneer franchisee Bill Divine presenting the Judy Divine Award to franchisee Frank Weddle at the Great Clips Convention in 1994.

Franchisee Ed Neumayr being escorted on stage by corporate staff members Marlene Oberste (left) and Ann Lateadresse (right) upon receiving the Franchisee of the Year Award at the Great Clips Convention in 1995.

Marlene came up with the title for this Great Clips history book, and Ann is one of Great Clips' earliest employees, starting her career in 1984.

Franchisee David Oliverio receiving the Franchisee of the Year Award from Rhoda Olsen and Ray Barton at the Great Clips Convention in 2004.

Mike DiCarlo, Franchisee of the Year, pictured with his wife Cheryl and their management team at the Great Clips Convention in 1999.

Rhoda Olsen at the Great Clips Convention in 1996, having fun with the Salon Performance Operating Tracking Report (SPOTR) that was first adopted by Great Clips in 1984.

Great Clips Hall of Fame franchisees recognized at the 2012 30th Birthday Convention (left to right): Mark Tucker, Clara Osterhage, Tim Lawless, Ed Neumayr, Pat Stevens, Ruth Saylor, Jim Hemak, Mary Lou Barton, (Great Clips' President Charlie Simpson, CEO Rhoda Olsen, David Rubenzer (Great Clips' Chairman Ray Barton), Marylu Ledebuhr, Roger Ledebuhr, Dan Washburn, Pete Schneider, and Tom Schneider..

Canadian franchisee Mark Tucker inducted into the Franchisee Hall of Fame by Charlie Simpson, Rhoda Olsen, and Ray Barton at the 2012 Great Clips 30th Birthday Convention.

Ray Barton and his "5th grade teacher," Mrs. Schlump, appearing together in a skit at the 1998 Great Clips Convention. Mrs. Schlump was quoted by Ray in a few of his convention speeches over the years.

Rhoda Olsen toasting thirty GREAT years at the 2012 Great Clips 30th Birthday Convention.

A Great Clips salon showing the Maple Leaf logo developed exclusively for the Canadian market in 2010.

A Great Clips salon in 2012, featuring the Relax design.

Victory! Kasey Kahne, driver of the Great Clips No. 5 car, celebrating his Sprint Cup victory at Bristol Motor Speedway on March 17, 2013.

Above: The Great Clips No. 38 car, driven by Kasey Kahne, at Phoenix International Raceway on November 10, 2012.

Right: The Great Clips No. 5 car, at Daytona International Speedway on February 23, 2013, sporting an updated paint scheme and a new driver lineup including Kasey Kahne, Jimmie Johnson, and Dale Earnhardt Jr.

PART SEVEN

A New Beginning

CHAPTER 57

Living with Creditors

It would have been tidy if Great Clips simply signed a note to repay the $15.5 million but, as noted earlier, nothing is that easy in the ethereal world of high finance. Instead, the deal was structured in two basic pieces: The company (1) signed a note for $6 million and (2) issued preferred stock to RFE with a par value of $9.5 million—*which Great Clips was required to buy back at a later date at two and a half times par value, or nearly $24 million!* In fact, if the buy-back was delayed past a specific date, the multiple increased to as high as four. Thus, for the privilege of borrowing $15 million to buy out the three other shareholders, the company has to pay $500,000 for RFE's expenses, $6 million plus interest on a note, dividends on the preferred stock, and a minimum of $24 million to buy back the preferred stock—or well over $30 million. And if the pay-back was delayed, the $30 million could be increased to as high as $44 million.

"We figured that the company was worth about $30 million," Ray explained, "which was why I offered $15 for half the stock. "But with this new obligation hanging over our heads, our own stock was mathematically worthless!"

"You have to give Ray a lot of credit," said Morris Sherman, Ray's personal attorney. "He worked hard for fifteen years to build up a sizable equity, and now he was putting it all on the line with one roll of the dice. These money guys—RFE and others like them—are pros. They cover all the bases when it comes to protecting themselves, and they'll take your firstborn child if you don't perform."

The exhilaration of victory was short lived. Now it was time to go to work. Ray and Rhoda knew that the pressure of having this much debt would force them to work harder than ever, and they wasted no time in rolling up their sleeves and tackling their jobs with a new sense of heightened responsibility. And there was another incentive for them to push harder: "We had a lot of franchisees and employees whose livelihoods depended on us to succeed," said Ray. "Rhoda and I both knew that we had to work hard for them because they were working hard for us."

Especially supportive during those gut-wrenching days leading up to the buy-out were Steve Overholser, Steve Hockett, and Dean Wieber from the employee ranks, and Jim Hemak, Pat Stevens, Roger Ledebuhr, Bill Divine, and Ed Neumayr from the franchisees. Bob Todd, then president of Salon Innovations, and Brad Hepp, who provided the insurance needs for the company and many of the franchisees, were likewise giving their emotional support.

Ray and Rhoda, who now owned all of the voting shares, immediately held a meeting to vote in a new Board of Directors. Pat Bradley, who had been an open ally of David and Steve, was out. So was Charlie Kanan. Shelby Yastrow remained on the board with Ray and Rhoda.

Jeff Elgin remained at the company as head of franchising for a short time, then left to start his own firm for brokering franchise sales. Great Clips, with which he maintained a close relationship, became one of his principal clients. Jeff's contribution to Great Clips has been tremendous. He kick-started franchise sales when they were stagnant; he was the catalyst for the settlement among the owners; he instigated the buy-out; and even after he left he brokered franchise sales for the company.

The loan documents provided that the primary lender, RFE, and the secondary lender, Merchants Capital, would have board seats until they were fully repaid. Mike Foster and Richard Goff were elected to those two seats, completing the new five-person board.

Peter Reiter from RFE also attended board meetings for a time in a non-voting role, as did Kirk Griswold of Argosy Capital, another participating investor. In fact, after the buy-out Ray reinstated a policy he initiated in the early 1990s to have certain advisors attend board meetings to act as a sounding board and lend counsel on matters within their expertise. The original Committee of Advisors included Jeff Keyes, Mike McKinley, Dennis Flaherty, and Tom Gegax. The current advisors who are regular attendees of and valuable contributors to board meetings and company decision-making are Brian Gustafson, Doug Donaldson, and Andrew Duff. And Morris Sherman, who has long given Ray and the company solid legal advice, attends board meetings when sensitive legal, financial, or governance issues are on the agenda.

Doug Donaldson has been deeply involved with Great Clips for almost twenty years, primarily to enhance the blend of technology and marketing. Even before he came on the scene, the company had been developing an innovative customer database. But Doug and his colleague, Scott Urling, took this to a new level of detail and sophistication that has been immensely helpful for customer tracking and as a platform for targeted marketing and direct mail.

Vital financial guidance is provided by Andrew Duff, who is chairman and CEO of Piper Jaffray, a global investment bank headquartered in Minneapolis. Further, Andrew plays a special and very important role in helping with ownership and management succession matters. Brian Gustafson worked for Great Clips for a time in the mid-1990s after a stint in the Peace Corps. He is now a portfolio manager in the investment industry and gives valuable advice to Great Clips in the areas of management succession and compensation.

Not only do these advisors give guidance in their areas of expertise, they all are helpful on other matters that come before the board. And they are always available for counsel when Ray, Rhoda, or others at the company call upon them.

The first official board meeting after the buy-out was the first that Ray could remember when there was no tension, bickering, or cross-agendas. All in attendance shared the same vision and strategy for growing the company, and they harmoniously worked to that end. If any one event signaled a new beginning, that was it.

Naturally, Ray was apprehensive that the investor representatives on the board might be a problem. *Would they oppose reinvestment of the profits that might otherwise pay down their loan? Would they unreasonably clamp down on expenses for the same reason? Would they constantly be looking over his shoulder on general management issues?*

All of these concerns quickly vanished. As Morris Sherman observed, "Sometimes these venture guys with all the money can be pains in the ass. They think that having the money makes them smarter, and they inject their own thinking into areas where it doesn't belong. But," he added, "these guys from RFE and the other investors were great. They asked a lot of questions, made a few suggestions, but basically stayed out of the way."

Richard Goff remained on the board for about a year, and Mike Foster stayed until 2007 when the RFE loan was fully paid and the equity components of the transaction were redeemed. During all of those years, there was never an executive or managerial decision that Mike and Richard didn't support. There was no second-guessing, no dunning for payment, and no interference.

Ray's respect for Mike's cooperation is illustrated by an incident that Shelby Yastrow will never forget. "Mike and I made up the Compensation Committee," he said, "and we had this meeting to consider Ray's and Rhoda's annual bonuses for that year. It had been one hell of a year. We added more franchisees and opened more salons than in any previous year, the customer counts were way up, and salon and company profits were above projection. I was for giving giant bonuses to Ray and Rhoda—even above the guidelines we had approved—but Mike refused to exceed the guidelines."

Shelby continued, "Some months later I casually mentioned to Ray that Mike could be a little tightfisted when it came to bonuses. It was the only time in nearly eighteen years on the board that Ray hammered me! He said, 'Mike is not tightfisted! He's been extremely fair and reasonable. Please don't push him to give us one dollar more than the guidelines provide.'"

Regardless of how a deal is structured, and regardless of the risks, there is always one overriding question that investors ask: *How do we get our money back?* If the borrowing company succeeds, the investors want to be able to collect their profits and go on to the net deal; if the borrower fails, they want pre-established rights to be among the first to start picking the meat off the bones. In either event, the borrower must be able to provide the investors with exit strategies, and the original business plan submitted for the loan has to address this issue.

In this transaction, four alternative exit strategies were proposed, discussed, and analyzed in depth. They were:

1. A public offering—the same thing that Ray resisted when it had been proposed by Steve Lemmon and David Rubenzer.

2. A sale of the company to another company or to a private equity group.

3. A recapitalization through the sale of stock to new shareholders, thereby raising money from new investors to buy out RFE and the participating investors.

4. A recapitalization through borrowing from other financial institutions, thereby avoiding the need to bring in new shareholders and dilute equity.

The first of the alternatives—going public—was never seriously embraced, but it was not totally ruled out for another two or three years. Ray had invited a few outside investment bankers to a board meeting, and they pointed to two financial facts of life that finally put the subject to bed. First, it was now the late 1990s and the country was in the midst of a technology boom. The only public offerings that got any attention at all were the dot. com ventures on the NASDAQ. Second, Great Clips was just too small. Institutional investors—not moms and pops—dominate the stock market and account for about 75 percent of all the public stock holdings. By law, most of these investors may not own more than 5 percent of the stock of any company. Even if Great Clips was three times larger than it was, it would have a market value of less than $100 million, and therefore an institutional investor would be limited to a $5 million holding. Chicken feed—not worth the time and money to bother with. After that meeting, the idea of going public was never again considered as a way to pay back RFE.

The second alternative—selling the company outright—never got any traction at all. Ray and Rhoda had worked hard to get to this point, and selling out would be the very last resort.

For similar reasons, there was no enthusiasm at all for the third option—raising money by bringing in new shareholders. Ray and Rhoda were undertaking this enormous debt for the purpose of buying out old shareholders, not bringing in new ones.

The exit strategy eventually pursued was the fourth—recapitalization through commercial borrowing. The prosperity of Great Clips over the next several years made it possible to take out commercial loans on terms far more favorable than those of the RFE deal. Indeed, the company did refinance its debt five times between 2001 and 2007, and that was how the RFE group in 2007 recovered their entire investment.

In the meantime, the pressure of a $30 million-plus debt reinforced the need for the growth that Ray had envisioned from the beginning. As he saw it, more salons than ever before were needed to generate profits to meet the debt as well as all other expenses. This became front and center on the agenda for the first meeting of the new Board of Directors.

One suggestion made to jump start new growth was to develop company-owned salons instead of focusing only on franchising. But this was a risky route, and Shelby voiced his opposition just as he had when it was proposed earlier by David and Steve, with the same reasoning. "We'll be asking for a lot of trouble," he said, "if we start competing with our franchisees for locations, managers, and stylists. If we *have to* do it, we should do it only in isolated markets where we have no franchisees." Shelby also reminded the board that such an initiative would require a separate division within the company with a separate budget and financial model, "all of which will be a major distraction to our main and proven business—franchising."

Peter Reiter totally agreed, pointing out further that such a move would jeopardize the company's strongest asset—the trust of the franchisees.

There was an even more compelling argument against having company-owned salons: They could be more of a liability than an asset, especially in the short term. As explained earlier, in most franchise systems company-owned outlets don't perform as well as franchised outlets, and it would be dangerous to assume that company-owned salons could produce enough profits in the foreseeable future to make them worthwhile.

Steve Overholser, who oversaw the company finances, also scoffed at the idea. "We'd have to own and operate at least 150 salons to make a difference, and that would take us completely out of our element. Worse, developing company salons would divert capital that we needed to implement our growth and expansion into new markets."

As it happened, the company did buy about twenty existing salons from franchisees as a way to "stick a toe in the water," but it didn't create much enthusiasm and the salons were later sold.

With the last of a series of favorable recapitalizations in 2007, Great Clips was able to pay off the RFE loan and buy back the entire investment made by RFE and its participating investors. Everyone was happy. The investors got their money back with a healthy profit, and Great Clips was left with a much more manageable debt.

Interestingly, the repurchase of the investors' common stock was to be at "fair market value," but this was an indefinite term since Great Clips was not publicly traded on any stock exchange. In ordinary circumstances, this could lead to lengthy—and possibly bitter—negotiations. However, owing to the solid relationship between Ray and Mike Foster from RFE, they were able to agree to the stock valuation in less than an hour.

CHAPTER 58

The Perfect Match

For the previous fifteen years, Ray had fought tooth and nail for greater growth in existing markets and expansion into new markets. Now he had a new board who not only wanted growth and expansion, *they insisted on it!*

As Great Clips geared up for the fastest growth in its history, Rhoda was promoted to president and Ray took the titles of CEO and Chairman of the Board of Directors. It was the perfect match—Ray providing the big picture and Rhoda connecting all the dots.

As well as their talents balanced, Ray and Rhoda don't always see eye to eye. What brother and sister do? But they do their best to resolve their differences by listening to each other with a willingness to compromise without the feeling of "losing." They both have that same attitude with franchisees—always prepared to listen and not a bit hesitant to compromise when it's the right thing to do.

Now, with the two of them sharing the driver's seat, Ray and Rhoda took the Great Clips system on a thrilling ride to the top. In the ten years

Ray Barton and Rhoda Olsen celebrate Rhoda's promotion to president at the 1998 Great Clips Convention.

following the buy-out, the number of salons more than tripled (to nearly 2,600), and system-wide sales more than quadrupled (to nearly $650 million).

This focus on system-wide growth has never distracted from the focus on the franchisees and their success. In fact, as Shelby Yastrow put it, "In our board meetings, we spend a great deal of time reviewing franchisee attitudes and performance, analyzing average salon sales and profits, salon customer counts, and "same salon" performance from year to year. The time spent on these discussions dwarfs the amount of time we spend on company revenues and profits."

Rhoda had already made it a point to visit every salon in the system, a practice she continued until there were about 1,800 salons. During each visit, she asked questions, answered questions, and showed a genuine concern for the stylists and managers. "Are you really the president?" one stylist asked. "I used to work at Supercuts, and when executives came into the salon they wouldn't even talk to us."

As Rhoda visited more and more salons, Ray visited fewer and fewer. Soon Rhoda was better known than he, a point he readily acknowledges. "When I go into a salon," he says with a grin, "I say, 'Hi, I'm Ray Barton from the home office.' I get a bunch of blank stares, and then someone will say, 'What do you do back there? Have you ever met Rhoda?'"

While Ray's goals and prophesies were sometimes overly ambitious, the one that he made at a convention in the early 1990s has proven true: He noted that IBM had been the Cinderella company of the 1960s, Xerox had dominated the 1970s, and McDonald's was the headliner of the 1980s, and he concluded with the proclamation that "the '90s belong to us!"

And indeed they did. As the twentieth century drew to a close, the company and its franchisees could look back over their seventeen-year history—and especially the decade of the 1990s—with pride. Great Clips was now

The pin Ray Barton created to promote the prophesy he made at a convention in the early 1990s: "The '90s Belong to Us."

on the brink of becoming the largest and fastest growing salon brand in the world, a title it would achieve in 2001—and the 3,000th salon was not far away.

The 1999 convention was chosen to congratulate the system—franchisees, vendors, and staff—on their collective performance. The franchisees had special reason to celebrate: Among them there had been 900 weeks of record sales during the previous year!

Ray capped off the celebration—literally!—by arranging for bottles of 1989 Chateau Meyney to be passed throughout the crowd so everyone could toast their success. "I bought fifty cases of wine futures back in 1990," Ray says, "to have it to celebrate our 3,000th salon. But I couldn't wait."

The little company that started out seventeen years earlier in Steve Lemmon's backyard with nothing but a dream was closing the millennium with its major goals within its grasp—3,000 salons, plus being the largest salon brand in the world. But Ray and Rhoda were not complacent. The day after the convention they buckled up to attack the twenty-first century with renewed vigor.

CHAPTER 59

GCRC Phases Out

In early 1999, Ray opened his front door and found 220 salons on his doorstep!

Michael Connolly had decided to abandon the haircare business and liquidate his investment in GCRC. Of the four regions he had agreed to develop, he had surrendered Chicago before even putting a stake in the ground and had essentially walked away from the Mid-Atlantic Region after barely beginning to develop it. Northern California was struggling, and only the Northwest Region was holding its own.

In an effort to salvage a bad situation, GCRC had already sold all of its rights in the Mid-Atlantic Region in 1998 to Gerry Czarnecki, one of its investors and a franchisee in the Northwest Region. "To say I 'bought' the region isn't exactly accurate," Gerry said. "I just stepped in and took over all the liabilities. I like to think that we cleaned up the franchise support problems and set the foundation for the region to grow even beyond what we were able to achieve. Eventually, I got to the point where my other business interests forced me to make the decision to sell the region back to Great Clips in 2004."

Gerry went on to say, "It was a great experience to be a franchisor, and I learned a lot about the real nature of partnering in the franchise model. I realized that Great Clips had developed an excellent model for assuring brand integrity while supporting the profitable growth of the franchisees."

GCRC was having more trouble than ever running the remaining two regions. In 1999, GCRC sold both regions back to Great Clips, thereby ending its development venture.

Ray and Rhoda knew how difficult it would be to absorb 220 new salons. Fortunately, Rhoda had spent considerable time in the GCRC markets and had gotten to know many of the franchisees, and that made a difficult transition much more manageable. "It was a big pill to swallow," Ray remembers, "and it took a lot of time to smooth things out. But at the end of the day it was a good thing. We have those markets, and the franchisees are happy and making money." Then Ray adds, "And I appreciate the investment and hard work of everyone at GCRC. They helped make us the world's largest and fastest growing salon brand."

Indeed, it was through GCRC that Great Clips acquired an international presence. The Northwest Region extended into Canada, and in 1993 GCRC issued a franchise in Vancouver to Norman Chow. Norman opened his salon in December of that year, but in the following year, he sold it to Mark Tucker. Today Mark has eighteen salons—more than any other franchisee in Canada. He was inducted into Great Clips' Franchisee Hall of Fame

On December 18, 1993, franchisee Norman Chow opens the first Great Clips salon in Canada. On his left is Michael Connolly of Great Clips Regional Companies and Ray Barton is on his right.

at the convention in October 2012. Norman Chow is now a practicing attorney in Canada and represents Mark and many other Canadian franchisees.

CHAPTER 60

Reacting to Tragedy

No matter how well a company plans for contingencies, it can't anticipate everything. Some things are just not foreseeable. Such was the case of the terrorist attacks on September 11, 2001, only ten days before the 2001 Great Clips convention was scheduled to begin.

In the days following the attack, the nation was traumatized, confused and afraid. There was a particular fear of flying since commercial airplanes has been the terrorists' weapon of choice. In fact, commercial flights had been temporarily grounded by order of the federal government, and no one was sure when the order would be lifted. Conventions and other meetings were being canceled all over the country.

Rhoda's first act after the tragedy was to find out which company employees had been traveling or were scheduled to travel within the next week or two. She personally called every one of them, asking if they were alright and telling them to stay put. If they were stranded away from home, Great Clips would take care of all of their expenses.

Ray and Rhoda deliberated about whether to cancel the convention. They considered all the angles. In the end, after confirming that flights would be resumed, they decided to move ahead. The convention theme for that year carried the hauntingly ironic title, "Upward Bound."

A surprisingly large number of people showed up for the convention. In fact, there were only about fifty cancellations, and over 1,000 people attended. Phoenix franchisee Ed Neumayr, who owned multiple salons, voiced the same explanation that people were offering all over the country: "One flight out of so many gazillion—the odds of that happening again within the next few days on any given flight are astronomical. I bring many of my managers every year, and they look forward to it. Not one of them dropped out."

More than a few of the convention attendees opted to drive rather than fly to Minneapolis, with some coming from as far away as Texas

Sunu Cheeran, who was the company's office administrator, said, "There were a lot of mixed emotions at the convention, but everyone there was delighted that we went ahead with it." It turned out to be an extra special convention for Sunu. She was honored with the award for the Corporate Employee of the Year!

As anyone knowing Rhoda would expect, she made countless last-minute changes in the convention agenda in recognition of the national mood. She added a patriotic tone, which was woven into many of the talks and presentations.

By a remarkable coincidence, the keynote speaker was a military hero, Captain Gerald Coffee, Retired of the U.S. Navy. During the Vietnam War Captain Coffee, a fighter pilot, was shot down and held as a prisoner of war

A sample of the poster that was sent to all salons after the terrorist attacks on 9/11 on display at the Great Clips Convention in 2001.

in North Vietnam for seven years. As a younger pilot, he had received the Distinguished Flying Cross for flying low-level reconnaissance missions over Cuba during the Cuban missile crisis. His speech at the convention focused on the power of the human spirit and was not only timely but inspirational and motivating as well.

CHAPTER 61

"Stay Away from 'My' Customers!!"

In earlier chapters discussing market development, we pointed out that the definition of "market saturation" is a mercurial one and depends on who is doing the defining.

Franchisors are keenly aware of the importance of dominating a given market in order to strengthen the brand within that market, and to achieve that domination they look to open more and more sites. More sites mean more advertising dollars, greater brand awareness, and higher sales and profits for all of the franchisees in the market. And each new location is one that won't go to a competing brand.

On the other hand, nearby franchisees already in the market get nervous about new locations that might draw away their customers. The more new locations that are opened, the more nervous—and hostile—the franchisees become.

This supposed "drawing away" of customers to the new location is known by a variety of terms—"encroachment," "sales transfer," and even "cannibalism!" For consistency, we will refer to it as "impact"—that is, the adverse effect, or *impact*, that the new location has on one or more existing ones.

The debates over impact are never ending, and they take place in courtrooms as well as in boardrooms. "This is the bane of *all* franchise systems catering to the 'walk-in' or 'drive-by' customer," according to Shelby Yastrow. "I can't begin to describe the nightmares impact has caused for franchisors and franchisees alike. It is, and will always be, a subject that is never off the table. I look at impact as the unwanted child of growth."

Shelby goes on to say that the problem has so many facets that it defies a single approach. "For example," he explains, "if the new location goes to the same franchisee located a mile away, he may see having the second site as a wonderful thing. But if the new location goes to a *different* franchisee, with whom he will have to compete, he will scream bloody murder. So, opening a new location involves a *who* decision as well as a *where* decision."

Also, a dose of reality has to be injected into any discussion of impact. Let us assume that a franchisor goes into a brand new market—a completely virgin territory. Assume further that the market can support, say, twelve locations. Obviously, the dozen locations can't be developed and opened at the same time, so they will open one at a time. The franchisee who is awarded the first of these sites will have all of the "borrowed" customers who will one day be going to one of the eleven other locations, but in the meantime have nowhere else to go. He has the perfect monopoly! When the second location opens a few months later and is awarded to another franchisee, some of those borrowed customers will leave and take their business to the new location—and he, too, is likely to scream bloody murder.

Is that exodus of customers a result of *impact*? Yes, but only in a purely technical sense. This is clearly not a case where the first franchisee has a legitimate complaint or where the franchisor should apologize for adding the second location. "But there is a point," Shelby says, "when the franchisor can go too far. It might be with the fifth or sixth location, or maybe sooner if they get too close together. On the other hand, with careful site selection there may not be a problem until much later—if at all. In other words," he concludes, "every situation is unique and requires its own analysis."

Complicating the issue even further, there is no good way to define "too close together." In central Manhattan or downtown Chicago, for example, outlets two blocks apart may not have a competitive effect on each other; but, in a small rural community, two outlets on opposite sides of town may be arch enemies fighting for the same customers. "I've seen two McDonald's directly across the road from one another," Shelby recalls, "and both were thriving. How can that be? Because it was an interstate highway with a median down the center, so one of the McDonald's was capturing the eastbound traffic while the other one was getting the people driving west. Absolutely not one penny of impact, and eliminating one of them would not create any new business for the other." On the other hand, if a new McDonald's went in *thirty miles away* to the west, it could have a devastating impact on the one getting the westbound traffic. "No need to stop here," the driver may say to his family as he spots the billboard for the next McDonald's, "there's another one a half-hour away."

Notwithstanding the artificiality of "distance" as a criterion, many franchise systems continue to use it to determine new locations and protect existing ones. The Great Clips franchise agreement, for example, has always provided that no new salon may be opened within three-quarters of a mile from an existing salon. This is called a franchisee's "protected area" or "exclusive area." Over time, Great Clips began offering franchisees a "right of first refusal" within the one-mile circumference *beyond* the protected area so that there is an element of protection for one and three-quarters of a mile in all directions. However, the right of first refusal is conditional on the franchisee being "in compliance" with the franchise agreement and with the Great Clips operating procedures.

To add a practical overlay to the entire situation, Great Clips will recognize a right of first refusal even *beyond* one and three-quarters of a mile in locations where it would be fair to do so. Conversely, in high-density areas, the franchise agreement might reduce the "protected" or exclusive area to *less* than three-quarters of a mile.

How the application of these provisions works in real life will be examined later.

Whenever a franchisor gets aggressive and over-develops an area with too many locations on top of each other, the franchisees revolt. Conversely, if the franchisor is too conservative and passes up good sites in order to appease franchisees, the market will never be adequately developed and the brand will suffer. Worse, competitors will come in and take the abandoned sites.

Because impact is such a divisive and volatile subject, responsible franchisors do all they can to avoid it, minimize it, and, when necessary, make concessions to atone for it. The main obstacle is that the extent of impact is difficult to predict. *Will the new salon impact the gross sales of the old salon by 2 percent, 5 percent, or even 20 percent?*

Moreover, it's difficult to measure impact after it happens. *Did the sales of the old salon decline because of impact or was it bad weather, a closed street, road repairs, or an anchor tenant going out of business? Or, more realistically, was it because the impacted salon had poor management and lousy operations, or that it needed to be cleaned up and repainted?*

The problems of impact struck Great Clips clear back in its earliest days and led to an eventful meeting in July 1986. As already noted, ever since the first franchise was sold in 1983, the agreement defined a franchisee's protected (exclusive) area to be within three-quarters of a mile of his or her salon. But, according to the memory of some of the earliest franchisees, they were told by Great Clips people, "Don't worry, even though the contract says we won't put another unit within three-quarters of a mile, it's our practice not to place another unit within *two miles* of an existing salon." Naturally, all that the franchisees heard was "two miles," and to them that distance would forever define their protected territory. They pushed so hard that the company relented and in a spirit of compromise agreed at that 1986 meeting to extend the protected area to two miles for those early franchisees—but only until their ten-year franchise agreements expired, and that would begin in 1993.

This meant that 1993 would be a year of reckoning—the year when the protected area for the earliest franchisees would be shrunk back to three-quarters of a mile and the year that those franchisees would be up in arms. Dean Wieber, who had just come to Great Clips to take over the real estate department, went to his first Denver franchisee meeting in 1991. Ray and Rhoda had already briefed him on what to expect. This was quite an initiation. Dean was the corporate representative at the meeting and had to take all the heat.

Dean assured the franchisees that the company would be fair when it came to putting new salons in "never-never land"—the area just outside the three-quarters protected area but still within the two mile area that was being phased out. Yet, handling these situations on an *ad hoc* basis and without a formal process opened the door to problems.

The story that best illustrates the deficiencies of the process ended up, in all places, in Ray Barton's bedroom! Still new on the job, Dean received a call from Minneapolis franchisee Pat Stevens who suspected that a new salon was within his two-mile radius. Dean agreed to investigate and, sure enough, a measurement revealed that the new salon was *just barely* less than two miles from Pat's salon. As if that weren't enough, the owner of the new offending salon was none other than Mary Lou Barton, Ray's wife! And to add to the madness, Mary Lou was Pat's sister!

"Here I was, still the new kid on the block," said Dean, "and I had to go in and tell the CEO that his *wife's* salon was encroaching on his *brother-in-law's* salon." Even though Mary Lou had completed the build-out and had hired staff, Ray didn't hesitate once he heard the facts. "That salon goes to Pat, period. There's nothing to discuss." When he broke the news to Mary Lou, she was heartbroken. She herself had found the site in a high-end mall next to a Target, and she knew how successful it would be.

As their angst over the "protected area" issue intensified, the franchisees trained their cross-hairs on Dean Wieber who was the head guy on site selection. In 1994 he spearheaded a process to deal with remote sites outside the protected area that may nevertheless create significant impact. The "impacted" franchisees could complete a questionnaire about their customer base, trading area, and other relevant data in an effort to "kill" the new site or take it for themselves. While they were afforded a full opportunity to make their case, the final decision was still in the hands of the company. This was a temporary solution to a permanent problem. As we will see, a better and fairer solution was right around the corner. Nevertheless, this signified once again how the company listened and responded to franchisee concerns.

Predicting and measuring impact is at best an art and not a science. Still, there are companies whose business it is to predict impact in advance and to measure it after the fact. The processes used to do this are complicated, and the findings are often challenged. Back in the 1970s and 1980s, the customary process was very rudimentary. If the purpose was to predict the impact on salon A from the proposed salon B, one would go into salon A and ask customers where they lived. Their answers would be represented by dots pasted on a map of the area. One would assume that the customers represented by those dots would prefer to go to the salon nearest to them. Thus, if there were a large concentration of dots in the area near the proposed salon B, it would be strong evidence that salon A would be heavily impacted by the new salon.

However, where a person *lives* may not be relevant to where he or she shops, eats breakfast, or gets a haircut. Studies have shown, for example, that people who drive to work will more likely have a fast food breakfast near where they work and not near their homes. An impact study at such a restaurant will involve a "trip pattern analysis" to factor in where customers have been and where they are going as well as where they live.

The quest for national dominance led the company to set its sights on those larger markets with the most potential for growth. One result of this was that less attention was given to smaller markets that could support only a handful of salons.

In the late 1990s, Charlie Simpson, then vice president of development and now the company president, saw that the company was missing the tremendous opportunity these smaller markets could collectively offer. Charlie knew, however, that these markets could not be developed in the traditional way with multiple franchisees. There just weren't enough sites to go around! Instead, his plan was to select a single franchisee to develop each of these markets.

This led to the creation of the Market Development Agreement (MDA) by which a franchisee would agree to develop a specific market on an agreed-upon schedule. Each market selected had a potential of no more than twenty salons. The idea became a reality in 1999, and it is another Great Clips success story. There are currently forty-four Market Development

Charlie Simpson was named president of Great Clips in January 2011.

Agreements, and 195 salons have thus far opened in those markets. Rhoda credits Charlie with this idea which, she says, "has been core to our growth, and has produced some of our strongest franchisees."

And of course, a valuable by-product of this plan is that it avoids the endemic problem of impact.

CHAPTER 62

The Impact Crisis Is Averted

The growth rate at Great Clips exploded following the buy-out of David and Steve in 1997. This is what Ray wanted and the board supported, and it was helped by higher demand for franchises. The company would soon be opening over 200 salons each year for several years in a row. But as more salons are added the distance between them decreases. Increased impact, especially in the more mature markets, was inevitable.

In the eyes of the company, the impact was for the most part tolerable and was the natural collateral damage from needed expansion. But in the eyes of the franchisees it was becoming more of a problem. To some of them, their interests and the interests of the company were not aligned. Franchisees are great at math. They know that more salons mean more system-wide sales, and that means higher royalties for the company—even if the impacted salons are losing money. Furthermore, 200 new salons in a year would produce about $4 million in up-front franchise fees for the company. So, to some of the franchisees, the impact from more salons was attributable to nothing more than company greed.

As with all retail franchise systems, it's always the most drastic cases that get all the attention, and by repetition it seems there are more of them than is actually the case. And then there is always the story of the franchisee who never had a single case of *serious* impact, but cites many cases of *minor* impact, which collectively add up to "death by a thousand cuts."

By the beginning of the new century, the negative impact from new Great Clips salons had grown into a hot issue among franchisees, and they were not bashful about raising it at every opportunity. Emotions ran high, and the rhetoric was heated. Dean Wieber was the most obvious target, and he finally came to Ray and Rhoda to tell them that the issue was getting out of control. They decided to create a joint task force, with both franchisees and company people, to study the problem. Wisely, Ray and Rhoda did not want Dean to take a lead role on the task force since, from the franchisees'

point of view, he was so involved with impact issues that his objectivity might be questioned.

The company and the MARC, working together, created the task force and named it Network Expansion Conflict (NEC)—an extravagant euphemism for impact. The franchisees elected Jim Hemak to co-chair the task force, and the company appointed Charlie Simpson to co-chair from the company side. Both were excellent choices. Jim was thoroughly trusted by the company as well as by the franchisee community, and he had the keen ability to see issues from both sides. Charlie, who had been hired in 1999 to replace Jeff Elgin to head up franchising at Great Clips, was likewise open-minded and trusted by the franchisees. An added advantage was that both men had the dispositions and patience to keep the discussions on a high plane.

Charlie, who was later to become president of the company, had a special empathy with the franchisees because he and his wife had previously been Great Clips franchisees. Before that, he had been National Franchise Director at Southland Corporation, overseeing franchisee relations with the owners of about 3,000 7-Eleven convenience stores. "I had good credentials for this assignment," Charlie explains. "Having been a franchisee, I was able to put myself in the franchisees' shoes and see this impact problem as they saw it. That's vital for reaching a meeting of the minds, and without a meeting of the minds there can't be a solution."

Charlie and Jim were equally aware of the seriousness of the impact issue, knowing that it was on the brink of causing wounds that might never heal. Ray and Rhoda envisioned a national franchise system built on a foundation of trust, but nothing could destroy trust as much as a franchisee waking up one morning and seeing another Great Clips in what he considered his backyard. The two co-chairmen confronted the issue head on, with Jim recognizing that the company needed to grow and Charlie acknowledging that the franchisees needed to profit.

The NEC Task Force held its first meeting on January 24, 2004. There were eight franchisees on the Task Force—Jim Hemak, Pat Stevens, Clara Osterhage, Ruth Saylor, Ron Brooker, Dick Hagadorn, Baruch Toledano, and Ken Hand—but only five company representatives—Charlie, Dean, Jerry Spicer, Larry Timmerman, and Kavita Naimpally. This was a prudent move for Great Clips. It underscored the fact that the company wanted the franchisees to have a large voice on this sensitive issue that affected them and that the company had not proposed creating the Task Force with the intention of dominating it.

The agenda for the first meeting was to set goals, affirm beliefs, and establish ground rules. All agreed that a solution that did not work for one side could not possibly work for the other. Terms like "fairness," "mutually profitable," and "beneficial to the system as a whole" were centerpieces of the discussions. The Task Force met frequently for the next year and a half, methodically seeking facts and exploring ideas. "To help us," Charlie recalled, "we brought in people from other franchise companies, including Shelby Yastrow from McDonald's, to tell us how they dealt with the impact problem. We asked them hard questions, and we wanted facts and numbers more than impressions."

Appealing to hard data was crucial. Just as the franchisees mistrusted the company on location decisions, the company didn't trust the franchisees' own measurement of their impact. As already mentioned, declining sales can be attributed to a host of reasons that have nothing to do with the proximity of a new salon.

Since a site not taken may end up in the hands of a competitor, the Task Force had to deal with a central question: *Would I rather compete against a Great Clips salon or some other brand, such as a Cost Cutters or Supercuts?* Most franchisees believe they'd be better off competing against a different brand. This discussion was not merely an academic one, it responded to the risk of a site going to a competitor if Great Clips passed on it because of possible impact. Dean Wieber produced research to show that the impact from a competitive brand would be significantly lower than the impact from another Great Clips—by 40 percent. On the other hand, the new Great Clips salon would contribute dollars to the advertising fund, and this would benefit all the franchisees in the market through the building of greater brand awareness.

The NEC Task Force had good reason to be satisfied with the product of its labors. The franchisees (in compliance with Great Clips standards) were given a right of first refusal within a one-mile area *beyond* the three-quarter mile exclusive area. In addition, the Task Force supported the demographic process perfected by MapInfo, Inc. (now called Pitney Bowes Business Insight) to predict impact. That process thereafter became an integral part of the location review process at Great Clips; although Great Clips later perfected its own technology enabling it to conduct most impact studies in-house.

Coming out of the Task Force, the company acknowledged that it would not have a closed mind when considering sites beyond one and three-quarter miles. Thus, the company would take impact into consideration even if a potential site was two miles from an existing salon. Further, it was agreed that, regardless of the situation, an aggrieved franchisee might appeal any decision all the way up to the president of Great Clips.

Totally apart from the direct benefits of these new procedures, the process proved that the franchisees and the company could work arm-in-arm to solve even the most sensitive problems. This alone did more to reinforce trust than almost any other single event in the history of the Great Clips system. Las Vegas franchisee Dick Hagadorn, one of the franchisees on the Task Force, said, "This was a real triumph for the franchisees, and it would not have happened with any other company. But Great Clips isn't like those other places. Everything's on the table and open for discussion. In the end, a common understanding of the brand-building focus of Great Clips on the one hand, and the franchisees' investment risks on the other, produced a new framework to maximize mutual success. Brand dominance and salon profitability were co-important. It was truly a watershed collaboration."

How did the safeguards and procedures adopted by the Task Force actually affect the decisions on choosing sites? Clearly, the company was seen as more sensitive to the franchisees, avoiding the extreme sites that obviously would have caused fireworks and being willing to compromise on questionable sites. Conversely, the franchisees had a greater understanding of the company's position and were more tolerant of the less extreme cases. When there was an objection, it was voiced in a calmer manner and handled more fairly.

The NEC Task Force was another high-water mark in the franchisor-franchisee balance of power at Great Clips. Less than twenty years earlier, franchisees were passive investors who were asked to stay out of their own salons. Later, they took an active role in the management of their salons, but their influence never extended beyond those walls. Then, through the MARC, they were brought into the marketing process. Now they were given a genuine role in the process of site selection criteria, one of the most important—and contentious—areas of retail franchising.

The site selection process proves once again that, without a doubt, no franchise system in the country shows more respect for its franchisees than Great Clips.

Rob Goggins is the Great Clips senior vice president of real estate and development who succeeded Dean Wieber. Rob can attest that careful site selection and open communications with franchisees go a long way to ease the impact problem. He says, "We recently created a Real Estate Committee with five members—two from the company and three franchisees (Clara Osterhage, Bob Crowther, and Jim Petrowich)—to discuss any and all opportunities to improve the real estate processes, forms, and overall service to the franchisees. This kind of ongoing dialogue is very useful."

If we were to pick just two illustrations to put the impact bugaboo in perspective and demonstrate how the system survived it, we might look to Ron Brooker in North Carolina and Mary Lou Barton in Minnesota.

Ron had once lamented that he would eventually lose a lot of money over the years because of cumulative impact from other salons. Be that as it may, he has continued to open additional salons along with other franchisees in his market, and he now has fifteen. Ron's average sales and cash flow exceed national averages, and *those averages have grown as he and others in the market continued to open new salons.* Instead of being hurt by having more salons in the market, adding new ones has increased sales and profits at his existing ones. The explanation: More salons in the market—even when owned by other Great Clips franchisees —increase the awareness of Great Clips and, with the added marketing dollars, help to leverage the brand for the benefit of all.

Mary Lou Barton has four salons in the St. Cloud, Minnesota, area. Three are within one-and-a-half miles of each other, and the fourth is only about two miles away from one of the other three. According to Mary Lou, "I could almost cover them with a blanket!" Most franchisees would say these salons are too close together, and that the impact must be dreadful. Yet, three of them have been in the "top 25" salons in the entire system for many years, and one of them has led the entire system in customer counts for nearly twenty years. Has Mary Lou finally saturated that small market with those four salons? "No way," she laughs. "I've already started the fifth! I've proven to myself that Ray has been right all along—every new salon helps the others; and if we can dominate a market with a lot of great salons, *the customers will stay with us and the competition will stay away.*"

These two cases are not unusual. In market after market, Great Clips has proven that adding new salons is a "double whammy." New salons help old salons, and market dominance discourages the competition from trying to break in.

In short, some impact is an unavoidable by-product of growth, and brand-conscious franchisees understand that. John Marcotte, who owns multiple salons in Seattle and St. Louis, offers this perspective: "To grow the brand helps all of us, and to have that we have to accept the inevitability of impact. Too little is as bad as too much. The trick is to keep it under control."

A major point, alluded to above, deserves repetition: *Good salon operations are the best defense against impact.* When customers get the experience they want, they won't be inclined to go elsewhere at the first opportunity. Conversely, customers subjected to lackluster operations will bolt as soon as they see a new salon open a few miles away.

CHAPTER 63

Redefining the ABCs

As with all businesses, there were always challenging issues at Great Clips—marketing, real estate, financing, franchisee relations, human resources, and wrestling with governmental regulations, to name a few. Each was critical to the success of the system, but all were distractions to the most critical challenge of all—*operational excellence within the walls of each salon or, in the lingo of Ray Barton, "execution."*

"Execution" is a word that punctuates nearly everything Ray has to say about the business. One of his favorite quotes, taken from Don Beveridge, a popular business speaker and writer, is: "Businesses fail not because of lack of knowledge; they fail because of lack of execution." Another of Ray's oft-cited sources is *The Discipline of Market Leaders* by Fred Wiersema and Michael Treacy, which stresses that the most successful market leaders excel in operational excellence, product leadership, or customer intimacy, but not all three since each requires a different discipline. While Ray appreciates the importance of all three, the principal focus at Great Clips is operational excellence.

Soon after Great Clips celebrated its twentieth anniversary and had moved into the new century, the salons were experiencing disappointing sales and customer counts. As was to be expected, many franchisees blamed the two standard scapegoats—poor marketing and impact from other Great Clips salons.

Ray and Rhoda, however, pointed in another direction—*ineffective execution within the salons.* Owners of the better-performing salons agreed with them. John Marcotte, for example, a franchisee who exemplifies operational excellence, says, "Solid execution will produce good profits in a mediocre location, and maybe even in a C location, but poor execution will produce failure even in an A location."

The problems of poor execution were accentuated as markets became more competitive. In the early days, the competition was mainly from full-service, high-price salons, and Great Clips was able to differentiate itself—and attract customers—with low prices, no appointments, and being open on evenings and weekends. Great Clips offered much that the full-service salons could not match.

But as more and more low-cost salons moved in with evening and weekend service and no appointments, the competition became more direct—and more indistinguishable. Something new was needed for the Great Clips arsenal. "When we were the first mover in a changing industry," Ray explained, "we could be successful even if we were a little careless about execution. But as the category got more competitive with other brands using the same concept, we could only stand above the crowd by executing our jobs better. We were all doing haircuts, we were all in the same shopping centers, and we were all charging about the same price. That meant we had to do a better job at giving the customers what they want. *In other words, we had to execute better within the salons!*"

By no means was this a new rallying cry for Ray. Back in the early 1980s when his own wife, Mary Lou, and her partner blamed poor sales on the marketing, Ray countered by putting the blame on their slack operations. However, in the face of stronger competition, Ray came to realize that vague platitudes like "better execution" were no longer hitting home. He knew something else was needed—something *more specific* that could easily find its way into the salons. This "something" had to be adaptable and actually make a positive mark on operations. *But he didn't know what it was or where to find it!*

Rhoda, enlisting the help of Charlie Simpson and Terri Miller, vice president of marketing and communications, stepped in to pick up the ball. The three of them launched a full-blown process aimed at finding the right key that would open the lock to better operations. They engaged the entire executive team, business partners, consultants, and franchisees Dick Hagadorn, Ed Neumayr, and Pat Stevens. Feedback was sought from stylists, managers, and customers. There would also be an analysis of what was going on in the competitors' salons.

Upon hearing their plans, Ray had one small request: "Whatever you find must be easily adaptable, so let's not overcomplicate it. Whatever you recommend, I'd like to see it recapped on one page." He went on to say that he didn't want anything changed just for the sake of making changes. He often made this point, quoting Ferdinand Porsche, the automobile icon: "To change is easy; to improve is difficult."

Stellus Consulting, a Minneapolis agency specializing in branding, led the team through the process and carried out the research. Corky Hall, chief executive officer of Stellus, gave this assurance to Great Clips at that time:

"We will guide you and your team to instill the language, beliefs, and behaviors required to make brand-building a way of life in your company. We will help ensure that your processes get rigorously applied and deeply ingrained across your organization so they will outlive the inevitable turnover. This is how you sustain profitable growth."

A barrage of meetings, questionnaires, and focus groups explored the thoughts and feelings of everyone associated with Great Clips, from the customers clear up to the executives. The goal was to capture—and then crystallize into a few words—*what it would take to differentiate Great Clips from the rest of the pack and keep the customers coming back*. Ray and Rhoda both knew that repeat customers were the key. By coming back they were saying that their experience was a good one. And it's easier to have one customer come back twenty times than it is to attract twenty new customers.

The study was productive, and it proved that solid execution required far more than a good haircut. It was the entire *experience*, from the moment the customer walked in the door until he or she left. The research pointed to three ingredients for this experience: comfort, freedom, and connection. The customer had to feel *welcome and comfortable* in the salon, like a guest in someone's home; he or she should have the *freedom* to get a haircut when convenient without an appointment and without having to endure a long wait, without being charged a high price; and there should be a friendly *connection* with the stylist, from the greeting to the invitation to come back.

When Rhoda read the finding, she had a sense of *déjà vu*. The report focused on the same elements that David Rubenzer had been stressing since he began training Great Clips stylists. "David may not have used the same words," she said, "but he fully understood what the experience had to be for the customers to come back. He also understood that the overall experience trumps a good haircut." So, while David had been a stylist and identified with the stylists, his training methods were always geared to the needs of the customer.

Roxie Poliak, one of David's original trainees and now a Great Clips franchisee, said it well: "You can have a stylist who gives a mediocre haircut, but she has all the personality in the world and follows the five steps. The customers love her, and they keep coming back. And then you can have the stylist who gives the best haircuts ever, but who's a dishrag when it comes to personality, and the customers won't come back. The haircut is important, but it's only one part of the experience we have to deliver."

The final recommendations went into detail as to *how* to achieve the experience, providing, for example, staffing guidelines to reduce waiting time. They likewise provided ways to *measure* how well the experience was delivered by tracking such elements as repeat customers and wait times. The state-of-the-art technology already in the Great Clips salons made these "brand measures" easier to monitor.

Even though the entire project was referred to as "rebranding," Ray's *initial* reaction was vintage Ray: "There was nothing new here. The recommendations were that we had to staff properly and that the stylists had to go through the five steps with each customer, but we'd been talking about those things for over twenty years." Then, shortly after the rebranding initiative was complete, Ray spent a day with Phoenix franchisee Ed Neumayr and told him that there was really nothing new in the whole rebranding effort.

Ed replied, "Ray, if you present this as 'nothing new,' no one will take it seriously and nothing will change. But if you present it as something new, and something that will really boost sales and profits, you will change behavior."

Ray reflected on Ed's comment, and then it clicked. In a flash, he saw what others already understood: The rebranding was not simply a reinforcement of the past, but was to be an entirely new, simplified road to a more profitable future. Instead of broad, "feel-good" generalizations about customer care, there were now specific steps to follow, and there were specific measurements to determine if—and how well—these steps were working. The brand measures soon became a standard part of the Great Clips lexicon, and the continuous monitoring became an integral part of salon operations.

"Before the rebranding," Ray explains, "a franchisee could call three different people in the organization and ask, 'How can I improve my profits?' and he would get three different answers. One would say he has to hire more stylists, another would say he has to sell more shampoo, and a third would say he has to be open longer hours. And when a franchisee gets three different answers, what does he do? He does nothing!

"But the beauty of what we have today, after the rebranding, is that that same franchisee would get the *same answers from all three people.* They'd each say, 'Let's take a look at your brand measures; that will tell us what we have to do to improve your business.' For the first time we could solve each franchisee's problem on an individual basis, and we could do it with objective, fact-based data. No more of the 'one-size-fits-all' thinking. Better yet, every franchisee and manager could do the measurements daily or weekly, and keep everything finely tuned."

"Before the rebranding," franchisee John Marcotte relates, "all franchisees thought their operations were great, and it was impossible to convince them otherwise. But the new measurements removed any doubts, and we can now pinpoint any deficiencies and provide the tools to fix them without guessing."

If one were to describe the rebranding effort in one sentence, it might sound something like this: It took the ethereal, intangible concept of execution and reduced it into tangible, understandable, measurable elements which everyone could see in the same way and discuss in the same language. Not only is this rare in the business world, it represents a truly unique competitive advantage for the network of franchisees spread over an entire continent.

Branding consultants will testify that most companies undergoing a rebranding process do not follow through. The renovated brand for those companies may mean little more than a new logo on the company stationery and business cards, or a mission statement hanging on a wall somewhere. That would *not* be the case at Great Clips.

Rhoda, Charlie, and Terri Miller were determined to incorporate the key elements of the "new" brand—comfort, freedom, and connection—into the DNA of the Great Clips system, from top to bottom. It was not enough to define the brand; it had to be *implemented* into the system to be effective. Terri put together an internal Brand Action Group at the corporate office that met regularly with the goal of ingraining the brand into every sector of the company.

She said, "If we were serious about being the brand down to our core, then it had to touch every person in our business. Our Brand Action Group had a representative from every department—real estate, legal, marketing, development, operations, and human resources. The elements of the brand had to come to life everywhere. We even threaded it through our job descriptions, our performance reviews, and everything else we did."

Terri's point is a critical one, and it's one that many companies miss. *The misconception is that "the brand" is the concern of only the marketing department,* but the businesses that best deliver their brand do it throughout the organization. It's been shown, for example, that in the hotel industry, it's the doorman who, more than most any other employee, can deliver—or destroy—the image the hotel is seeking to convey. He's the first and last person the guest sees, the first and last to make an impression, and the first and last to lend a hand.

Once the company was convinced that the new rebranding concept was the key to better operations, the focus was on how to best implement it at the salon level. Ann Latendresse, Director of Brand Marketing, tailored the process to the stylists and managers through DVDs, fun-filled training camps, and special sessions at the 2006 convention. The stylists got the message loud and clear: *Your mission is to make the connection to build brand loyalty so the customer comes back. The haircut is only a small part of that.* The stylists were quick to adapt, and in no time they were delivering the newly-created "five-step customer connection" regularly and flawlessly.

Anyone doubting the benefits of the rebranding program—and the effect it has had on salon operations—should be reminded that, *since it was launched in 2006, average unit volumes across the entire system have risen every quarter!*

What the NEC Task Force did for franchisee relations, the rebranding program did for franchisee profitability. Almost overnight the franchisees began to incorporate the brand measures into their routine evaluation of their operations, and each year the number of disciples grew.

David Oliverio, a franchisee who owns twenty-six salons in the Phoenix market, captured the importance of execution in a single sentence: *"A good plan executed very well is far better than a great plan executed poorly."* David expands on that thought to point out that the execution must be universal; that is, *all* of the franchisees within the system must execute the plan well. As he explains, "The key to maximizing *all* of the franchisees' success is for *each* to realize that he or she is a part of a larger, proven system. If there are parts of it with which they don't agree, they should work *within* that system to change them. At Great Clips, dissent is welcome."

CHAPTER 64

"Relaxing" the Salon

By 2004, there was a growing feeling at Great Clips that the salons needed updating. The Classic design and décor originated from more than twenty years ago, and it was becoming stale and outdated. Perhaps this was the time to refresh the salons, to come up with a new look.

While this was being considered, the rebranding effort was confirming the need for having the customer feel more *welcome, comfortable, and free* from the stress of waiting and high prices. If one word were used to describe the message of the rebranding program, it would be "relax." Nearly every item in the rebranding report centered on the importance of a relaxed atmosphere in the salon. Words such as "comfort," "friendly," "connecting," and "freedom" are easily wrapped into the label of relaxation.

Seizing upon this learning, the company had some

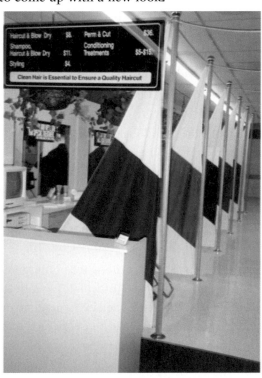

This Classic salon interior from the early 1980s shows the first price board design.

informal conversations with a few franchisees—Jim Hemak and Minnesota franchisees Kim Vosika and Carla Fryar—in the spring of 2004 to test the idea of a new décor for the salons.

Getting a favorable response, Dean Wieber and Tom Schuenke met with an architect in July to explore a salon redesign that would blend in with the new branding and deliver a feeling of relaxation. Almost immediately the intended new look was labeled the *Relax* design.

The sails, long identified with Great Clips, had to stay, but everything else was on the table. An exciting ambiance emerged from this process featuring raised ceilings, wood floors, more trim, and stylish, hard-panel sails between the chairs to replace the cotton and nylon fabric of yesteryear. The colors went from "harsh primary" to "soft muted."

But when the developing concept of the *Relax* design was later unveiled at a MARC meeting, the reception was less than enthusiastic. Most of the resistance had to do with the higher-end "feel" of the new design as well as the cost—a cost that would be hard to recoup because the salons were in rented space with short to medium-term leases. Another objection was that a franchisee would feel pressured to make the changes if a new or neighboring salon had them, and no one likes to be pressured. By the end of the session, the Council balked at endorsing the re-design.

Undaunted, in January of 2006 the company regrouped to push for the new design, but this time they wisely invited the MARC to be an integral part of a joint task force, and "affordability" became a key goal. The Salon Design Task Force was co-chaired by Dean Wieber and Ohio franchisee Ruth Saylor, and included franchisees Keith Chalmers, Ed Neumayr, Michael Reynolds, and Hunter Hughes. The breakthrough came when Tom

The Relax salon interior design was developed in 2006.

Schuenke came up with the idea of modular, separately-priced elements of the re-design, permitting a franchisee to do only parts of the new *Relax* design that would still blend in nicely with the former Classic design. Thus, a franchisee could re-do only the lobby, or the sails, or the floor, and still achieve a refreshed look without spending more than they could afford.

There was a corporate sigh of relief when the MARC voted to approve the reconfigured design. Prototypes of the new décor were incorporated into salons through July 2006, and in October 2006 Mike McCord in Cincinnati was the first franchisee to upgrade to the official *Relax* design. All new and relocated salons were required to adopt the new look. Today, over 2,100 Great Clips salons—or about two-thirds—have some degree of the *Relax* design.

Once again, the importance of consulting with—and listening to—the franchisees was confirmed. The franchisor-franchisee relationship has something in common with a marriage: The more people talk, the less they argue. By not being more collaborative with the franchisees at the earliest stages of the re-design process, the company was unwittingly acting like the husband who came home one night and announced to his wife that he decided to remodel their home without asking for her input—*and that she would have to pay for it!* However, franchisors do those things all the time. Even the best ones, like Great Clips, can sometimes forget to touch all of the bases.

In 2007, the Great Clips system adopted a new advertising tag line: "*Relax*. You're at Great Clips.®" The music for the new advertising campaign, taken from a Top 40 hit made popular in 1962 by the Rooftop Singers, was the perfect choice:

> *Walk right in, sit right down,*
> *Baby, let your hair hang down.*©

Those two lines said it all: No appointments needed; no waiting; no formalities; no hassles; and the perfect metaphor for relaxation—*let your hair down.*

"Relax" became the buzzword throughout the system, and hats and t-shirts with RELAX emblazoned on the front were circulated at meetings, outings, and conventions.

CHAPTER 65

From Gorillas to Cyberspace

Trying to define "marketing" is as frustrating as trying to nail Jell-O to a wall. The man on the street will define marketing as advertising, and in his mind he'll see little more than newspaper ads or television commercials. To a marketer, the term will conjure images of demographic trends and studies, promotions, websites, Internet presence, alliances with other companies and brands, games and contests, team and event sponsorships, billboards, and even product placement—paying to have your breakfast cereal sitting on a table in a movie set.

As we saw, the first Great Clips marketing plan, launched in 1982, consisted of a guy out in the street in a gorilla costume hawking free haircuts. Currently, the company spends about $46 million annually on marketing, the amount coming primarily from franchisees' payments into the advertising fund (5 percent of their sales). Over one-third of that amount is split between local radio and television commercials, and is allocated to the markets roughly proportionate to advertising fund dollars generated from those markets. The balance is devoted to NASCAR and Bowl Championship Series sponsorships, in-salon media, local promotions and sponsorships, direct mail, print campaigns, and, of course, the digital marketing so necessary in today's world. None of this includes the money spent independently by franchisees for their individual salons or by local co-ops for local promotions and sponsorships.

In 2008, the company encouraged its franchisees to hook up to broadband Internet in their salons. At the time, only 12 percent of the salons were connected, but within three years the number reached 86 percent—an amazing increase considering the cost factor and also considering that the franchisees either didn't at first see or understand the need.

The value of Internet accessibility throughout the system is enormous. There is now faster data transfer and better data protection. Sales data and other information are now communicated more frequently between the salon and the company, negating the need for the slower mail and faxes. Also, all data can now be easily stored and backed up to a remote server—an essential precaution in today's world.

But it isn't only the franchisee and the company who benefit from these advancements. The broadband technology facilitates credit card and gift card transactions, a significant convenience for the customer.

Having high speed Internet in all Great Clips salons paved the way for a new program called Online Check-In, a capability that many franchisees had been wanting. This innovative program was independently conceived, but it had a certain resemblance to the Call Ahead program championed by David Rubenzer years before. That original idea, which David tested in a few salons, would invite customers to telephone a salon to get on a waiting list. This provided a convenience to the customer who could now better schedule his or her haircut with other errands. However, there were drawbacks that prevented the program from being widely accepted, drawbacks that convinced Ray that the program should be abandoned. First, the phone calls would take the stylists away from their customers unless a full-time receptionist was hired to take the calls. Second, customers already in the salon and waiting for a haircut would resent it when someone came in and was called to a chair before them as if they were cutting in line. Online Check-In avoids these problems. No one needs to leave a customer to take a phone call because the customer checks in online. And there is no confusion as to whose turn it is because the waiting list is displayed on a visible electronic screen; therefore, waiting customers can plainly see that someone may be coming in ahead of them.

Online Check-In, which was developed for Great Clips by Innovative Computer Software (ICS), was tested for about a year before it was launched system-wide in 2011. Customers wanting to use it would log onto the Great Clips website where a "real-time" map was displayed showing the locations of nearby salons and their approximate wait time. To make the program accessible for users of smartphones, an Online Check-In app was created for iPhones and Androids. This high-tech innovation was so impressive that it was featured in the *Wall Street Journal* with an interview of Rob Goggins.

Many Great Clips customers attest to the value of Online Check-In, and, not surprisingly, they do so online! For example, a customer named Scott in Lubbock, Texas, submitted the following message online:

> Do you know why I go to Great Clips? It's because of the Online Check-In. I love checking in on my iPhone. It is the BEST. I'm a 38-year-old male. I can get a fast haircut anywhere in town, but

your Online Check-In helps me with my daily schedule. Also, I love the fact that you have my previous hair style comments already logged into the computer. The Online Check-In AND the computer style records will keep me coming back AGAIN & AGAIN. Thanks for doing an A+ job in customer service!

Online Check-In provides important information to the salon as well as the customer. This was observed by Stacy, a customer in the Fayetteville area of Arkansas, who provided this feedback:

I felt I needed to tell someone about the service my husband got at one of your locations last night. He went in to get a haircut at 8 P.M. and was surprised to hear he had a 45-minute wait. He decided to stay because he needed a cut. Ten minutes after he sat down two women hurried through the door and started helping customers. His forty-five minute wait had now turned into only ten minutes. When he asked about the two employees showing up, he was told that they were managers already off for the day, but they had seen the wait online and rushed in to help their coworkers. It is nice to see people who care about their coworkers and customers.

There was a time when a business's legitimacy was established by being listed in the Yellow Pages. In more recent years, a business could hardly exist without having its own website. And even having a website is no longer enough. Today a company's legitimacy requires a Facebook page, a Twitter account, and other connections with the new explosion in social media.

To stay on the cutting edge, Great Clips in 2010 went full bore into this ever-changing world of cyberspace. The significance of this venture is astounding. Consider the following: *The Great Clips website, www.greatclips. com, averages 1,000 visits every hour! And its Facebook page has more than 70,000 fans or "likes."*

Social media is still in its infancy. How—and how long—it will be used is still open to conjecture. However, we have already seen these avenues used for interfacing between customers, franchisees, and the company. The company has a full-court press in play to take advantage of this new technology.

Of course, social media also has a downside. No one can prevent the unpleasant postings of an unhappy customer or a disgruntled employee, and anyone with a cell phone can videotape from inside a salon and post it on YouTube. The good news is that people also post positive comments and complimentary videos. As Rhoda said at the 2010 Zone Meetings, "Every salon is a stage and every employee is an actor." It is yet another reason to make sure the customer is comfortable, relaxed, and made to feel like a welcome guest.

It is impossible to get ahead of the technology curve. Software and hardware become obsolete almost by the time they are installed. Just keeping up means constant updating, training, and tweaking—some major and some minor. There are new things being done, and old things being done better.

There is no program or process that Great Clips takes for granted. Even the customer tracking system, initially introduced many years ago, is constantly being enhanced to provide new and more relevant data: Which other Great Clips salons has the customer visited? How long between visits? What specific services were provided? Which products were purchased? How long did she wait? How long did his haircut take? Did she use Online Check-In or take advantage of a discount?

Even the process for scheduling stylists is constantly being re-examined. The latest iteration, aptly named the Scheduler, was introduced in 2008 to make scheduling more efficient, more responsive to customer demands, and more convenient for the stylists themselves. The process was developed by Innovative Computer Software (ICS) with Mari Fellrath, Great Clips' vice president of business intelligence, and is continuously being refined. Its benefits are enormous. Using the Scheduler, a salon can actually have increased hours of operation with a smaller payroll, and the customers will have less wait time—a win-win-win!

The variety and sophistication of the technological advances at Great Clips are hard to describe. Great Clips was the first in the industry to utilize a sophisticated algorithm to monitor and reduce customer wait times and a program to increase the consistency and efficiency of stylists by providing technical information in a "tree" form.

ICS was the midwife for virtually all of these innovations, as well as with Online Check-In, scheduling, wait-time monitors, and enhanced customer tracking. Great Clips has maintained an exclusive relationship with ICS and, according to Rhoda, "It has been one of our major competitive advantages."

"For a period of time," Shelby Yastrow said, "I was hosting think-tank sessions with several franchise companies. The president or CEO of each company attended, and Rhoda was there for Great Clips. Those other guys were in awe when she told them what she was doing with technology. They were just starting to work on things that Great Clips had already considered obsolete. And Rhoda, being Rhoda, scolded them for being behind the times!" Shelby laughed and added, "I never told those other guys that, not that long ago, Rhoda's brother resisted having a fax machine in the office."

Totally apart from the social media and web-based arenas, Great Clips has the best and most comprehensive data in the industry. The company currently has 335 million customer transactions on record, and records 75 million additional transactions every year. More important, that data does not remain in old files collecting dust. Great Clips is constantly developing more refined tools to make that data actionable.

In the future, these accomplishments may seem "ho-hum" in the context of the always developing electronic world. Who knows what the future holds? It's a safe bet that, whatever is happening, Great Clips will still be on the cutting edge.

The subject of Great Clips' technology deserves an additional comment, and it too has to do with Rhoda.

By now, the reader is likely to have the impression that Rhoda is an infallible Super Woman. But in fact she constantly wrestles with—and is frustrated by—issues which, to her, are serious shortcomings. "I have my own failings," she admits, "and, as hard as I try, I don't deal with them very well. I think I'm getting better at it, but I'm still not as collaborative with others as I'd like, I'm often guilty of micro-managing, and I tend to get too wrapped up in details. I'm sure these flaws have reduced my effectiveness."

But as hard as Rhoda can be on herself, there is one area where she openly takes pride—the technological supremacy of the company. "We've always known that the company's success depended on the franchisees' success," she says, "so we have to do everything within our power to help them. Several years ago, I began to see that fully supporting the franchisees demanded that we take advantage of the electronic breakthroughs that were popping up all around us. The more I looked into it, the clearer it was. The ability to collect and use data was staggering. Interactive, digital, and social media were becoming commonplace. Specific consumer groups, such as the twenty- to forty-year-old male, could be targeted like never before. I became relentless in driving our staff and our vendors to be leaders in this new ballgame, and it paid off. Moreover, it's given us a competitive edge going forward, and that doesn't bode well for the other brands out there."

CHAPTER 66

Tough Love

The strong bonds of trust between Great Clips and its franchisees can't be overstated. But that should not be taken to assume that the company will tolerate shoddy operations in the salons or anything else that can taint the brand. The reputation of the company is sacrosanct, and woe is the franchisee who jeopardizes it by cutting corners or mistreating customers.

We have already seen that the franchisee's opportunity to acquire additional salons is conditioned on him being in compliance with the franchise agreement and company procedures. Those procedures are embodied in manuals, policies, training videos, bulletins, and other communications which the franchisee has committed to follow. But how is that compliance monitored?

Franchisee submissions such as royalty payments and sales reports are easily tracked at the company's home office. The more subtle requirements that have a huge impact on the customer and the brand—minimizing wait times, giving a great haircut, having well-trained stylists, providing the right ambiance in a well-maintained, clean facility—are overseen by the field staff. Non-compliance, depending on the severity and frequency, is met with serious discussions, written warnings, and follow-up monitoring. Sanctions for continuing violations of standards range from "non-expandability"—a loss of the opportunity to acquire additional franchises—to loss of the opportunity to renew the franchise when it expires. In an extreme case it could result in termination of the franchise. It is a mark of Great Clips' commitment to work with its franchisees that it rarely resorts to the extreme step of termination.

Since the company gave its first haircut in 1982, it intuitively was understood that the brand is directly influenced by the customer's experience within the salon. But that was empirically confirmed beyond doubt through the previously discussed rebranding initiative launched in 2006. Using that learning as a platform, the company created a task force to modify the compliance program by centering it on *measurable* customer experiences. This task force was co-chaired by Sandra Anderson, the company's chief legal officer, and by Tennessee franchisee Michael Reynolds, and it included franchisees Mike DiCarlo, Jean Hamilton, Howard Kratzert, Ruth Saylor, Ken Smith, and Randy Wakefield. One of the many outcomes, in addition to analyzing quantitative data on the customer experience, was to scrutinize and consider all customer complaints (and compliments). This gave the company a much better—and more accepted—process to determine whether a franchisee was in compliance and strengthening the brand.

"Refining the compliance program was a major step for the system, and an accomplishment in which I take a lot of pride," Sandra Anderson notes. "But we needed a thorough and fair implementation process to bring it to life and to ensure a fair and consistent application." That responsibility was assigned to Carolyn Bastick who reports to Sandra Anderson.

Carolyn has played a key role in that process, from receiving non-compliance reports, to sending notices, and to monitoring all remedial and enforcement measures. She sees her responsibility as follows: "Our compliance program serves to protect the brand by ensuring that only franchisees who are following the system are the ones who are growing. I like nothing better than seeing evidence that a previously non-compliant franchisee has resolved an issue and now has the go-ahead to put in a new franchise application or exercise a right of first refusal. I look for ways to make the compliance program work for all concerned. Ultimately, we all want the same thing—a strong brand represented by solid, growth-oriented franchisees. We're always in search of that win-win."

A book written about any company engaged in franchising would ordinarily include several chapters devoted to its legal problems. The dockets of American courts are loaded with cases of franchisees suing franchisors and vice-versa. Whenever a franchisee earns less than he expected, he will have no problem finding a lawyer eager to take his case. The usual allegations include misrepresentation of expected profits, lousy site selection, ineffective marketing, inadequate training, lost sales due to impact from new outlets, and, of course, some technical error in the voluminous disclosure statements. The number of such cases has increased dramatically since the economy turned south in 2008, and the number of trial lawyers representing both franchisors and franchisees continues to grow.

There are, to be sure, cases filed by franchisors against franchisees, but they are few by comparison. Those cases mostly involve franchisors trying to terminate a franchise because the franchisee has not met operational standards, has not paid royalties, or has underreported sales.

But as in so many other areas, Great Clips is an exception. Perhaps it relates to the company's universally fair attitude to its franchisees, but, whatever the reason, the incidence of franchisee litigation in the system is extremely rare. In fact, during the recent economic downturn when franchisee lawsuits were rampant, *there was not a single case of Great Clips being sued by a franchisee!*

The entire legal department at Great Clips has only one lawyer, Sandra Anderson, the chief legal officer. Sandra has an explanation for the litigation-free environment. "In a nutshell," she says, "our franchisees know that we treat them fairly and with respect. And, when we do have that rare problem, we're all able to sit down at the table and work things out. We all understand that once the courthouse comes into the picture, calm and productive discussions become impossible. On the other hand," Sandra adds, "our franchisees know that we will not compromise our standards, and if necessary we will go to court if that's what we have to do to protect our brand."

Sandra's management of the legal affairs of the company is noteworthy. While she has been the only lawyer in the company for more than twelve years, legal issues continue to multiply as the Great Clips system continues to grow. Every day presents new legal challenges over real estate sites, employment issues, trademark protection, franchisees' problems, filings and registrations, advertising claims, and antitrust compliance. One would think that she would be calling on more outside lawyers to help meet these demands, but incredibly outside legal fees have fallen by 50 percent from 2004 through 2012! Great Clips is committed to working with franchisees to address and ultimately resolve issues. There have only been about nine occasions in the company's history when Great Clips has felt obligated to initiate legal action to protect the brand. In all cases, Great Clips prevailed. Lawyers representing franchise companies should be judged not by the number of cases won, but by the number of cases averted. Using that test, Sandra Anderson has played a starring role in the story of Great Clips.

PART EIGHT

Time to Smell the Flowers

CHAPTER 67

Recession? What Recession?

By 2009, the country was in a deep recession, certainly the worst since the Great Depression that struck eighty years earlier in 1929. Employment and the markets plummeted as bankruptcies and home foreclosures soared. Personal investment portfolios took beatings, businesses suffered in every sector of the economy, and many solid companies—including large banks and financial firms—had to close their doors.

By contrast, the entire Great Clips system enjoyed record years during these tough times. Since Great Clips prefers to measure success by how its *franchisees* are doing, a look at salon performance from 2007 to 2012 is instructive. According to the financial reports submitted by the franchisees, the average salon had increased sales, profits, and customer counts *in every single quarter* during those bleak years. Furthermore, the average cash flow per salon during the same time increased by approximately 33 percent!

Over those same years, and based on available records, Great Clips opened far more salons than Sport Clips, Supercuts, and Fantastic Sams *combined*!

More important, Great Clips has been averaging about ninety new franchisees each year since the onset of the recession. As any student of franchising will attest, increasing the number of outlets is good—but increasing the number of franchisees is *very* good! New franchisees tend to be younger and therefore help ensure the future; they also tend to bring new energy, vitality and ideas to a system that thrives on these attributes.

That future looks even brighter! In 2012, Great Clips had over 1,000 signed franchise agreements for salons that had not yet opened. That kind of pipeline assures strong growth for the foreseeable future, and the sale of *additional* franchises is still continuing at a good pace. Further, franchisees coming into the system are seldom satisfied with only one or two salons. Currently, the average franchisee who has been in the system for more than five years owns between five and six salons.

These figures could give the impression that potential franchisees are standing in line for salons. That is definitely not the case, especially when it comes to *qualified* applicants. Even a successful system like Great Clips has to work hard to find and screen franchisees. Rob Goggins, the senior vice president of real estate and development, scheduled a well-advertised informational seminar in Boston a few years ago to open that market for prospective franchisees. "I expected that as many as thirty prospects would attend," Rob related, "and we had a glitzy presentation ready to go. I figured we'd recruit up to five new franchisees. To my dismay, a grand total of two people committed to show up—one of whom was already on our applicant list, and the other was with a competitor, Fantastic Sams, who came only to check us out." Rob can now laugh when he tells the story, but he says, "At least the one guy who was already an applicant signed up. I still tell him that he's our most expensive franchisee in the entire system. That meeting cost us $30,000!"

Despite that inauspicious start, the Boston market has had solid growth, and in only four years Great Clips was the second largest brand in that market.

As for Ray Barton's grandiose aspirations for $1 billion in annual sales, his dream is about to come true. System-wide sales are projected to reach that amount for the first time in 2013.

It is noteworthy that the two franchising companies that have led their industries for several years—McDonald's and Great Clips—extended their leads even further during the recent dark days in the business world. Each of them, as well as their franchisees, were shattering records while others were shrinking or closing their doors. How could this be?

There is, of course, no magic elixir. And it isn't enough to say that both systems offer low prices, good value, accessibility, and efficient service. There has to be something else.

When Vince Lombardi, the famous football coach, was asked to explain his incredible success, he reportedly said something like this: "Well, we all start out even—the same equipment, the same rules, the same number of players, and a draft system designed to promote equality. So, in theory every game should end up in a tie score. Therefore, as a coach, my job is to get *just 1 percent more out of each player on my team*—whether it's a fraction of a second coming off the ball, or just a tiny bit better at reading what an opposing player will do. And if I can do that, then it will be a rout. Those other guys won't have a chance!"

So, too, the best-performing companies strive to get that extra 1 percent out of everyone on the team. Considering the number of "players" in a company's squad, that can add up to a powerhouse. Vince Lombardi didn't use the word, but, like Ray Barton, he was talking about *execution*!

Jim Johannesen, chief operating officer of McDonald's USA, has his own take on the success of Great Clips during these turbulent years. "I've been a close friend and colleague of Shelby Yastrow for over thirty-five years, and it was only natural that I'd follow Great Clips after Shelby joined the board. It's clear from what I can see, and from what he tells me, that Great Clips has followed the same path to success that we've followed at McDonald's. The credo of both companies is the same—*listen to the customers, find out what they want, and give it to them better than anyone else.* And, like McDonald's, Great Clips sticks to that simple philosophy without getting sidetracked or overcomplicated. Everyone has to execute—the company, the franchisees, and even the suppliers." Jim Johannesen and Ray Barton have never met, but they sing the execution tune like a well-practiced duet.

Unquestionably, there is much in common between McDonald's and Great Clips—not surprising since Ray, even before getting into the hair-care business, considered the fast food giant to represent the epitome of franchising. Since his early days with Century 21, he followed McDonald's models of simplicity, consistency, value, and convenience, and his decision to ask Shelby Yastrow to sit on his board was undoubtedly influenced by the McDonald's connection. Rhoda, however, is quick to point out, "While we share many of McDonald's philosophies, we would never pretend to imply that we have achieved what they have. As much as we are flattered by the comparison, we are nowhere near the iconic level of McDonald's."

Ray Barton would be the first person to credit the entire team for Great Clips' success, and the first to discount the importance of any one person. "We would have no Great Clips at all," he explained, "if it weren't for Steve Lemmon and his belief in the concept, or for David Rubenzer who gave that concept a unique personality. But," he added, "if it were only the three of us, the business would have fallen flat on its face. From the very beginning we received enormous help from our franchisees, staff, vendors, bankers, lawyers—you name it—and without their collective help we would have been lost."

Ray went on to mention specifically the magic performed by Jeff Elgin in selling franchises and instigating the owners' settlement and buy-sell agreements, the financing provided by RFE and Mike Foster, the handshake deal with Salon Innovations to deliver product to the salons, and Jim Hemak and Pat Stevens who were so instrumental in building the relationship between the company and the franchisees.

And, of course, there was Rhoda! She was the glue that held everything together and the lubricant that kept the parts moving smoothly. Most importantly, she and Ray supplied the conscience that every successful enterprise needs to survive long term.

It would be unfair to both Ray and Rhoda to say that Ray was the brain and Rhoda was the heart of the company, because the presence of both is so obvious throughout every corner of the Great Clips system. Perhaps a better analogy would be the commanding of an army. Ray would be conferring with the generals, checking the supply lines, and getting intelligence from the field; Rhoda would be in the trenches lobbing grenades, tending wounds, and encouraging those around her to fight harder.

Ray is also the visionary of the duo, and some even called him a dreamer when he was predicting 3,000 sa-

Rhoda Olsen, CEO, and Ray Barton, Chairman of the Board, pictured in 2012.

lons by the year 2000. But businesses need dreamers—*people who set goals higher than anyone else*. In that respect, he had much in common with that "other" Ray—Ray Kroc who founded McDonald's, and whose stage name when he played the piano in a saloon as a young man was, ironically, Danny Dreamer. A reporter interviewed Kroc when McDonald's sold its one-millionth hamburger and asked if he ever envisioned that he would sell a million burgers. "Hell," he answered without missing a beat, "I figured we'd sell a *billion* by now!"

Ray Barton's vision was telescopic, with the lens always set far into the future. When his partners were aiming for seventy-five salons, he was predicting 3,000; while they were focusing on the Twin Cities, he had his sights set on a national system; when they wanted to take out their hard-earned profits, he wanted them reinvested for long-term growth; he stuck to the long-term "rifle" approach to expansion over the short-term "shotgun" approach. And in the very early days he even returned a badly-needed $10,000 check for a franchise because the location did not fit his long-range plans.

Ray knew that the franchise graveyard was filled with the get-rich-quick artists who grab upfront fees before they have anything to offer and who depend on those payments to survive. "It takes time to build a strong house that will survive the elements," he says. "If you get in a hurry and build it too fast, it'll crash down on you with the first storm."

In recent years, Ray has kept his focus on "the big picture" and long-term planning, and he has stepped back from many of the day-to-day management issues. Nevertheless, he continuously reminds everyone in the Great Clips system of the importance of his main passion—*execution*. "Today, we have more than 3,000 salons and 30,000 stylists giving over 70 million haircuts a year. Every change in our system must be one that can be easily replicated. We have to beware of the dangers of over-complication. A difficult new procedure may be fine for one or two salons, but it could be a disaster for a system extending throughout the United States and into Canada, where operational consistency is the name of the game. In short," he concludes, "We have to do a better job than the competition with *every single* customer in *every single* salon. That's execution."

CHAPTER 68

One Big Happy Family

It's impossible to discuss Great Clips without the word "family" weaving in and out of the conversation. In the early days, it was family that sustained the company—David Rubenzer's brothers-in-law came up with some of the seed money, Steve Lemmon's parents bought a franchise, and Ray's wife, mother, sister, and brothers-in-law bought franchises. In later years, many franchisees have brought their children on board, introducing them to the business through management roles, then turning over salons to this next generation. In fact, Ray's and Rhoda's mother, Alice, was one of the early franchisees and now Ray and Mary Lou Barton's three children, Katie, Jason, and Annie, are the first third-generation franchisees in the system.

Great Clips is proud of having helped facilitate these family legacies for their franchisees. Over the past five years, the company has embraced the next generation of franchisees by providing a formal process to educate both the outgoing and incoming generations through its Gen 1/Gen 2 Family Business Seminar Program. As additional encouragement, Great Clips also financially supports generational transfers by waiving the standard transfer fee in those cases.

The focus on encouraging such family legacies is evident throughout the organization. New franchisees are urged from the earliest stages of their journey with Great Clips to think of their commitment to the long-term, family strategy; in fact, the initial training program is aptly named "Building Your Legacy." The company's own commitment to this end accentuates that the business is ultimately about people, family, and building financial independence.

"Legacy" is a word heard often within the Great Clips system, but its meaning takes on different nuances depending on the context. It refers to more than generational transfers of franchises, as from parents to children. It also contemplates evolution of the brand, an ongoing refinement of the system's culture and its attitude toward customers, stylists, company staff, and franchisees, and even to management succession.

By the time Great Clips celebrated its thirtieth birthday, the family had extended well beyond its 30,000 stylists, 1,000 franchisees, and 200 company employees. There were countless others in the supporting roles of real estate brokers, insurance agents, lawyers, advertising agencies, consultants, bankers, and vendors. Considering all of these people as family might sound like a stretch—but not to any of *them*! The bonds are felt in every meeting, whether it's two people in a room or thousands of people in a convention hall.

Tim Lawless, who became a franchisee in 1985 and is now one of the system's largest operators, describes the attitude this way: "When I talk to new or prospective franchisees, I tell them that they are joining a family, that they will never feel alone. In addition to the corporate staff, there are dozens of franchisees who can help walk them through any situation. There is always someone who has faced the same problems that they are facing."

Mike DiCarlo was one of the franchisees who was on the receiving end of such help when he first joined the Denver co-op. Mike, who subsequently owned as many as twenty-six salons, and today owns sixteen, has returned the favor by helping guide new franchisees through their own trials and tribulations.

The entire atmosphere from the corporate offices to the salons is conducive to friendly, comfortable relationships, and the symbols of power are never flaunted. Even Ray Barton gets his own coffee, and he'll make his own copies of documents (when he can do so without the help of his executive assistant, Dianna Anderson). Executive offices are relatively modest in size and furnishings, and there are no executive bathrooms or dining rooms. Last names are not used, and birthdays are celebrated.

To be sure, any organization with over 200 employees will have those who are not entirely happy. Inevitably, there will be those who feel overworked; others will feel underpaid. Some will feel that they've been unfairly passed over for promotions, and some will resent those who were awarded those promotions. Great Clips is no exception. Nevertheless, employee surveys reveal that overall morale and satisfaction at Great Clips is high and discontent is low when measured against other workplaces.

There is no better example of the convivial atmosphere at Great Clips than that provided by Steve Overholser. Steve, the company's chief financial officer, is forever buried in spread sheets, financial statements, loan doc-

Steve Overholser, Chief Financial Officer (aka The Count), speaking at a 2011 Zone Meeting.

uments, tax returns, projections, and benefits plans—all serious and not particularly "fun" stuff. Yet, in company-wide voice messages, especially each October 31, which previously ended the company fiscal year, Steve will often take on a persona known to all as "The Count." This is a clever *double entendre*—as the financial head of the company his job is "to count," and in his communications he flawlessly impersonates Count Dracula. In that role, he evokes the image of a vampire who, with fangs and a black cape, spews his numbers and figures. What could otherwise be a dull message becomes an effectively delightful means of communicating important financial information to an eager and receptive audience.

More than anyone else, Rhoda inspires by example the togetherness and unity among the people at Great Clips. Dee Tabone, Rhoda's executive assistant, relates a particularly touching illustration: "When my dad died a couple of years ago, Rhoda rounded up seven of my closest friends in Minneapolis, and she and they flew to Kansas for the funeral—at no expense for my friends. As soon as I saw them, I turned into a puddle of tears, and my family was blown away to see that my boss would do this for us. Actually, that was not an unusual event for Rhoda. In spite of her hectic schedule, she regularly attends meaningful events—whether they be funerals or happy celebrations—for employees, franchisees, and their families."

Dee also tells of an employee who was having trouble selling his mother's car. "Rhoda decided to kill two birds with one stone, so she bought the car from him and then turned around and gave it to the pastor of her mother-in-law's church whose own car was falling apart." In another instance, Dee recalls, "Rhoda overheard an employee mentioning that he missed getting an Easter basket as he did when he was a kid. He now gets one every year—from Rhoda!"

Continuing with her heart-warming stories about Rhoda, Dee adds, "She makes midnight shopping runs to buy Christmas gifts for our Adopt-A-Family program, and she does the shopping and cooking for the employee pancake breakfast before our convention. Her kindnesses have become contagious at Great Clips and are emulated by other employees in so many ways."

Even in the routine of her day-to-day workload, Rhoda's thoughtfulness is apparent. "There have been times," Dee says with a little embarrassment, "when, without even asking, she will bring me lunch when I'm frantically racing to get out documents or making meeting arrangements. Keeping up with her is a real challenge, but she never fails to show her appreciation. I can't describe how wonderful it is to be with Great Clips and work with Rhoda."

The franchisees likewise are universal in their praise for Rhoda. One of them is Clara Osterhage, who now owns twenty-seven salons in Ohio and Indiana. Clara is famous for breaking customer count records, and in fact holds the official Guinness World Records for both the most haircuts given by a team of ten stylists in twelve hours, and the most haircuts given by a team of ten stylists in seven days. She also owns the salon that has broken the Great Clips record for the most haircuts done in one week—3,255! "Every time we break a record," Clara says, "Rhoda flies to Ohio to take the staff to dinner, and she takes the time to visit my family when she is here. I love her with all my heart, and I credit her for improving the lives of so many people, including mine." Clara paused, and then added, "And she never forgets my birthday."

Ray offers a special brotherly tribute to Rhoda: "Nepotism means that one person in a family owes his job to another family member. Then we must have it because I owe my own job at Great Clips to the wonderful work Rhoda does for the company!"

The Great Clips family had a scare in the fall of 2004. Rhoda underwent surgery for cancer, and the post-operative recovery and treatment were difficult. Even the indefatigable Rhoda wasn't up to returning to work for several months. Happily, she has had a marvelous recovery and is back to her frenzied, demanding schedule—including squeezing in time for her daily exercise regimen. As anyone knowing Rhoda would expect, she has used her health scare to help others. She now actively promotes the Great Clips wellness program where she issues challenges to the staff in every category from walking to push-ups.

Nearly all enterprises today have mission statements and vision statements, and in virtually all of them we will find references to building sales, beating the competition, and making money. Great Clips, on the other hand, being true to its ideals, *directs its goals toward the dreams and opportunities of its franchisees*. Its formal vision is:

"Working together to build the most profitable salons by delivering the most powerful and enduring brand."

The opportunities provided through the Great Clips system are immeasurable, and are beautifully captured in the many letters and e-mails sent by franchisees after the 2012 convention.

Typical was one sent to Ray and Mary Lou Barton from Nancy and Dennis Stevens. (Dennis is Mary Lou's brother.) Today Dennis and Nancy own twelve salons, an accomplishment that required tremendous effort. But they don't see it that way. "We don't feel that we've worked a day since becoming franchisees," they wrote. "It has been sheer joy."

Another came from Tennessee franchisee Ken Roberts who complimented Ray not only for improving the lifestyle of franchisees, but also for building a business *that permitted those franchisees to do the same for their employees*. He concluded by writing, "So, thank you so much for allowing me to build a long-term business and to bring jobs, opportunities, fulfillment, and improved economic circumstances to many others along the way."

Ken's theme of how Great Clips franchisees have "paid it forward" by creating opportunities for their employees is a recurring one throughout the system. We've seen examples in earlier chapters of how stylists have become general managers, co-owners, and franchisees in their own right. But a more touching example is provided by Dennis and Nancy Stevens: A mother who was basically homeless applied to them for a job, and today she is the manager of one of their salons in Laramie, Wyoming. The lives of both her and her son have been changed beyond description through this sharing of good fortune.

CHAPTER 69

Giving Back to the Community

On national, local, and individual levels, the Great Clips system from top to bottom has followed a pattern of giving back to the community, especially to benefit children in need.

For the last twenty years, the Great Clips franchisees in the Twin Cities have participated in a Cut-A-Thon program through which Children's Hospitals and Clinics of Minnesota receives a portion of the proceeds from all haircuts on a given day each year. Today this program raises about $60,000 per year, and since inception it has raised over $1 million for this important health provider (which is often referred to simply as Children's). These funds are earmarked to help kids with serious illnesses, such as cancer, to make the transition back to school by providing, for example, "child life specialists" to work with the kids and their families and schools.

Beginning in 1996, Great Clips has sponsored an annual golf outing and auction to raise money for Children's. To date, the event has generated nearly $3 million, and each year surpasses the previous one. These proceeds are funneled into the Family Needs Fund, which helps provide housing and covers expenses, such as parking, transportation and meals, for families with children receiving treatment. All of these funds support the hospital's philosophy of "family-centered care" to help ease the stress on families during a child's critical illness.

In 2002, the company decided to leverage the system to maximize the charitable good that could be done, and October was chosen as "Cause Branding Month." This effort was carried out under the banner of "Great Needs. Great Deeds®." At first, different charitable partners were selected for each year, and these included recipients such as the American Red Cross and the Salvation Army. In 2005, the decision was made to have an ongoing relationship with a charity that again had a more direct focus on children and one with a presence throughout North America to correspond with the presence of Great Clips salons in the United States and Canada.

After considerable research, the system teamed up with Children's Miracle Network, a network of 170 children's hospitals in the United States and Canada (and now expanding into Europe). Every October, each franchisee has the option to participate in a program by which customers contribute whatever they wish and sign paper balloons that are hung in the salon. In return, the customers receive a coupon that can be used toward a later haircut. Currently, about half of the Great Clips salons participate in the Children's Miracle Network balloon campaign, and the number increases each year.

In addition to the simplicity of the program, one of its attributes is that 100 percent of all funds collected go to the hospitals, with all administrative expenses being underwritten by others. Better yet, every dollar collected goes right back into hospitals in the same area where those dollars are contributed. In 2012 alone, this program generated nearly $500,000 for this important charity, and the amount grows every year. (In fact, a portion of the proceeds from the sale of this book has been earmarked for the Children's Miracle Network Hospitals.)

Another very worthwhile charity that benefits from the Great Clips system is Locks of Love. Through this program, customers may donate their cut hair to Locks of Love, where the hair is made into custom-fitted prosthetic hairpieces for financially disadvantaged children. Most of the children helped by Locks of Love have lost their hair due to a medical condition called alopecia areata, which has no known cause or cure. The prostheses help to restore their self-esteem and their confidence, enabling them to face the world and their peers. The vast majority of Great Clips franchisees participate in Locks of Love. The program encourages free haircuts to customers donating ten inches or more of their hair.

The Great Clips system is also the premier sponsor of Cut It Out, which is associated with the Salons Against Domestic Abuse Fund. This fund is dedicated to fighting domestic abuse, mobilizing and training salon professionals to recognize warning signs and refer victims to local resources. As with Locks of Love, this initiative involves stylists and managers and gives them, as well as the franchisees, an opportunity to give back to the community.

In addition to the charitable efforts of the system and the company, the franchisees in the individual local markets, working through their co-ops, continuously implement programs that benefit local charities. For example, the franchisees in St. Louis will on a given day offer free haircuts during ball games at Busch Stadium with the "customers" being asked to make voluntary contributions to a local charity. This program is repeated by other co-ops in other stadiums and arenas around the United States and in Canada.

In the Chicago market, the franchisees collectively sponsor events to benefit the Ronald McDonald House, a charity that provides convenient and comfortable housing for families with children while those kids are being treated in hospitals for serious diseases.

The individual employees at Great Clips themselves add considerable heft when it comes to giving back to the community. Under the leadership of Nancy Uden, vice president of franchise services and human resources, the employees have a Community Engagement Committee to plan and coordinate volunteer opportunities to benefit such organizations as Feed My Starving Children and Habitat for Humanity.

Great Clips further encourages employees to support the charities of their choice in a couple of other ways. First, there is a matching gift program through which the company will match monetary gifts; second, every employee is given a day off with pay each year to enable them to help out a cause of their choice by rolling up their sleeves and lending a hand.

The good citizenship of Great Clips has been recognized by civic associations and community leaders.

As noted earlier, Great Clips decided to hold its 2001 convention only days after the infamous terrorist attacks on September 11 of that year. In recognition of that bold move, the Minneapolis Convention Center presented an award to the company to honor its commitment to press on in the face of adversity.

In May 2010, Great Clips was named as the winner of the Minnesota Business Ethics Award for mid-sized companies. That honor was to recognize that business which "best exemplifies and promotes ethical conduct for the benefit of the workplace, the marketplace, the environment, and the community."

MINNESOTA BUSINESS ETHICS AWARD

MBEA

2010 RECIPIENT

In that same year, the Minneapolis *Star Tribune* included Great Clips on its "Top 100 Workplaces" list. And for the past four years the company received the Hennepin County Wellness by Design award that recognizes various attributes of health and wellness initiatives.

Several years ago, the company created the Alice Madden Barton Scholarship program, named for Ray's and Rhoda's mother, to award scholarships to students at cosmetology schools. John Halal of the Tricoco University of Beauty Culture has cited this program for the assistance it provides to aspiring cosmetology students and adds, "Even in other ways, Great Clips has always supported the American Association of Cosmetology Schools and other industry associations. We couldn't do it without Great Clips."

Mez Varol, founder and president of International Academy, echoes this sentiment: "In addition to the Alice Madden Barton Scholarship program," he says, "the Great Clips franchisees have stood up to the plate to support cosmetology education. For example, Dan Washburn, who owns several Great Clips salons in Florida, has been extremely generous in providing scholarships to our students. Dan puts his money where his mouth is. He's always calling us to say, 'If any of your students need some help, let me know.'"

In 1994, Ray and Mary Lou Barton's daughter Annie was a patient at Children's Hospitals and Clinics of Minnesota. After seeing the wonderful care Annie was receiving, Ray and Mary Lou made a decision to support this fine institution to the extent that they could do so. As the fortunes of Great Clips grew, so did their commitment to Children's.

An example of the Bartons' personal generosity toward Children's is evident in the expansion and redevelopment of the Children's Family Resource Center. This is a place where families can learn more about their children's illnesses, obtain advice about financial assistance, access computers, or simply come for a quiet break and conversation. The center, which includes a supervised play area for the siblings of patients, proudly bears the names of Great Clips and Ray and Mary Lou Barton.

Ray was asked to join the Board of Trustees of Children's Hospitals and Clinics in 2005, where he has served as chairman of both the hospital board and the foundation board. According to Alan Goldbloom, M.D., president and chief executive officer of Children's, "Ray is passionate in his commitment to Children's. He 'flies the flag' as our ambassador throughout the community, attracting donors, raising money, and supporting the institution far beyond the call of duty. And as a businessman he is incredibly helpful with management and governance issues. When any key issue comes before the board, Ray will always ask the most important question: 'How will this decision affect the quality of the care we deliver?'"

As evidence of Ray's dedication to health care, he was named the Hospital Trustee of the Year in 2012 by the Minnesota Hospital Association, an organization representing all of the state's 150 hospitals.

Ray is also an active supporter of Operation Second Chance, an organization dedicated to the needs of disabled veterans, and he sits on the Board of Trustees for the University of St. Thomas.

Mary Lou summed it up like this: "Ray and I have been blessed more than we had any right to expect and probably more than we deserve. It's only right that we share our blessings, not only with our family but with the community as well."

Ray Barton was recognized at the 2012 Great Clips 30th Birthday Convention for his volunteer work with Operation Second Chance.

CHAPTER 70

What Do the Customers Say?

From the first stylist trained by David Rubenzer in 1982 to the most recent stylist to go through the Great Clips Academy for Hair training program, the *paramount consideration is the customer.* The customers must be treated like welcome guests, they must get the haircuts they want, and they must be made to feel that *low cost and fast service does not mean low quality.*

The system-wide rebranding effort launched in 2006 provided quantitative processes for measuring customer satisfaction, and this was a milestone in the evolution of the Great Clips brand. But as important as that is, there is one other measure that trumps all of the others: *What do the customers themselves say?* Do the customers see Great Clips as something special? Do they consider Great Clips as a suitable substitute for the higher-priced, full-service salons? Take a look at a sampling of the customer feedback received by the company online to see what they are saying:

> In the past I would never go to those low-cost salons. I was a salon snob. Today, I decided to say what the heck. I went to Great Clips. *I am beyond impressed!* This was the cut I have wanted for thirty years, awesome long layers. Hats off to Kim [the stylist]. I am a believer and will be going back and sending friends (**Maria R., Lexington, Kentucky**).

> Today I got the best haircut and style EVER. I actually decided to make plans to go out tonight because my hair looked so good! (**Angela K., St. Louis, Missouri**).

> I went to the Newport Highway store recently and had the best haircut of my life from a woman called Stephanie. I can't wait to go back! She was quick, efficient, *and made me feel like I was the prettiest sixty-year-old woman in the world!!!!* Thank you so much. I am your customer forever!! (**Brenda H., Spokane, Washington**).

> I'd gone way too long without a cut, and I was in a hurry. I didn't know anywhere else where I could get a quick walk-in, so

I apprehensively went to Great Clips. So glad I did! I've gotten $60 cuts routinely in the past, but Debbie made my cut look just as good for $15! Plus, I checked in on Facebook as a newbie and got $5 off! (**Katie B., Chicago, Illinois**).

I've always felt that I needed to go to a full service salon to receive a top quality haircut. With the economy as it is, I decided to try a local Great Clips. The lady who cut my hair did a BETTER job than my $140 salon visits, and she was a pleasure to talk to. Thank you, Great Clips, for changing my perception on quality (**Victoria S., Baltimore, Maryland**).

I have a twelve-year-old son who is autistic. Today, we had a wonderful stylist named Sheree, and I have to say, she was the sweetest, most caring and concerned stylist ever!! I am happy to say that we have finally found someone who is sensitive to my son's needs and for that I am extremely grateful. Thank you from the bottom of my heart for employing people like her. P.S. My son said after we left, "Mom, if I could pick the best hair person in the whole wide world, it would be her!!" (**Becky P., Lexington, Kentucky**).

My hair had gotten butchered at another salon. Snovia did such a wonderful job of making my hair look great! She also made me laugh the whole time to make me feel comfortable and confident that all would be okay. Her talents and customer service were absolutely wonderful! I have since received so many compliments about my hair. Snovia made my horrible day great (**Lindsay T., Washington, D.C.**).

I'm not usually the kind of person to write a company just to sing their praises, but I've spent upwards of $70 a cut trying to find a stylist that can give me what I was looking for, and your incredibly talented staff did it for less than $20. I am writing this because I think great people and great services deserve to be rewarded. Every morning I do my hair I not only get to smile about how great it looks, I get to feel great about the amazing deal I got. That's a rare combination (**Lizzy L., Augusta, Georgia**).

Reprise—October 2012

To the surprise of no one, the 2012 Great Clips 30th Birthday Convention exceeded all expectations. The final number of attendees came to 3,034, making it by far the largest gathering in the history of the company, and certainly the most enthusiastic.

To constant ovations, awards were announced for franchisees, their managers, and system suppliers in a broad array of categories. There were likewise awards for Franchisees of the Year and Managers of the Year, inductees into the Franchisee Hall of Fame, and recognition for excellence in the field of community service.

Even with all of the speeches, awards, and hoopla, everyone agreed when it came to naming the highlight of the convention. It occurred shortly after Rhoda took the stage and introduced David Rubenzer! Although relatively few of the current franchisees and staff have met David—the system is now more than four times larger than when he left management—his contributions as a founder, visionary, franchisee, and *stylist extraordinaire* are legendary.

David had not attended a Great Clips convention since he left in 1997, but he came with bells on for the thirtieth birthday bash. When Rhoda beckoned, he leapt onto the stage to thunderous applause. Tall, well-built, and mustached,

Founder David Rubenzer being inducted into the Great Clips Hall of Fame at the 2012 30th Birthday Convention.

David was beaming as he hugged Rhoda and waved to the crowd. It was like a myth had come to life! Then he and Rhoda sat in a make-believe salon and, as if they were all alone, they engaged in a chat recounting special memories. The segment ended with the two of them performing a hilarious—and suggestive—skit that had the crowd howling.

During the awards ceremony, David was once again called to the stage for his well-received induction into the Franchisee Hall of Fame as both a franchisee and founder of Great Clips, Inc.

That final night of speeches and awards presentations was punctuated with two other highly charged segments. First, and certainly the most touching, was when representatives of Operation Second Chance presented Ray Barton with an award for all he has done for disabled veterans wounded in combat. To see the presenter express his gratitude, while making light of his missing limbs, left no dry eyes in the house. For a complete change of pace—and emotion—the audience was then treated to a surprise appearance by Kasey Kahne and Brad Sweet, the championship drivers of the NASCAR race cars sponsored by Great Clips.

Anyone familiar with Great Clips will see a series of continuous threads woven together into a tapestry that reveals a special culture. One such thread is "community," another is "inspiration," a third is "vision," and still another is "legacy." There are other threads to add color and strength—threads for fairness, helping, respect, commitment to basics, giving, and pride.

These are not short, temporary threads; indeed, each is thirty years long and, no matter how much has been woven into the tapestry, its end is nowhere in sight.

Each convention speech and presentation, whether at a general session or in a breakout session, was anchored by some or all of these threads.

Clearly, Great Clips does not reinvent a new culture or mission *du jour* for each meeting and convention. It uses the very same threads to weave each new segment of its history and create every one of its successes. This is what binds the system together.

So, when David Rubenzer came to the 30th Birthday Convention after being away for fifteen years, and looked at the people and listened to the presentations, he didn't really see things were remarkably *different*—he simply saw them *bigger*.

As with all previous company conventions, this most recent one symbolized another phenomenon that is part of the Great Clips DNA. While it was organized, managed, and staffed *by* the company, it was undisputedly *for* the franchisees and their managers. All of the awards and accolades were for the franchisees and their staffs. All of the breakout sessions were to help the franchisees and their managers run their salons better. All of the record-breaking announcements related to salon performance. Nothing was said about company earnings.

As everyone filed out of the convention hall after the final session, and as they prepared to resume their workaday world, there was a common feeling that everything was well, all systems were "go," and the future was brighter than ever. And while the theme of the convention, "It's Gonna Be Great," was reassuring, it may have been more accurate with the addition of two more letters:

"IT'S GONNA BE GREATER!"

A Thank You Message from Ray Barton

Steve got us started, David gave us a soul, Rhoda gave us a heart, and the story began.

Today, Great Clips is the world's largest and fastest growing salon brand. Being involved with Great Clips has changed the lives of thousands of people. At our 30th Birthday Convention, I was overwhelmed by stories people told me about how Great Clips had changed  their lives—how they started with little capital and a lot of hard work and hope. I was humbled as they expressed their gratitude for being involved with Great Clips. They also told me of the sacrifices, hard work, and sleepless nights. While I have always known and appreciated it, these stories brought home to me, once again, what a tremendous team effort has gone into building Great Clips.

It was hard work and hope that built Great Clips. Thank you to everyone that helped make Great Clips into the success story it is today. Thank you to those who shared their stories.

Looking back and remembering all those tough days and challenges we faced, I see the people who stood and led, who spoke their minds with courage, who consulted me with wisdom and challenged me with a positive, professional attitude. People like Jim Hemak and Pat Stevens were never afraid to pull me aside and say: "Ray, you are wrong. Please listen." Jim spent countless hours talking to prospective franchisees and mentoring new ones. Ed Neumayr guided me to see the incredible opportunity to improve our business with our rebranding effort. Charlie Simpson and Terri Miller focused our organization like a laser on brand delivery and our brand measures. In 1997, when we were a barely profitable company with big dreams and not much else, Steve Overholser stood by me and helped me organize a presentation to tell our story and successfully sell it to professional investors. Rhoda led us through some of the toughest times in our history with her caring, courageous style. And my family: Mary Lou, Katie, Jason, and Annie. Their love and support gave me the freedom to be completely obsessed with Great Clips for over thirty years.

I am proud of Great Clips and what we have become, but most of all, I am grateful for having had the opportunity to be part of it. Thank you, Dave and Steve, and all of the people who worked so hard and sacrificed so much to build Great Clips into the world's largest and fastest growing salon brand. Thank you! Thank you! Thank you!

Most exciting, this is only the beginning. We have a tremendous opportunity to continue our growth and success. We have a new generation of leaders ready to take the helm in our quest for 6,000 salons, serving 600 customers a week—people such as Steve Hockett, Rob Goggins, and Sandra Anderson. And, we have a great team of newer franchisees—including second and even third-generation franchisees. They are smart, aggressive, experienced, and are ready to lead us to the next level. As good as it's been, IT'S GONNA BE GREAT!

Acknowledgments

The authors would like to acknowledge the many Great Clips franchisees, employees, vendors, cosmetology school executives, and others who provided their recollections and suggestions so vital to the story that follows. There are far too many to name, but it would be unforgivable not to mention a few. Jim Hemak and Pat Stevens are among the earliest and most contributive franchisees in the system, and both played various roles—sometimes openly and sometimes behind the scenes—in helping shape its success. Further, these gentlemen were two of the very few people who saw these pages before they were printed; their keen memories and editorial comments were valuable to us and to the story.

We would also like to thank Marlene Oberste, a Great Clips real estate manager, who named this book. In keeping with the Great Clips culture of teamwork and employee involvement, it was decided to have a contest among all company employees to come up with a title. Of the hundreds of submissions, the title suggested by Marlene—*Vision to Legacy: The Great Clips Story*—was selected for capturing perfectly what the company and the story are all about. What started as a distant vision has produced meaningful legacies for so many.

Carolyn Bastick has been incredibly helpful in making this book happen. Carolyn joined Great Clips in 1988 and has served in a variety of important roles. In addition to her tireless research and verification of facts and quotes, she has not been the least bit hesitant to offer solid suggestions on grammar, punctuation, sentence structure, and organization of text. Most important, Carolyn has been a priceless sounding board on matters of substance.

Last but certainly not least, we join everyone in the Great Clips system in acknowledging David Rubenzer and Steve Lemmon, without whom this story could not be told. These two heroes founded Great Clips with only a few dollars—but with loads of vision, courage, and energy.